MONKEY BRAIN SUSHI

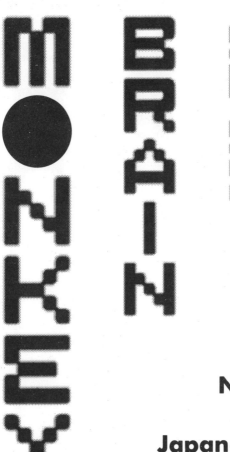

MONKEY BRAIN SUSHI

New Tastes in Japanese Fiction

Edited by Alfred Birnbaum

KODANSHA INTERNATIONAL
Tokyo • New York • London

Distributed in the United States by Kodansha America, Inc., 114 Fifth Avenue, New York, NY 10011, and in the United Kingdom and continental Europe by Kodansha Europe Ltd., Gillingham House, 38-44 Gillingham Street, London SWIV 1HU. Published by Kodansha International Ltd., 1-17-14 Otowa, Bunkyo-ku, Tokyo 112, and Kodansha America, Inc.

Library of Congress Cataloging-in-Publication Data

Monkey brain sushi: new tastes in Japanese fiction/edited by Alfred Birnbaum.—1st ed.
p. cm.
ISBN 4-7700-1543-7 : v3,000 ($18.95)
1. Short stories, Japanese—Translations into English. 2. Short stories, English—Translations from Japanese. 3. Japanese fiction—20th century—Translations into English. 4. English fiction—Translations from Japanese. I. Birnbaum, Alfred.
PL782.E8M66 1991
895.6'3010805—dc20
90-25938
CIP

Grateful acknowledgment is made to The New Yorker, where the story "TV People" first appeared.

CONTENTS

Introduction

Japan is a strange place for a writer: this rigorously group-think society turned relentlessly mass-sell society tends to drown out the lone voice. No laughing matter—that at least was the dark and humorless image of the Japanese artist until recently. Still stranger things have happened.

Starting from the early 1980s, a new generation of Japanese writers has emerged to capture the electric, eclectic spirit of contemporary life in Japan's mega-cities. Choosing to speak through the medium of popular magazines—rather than literary journals, as did the preceding generations —these young authors have shunned such traditional labels as *jun bungaku*, pure literature, opting instead for the Anglicism *fuikkushon*, fiction.

The choice of a Western epithet is telling: these voices bear little resemblance to Kawabata, Tanizaki, and Mishima, or even Abé, Endo, and Oé—staples of the older diet. If anything, the new writers look to the American "city novel" for their style and approach. They were all born and raised in an Americanized postwar Japan. The Japanese lifestyle they know has as much to do with jeans and hamburgers as *tatami* mats and *miso* soup; their romancing and nuclear-couple apartment living likewise only tenuously resemble the arranged marriages and extended households that were the mainstay of the highly involved family saga or the thinly veiled autobiographical *watakushi shosetsu*, "I novel", of the past. To them, prewar Japan might as well be fiction—a period piece on TV.

Today's Japanese writers grew up with omnipresent media. Steeped in Hollywood movies and television series, their imagination is less emotive than scenic. Their writing reflects a world-as-seen, not a world-as-felt through what Westerners have come to recognize as peculiarly Japanese shades of sensibility.

Furthermore, the Japanese language itself is changing. Trade imbalance notwithstanding, the Japanese have been enthusiastic importers of Western language. Not only is the Japanese language constantly acquiring foreign words—whole dictionaries of new vocabulary are published every year—but leanings toward foreign pop music and "lite" writing in translation are actually reshaping Japanese syntax. Writers of *fuikkushon* are more apt to use complete sentences with clearly stated subjects and objects—closer to translated forms than the atmospheric nuances and poignant silences of their parents' speech. Or again, they might shift into commercialese—the copywriter's flair for chopped, quirky phrasings that don't add up to sentences at all.

At the same time, the mass consumption of images has influenced their choice of themes and subjects. The vision they offer is of Japan, the perfect semiotic nation—though not *The Empire of Signs* described by Roland Barthes more than twenty years ago. The background noise running through their writing attests to the incredible speed and volume at which anything "new" and "different" is now sought out, reprocessed, and marketed for mass dissemination, flattening entire cultures into appealing designs in the Japanese consumer mind. To read these contemporary Japanese authors is to see the whole world become a cartoon —*manga*—clever, compact, disposable.

Which is not to reduce the argument to surface-over-substance. Rather, the Japanese *manga* is foremost a theatre of types and recombination. Parody is the paradigm. Originality—as distinct from creativity—has never been a Japanese obsession; the society works best within found forms. Japanese artists have always tended to describe their daily circumstances, altering details but never questioning the big picture. Today's infomaniac Japanese author, however, as showcased here, fictionalizes much more self-consciously—*in spite of* the big picture. Because by now, everyone knows the big picture is just a screen.

As in a cartoon, perspectives are thrown for a loop. Immediate surroundings are sketched with an inverted sense of detachment; everything seems mutually interchangeable. Any particular gives the feeling it could have been something else. Laid out in plain view like a fashion spread, the subject material is exactly *not* what it seems. Sex is less a commodity than a window display; electronics substitute for dreams; ambitions shuffle by like digital samples. The once-cherished ideals of the the early-seventies' Student Left are glossed over as easily as romantic stereotypes on *karaoke* sing-along videodisks. The salaryman's passion for work is played as patently ridiculous as the mock-heroic computer games of their kids. Gender takes a station-break; women authors exchange slants with their male counterparts to pen tougher prose and let the menfolk fret and stew.

Never hesitant or tentative, this new *fuikkushon* nonetheless bears witness to impermanence, the image of Tokyo's frenetic boredom. Kitsch and hype are everywhere on the page. Noticeably absent is any mourning for lost innocence; gone are the conflicts between traditional and contemporary values. The younger crowd no longer misses *saké* when drinking beer, and all that was emotionally "wet" has turned ambivalently "dry."

Understandably, these new tastes in writing have split the Japanese reading populace: older critics dismiss the stuff as "not serious literature" or, even, "not Japanese." It is a distaste for a way of life as much as its fictional projections. All the same, this new generation of writers has won over an under-forty readership in numbers that cannot be ignored. As they say: "We may not know serious literature, but we know what we like." Neither ponderous tomes nor throwaway pulp, this is popular writing fresh from the cultural chopping block. At once *haute* and irreverent, Japanese writers today are serving up slices of verbal *sushi* that bite back. Here at last we find sharply honed wit in the face of everyday non-sense, human comedy for the information age—the dazed adventures of the post-Zen "monkey mind" as it leaps from channel to channel toward a future that looks suspiciously like your favorite late-night rerun.

This collection of eighties-onward Japanese short fic-tion—the first time these authors have appeared together in one volume, even in Japan—cannot pretend to be compre-hensive. Unabashedly subjective, it sides with the most inno-vative, the most dynamic, the most fun—and with what most people really read. These are Japanese authors who will go on to cater to the nineties. Enjoy your first helping!

Alfred Birnbaum
Prague
December 1990

TV PEOPLE

Haruki Murakami

It was Sunday evening when the TV PEOPLE showed up.

The season, spring. At least, I think it was spring. In any case, it wasn't particularly hot as seasons go, nor particularly chilly.

To be honest, the season's not so important. What matters is that it's a Sunday evening.

I don't like Sunday evenings. Or, rather, I don't like everything that goes with them—that Sunday-evening state of affairs. Without fail, come Sunday evening my head starts to ache. In varying intensities each time. Maybe a third to a half of an inch into my temples, the soft flesh throbs—as if invisible threads lead out and someone far off is yanking at the other ends. Not that it hurts so much. It ought to hurt, but, strangely it doesn't—it's like long needles probing anesthetized areas.

And I hear things. Not sounds, but thick slabs of silence being dragged through the dark. *KRZSHAAAL KKRZSH-AAAAAL KKKKRMMMS*. Those are the initial indications. First, the aching. Then, a slight distortion of my vision. Tides of confusion wash through, premonitions tugging at memories, memories tugging at premonitions. A finely honed

razor moon floats white in the sky, roots of doubt burrow
into the earth. People walk extra loud down the hall just to
get me. *KRRSPUMK DUWB KRRSPUMK DUWB KRRS-
PUMK DUWB.*

All the more reason for the TV PEOPLE to single out Sunday
evening as the time to come around. Like melancholy moods,
or the secretive, quiet fall of rain, they steal into the gloom of
that appointed time.

Let me explain how the TV PEOPLE look.

The TV PEOPLE are slightly smaller than you or me. Not
obviously smaller—slightly smaller. About, say, twenty or
thirty percent. Every part of their bodies is uniformly smaller.
So rather than "small," the more terminologically correct
expression might be "reduced."

In fact, if you see TV PEOPLE somewhere, you might not
notice at first that they're small. But even if you don't, they'll
probably strike you as somehow strange. Unsettling, maybe.
You're sure to think something's odd, and then you'll take
another look. There's nothing unnatural about them at first
glance, but that's what's so unnatural. Their smallness is
completely different from that of children and dwarfs. When
we see children, we feel they're small, but this sense of
recognition comes mostly from the misproportioned
awkwardness of their bodies. They are small, granted, but
not uniformly so. The hands are small, but the head is big.
Typically, that is. No, the smallness of TV PEOPLE is something
else entirely. TV PEOPLE look as if they were reduced by
photocopy, everything mechanically calibrated. Say their
height has been reduced by a factor of 0.7, then their
shoulder width is also in 0.7 reduction; ditto (0.7 reduction)
for the feet, head, ears, and fingers. Like plastic models, only
a little smaller than the real thing.

Or like perspective demos. Figures that look far away even
close up. Something out of a trompe-l'oeil painting where the
surface warps and buckles. Where the hand fails to touch

objects close by, yet brushes what is out of reach.

That's TV PEOPLE.

That's TV PEOPLE.

That's TV PEOPLE.

There were three of them altogether.

They don't knock or ring the doorbell. Don't say hello. They just sneak right in. I don't even hear a footstep. One opens the door, the other two carry in a TV. Not a very big TV. Your ordinary Sony color TV. The door was locked, I think, but I can't be certain. Maybe I forgot to lock it. It really wasn't foremost in my thoughts at the time, so who knows? Still, I think the door was locked.

When they come in, I'm lying on the sofa, gazing up at the ceiling. Nobody at home but me. That afternoon, the wife has gone out with the girls—some close friends from her high-school days—getting together to talk, then eating dinner out. "Can you grab your own supper?" the wife said before leaving. "There's vegetables in the fridge and all sorts of frozen foods. That much you can handle for yourself, can't you? And before the sun goes down, remember to take in the laundry, OK?"

"Sure thing," I said. Doesn't faze me a bit. Rice, right? Laundry, right? Nothing to it. Take care of it simple as *SLUPPP KRRRTZ!*

"Did you say something, dear?" she asked.

"No, nothing," I said.

All afternoon I take it easy and loll about on the sofa. I have nothing better to do. I read a bit—that new novel by García Márquez—and listen to some music. I have myself a beer. Still, I'm unable to give my mind to any of this. I consider going back to bed, but I can't even pull myself together enough to do that. So I wind up lying on the sofa, staring at the ceiling.

The way my Sunday afternoons go, I end up doing a little bit of various things, none very well. It's a struggle to concentrate on any one thing. This particular day, everything seems to be going right. I think, Today I'll read this book, listen to these records, answer these letters. Today, for sure, I'll clean out my desk drawers, run errands, wash the car for once. But two o'clock rolls around, three o'clock rolls around, gradually dusk comes on, and all my plans are blown. I haven't done a thing; I've been lying around the whole day on the sofa, same as always. The clock ticks in my ears. *TRPP Q SCHAOUS TRPP Q SCHAOUS.* The sound erodes everything around me, little by little, like dripping rain. *TRPP Q SCHAOUS TRPP Q SCHAOUS.* Little by little, Sunday afternoon wears down, shrinking in scale. Just like the TV PEOPLE themselves.

The TV PEOPLE ignore me from the very outset. All three of them have this look that says the likes of me don't exist. They open the door and carry in their TV. The two put the set on the sideboard, the other one plugs it in. There's a mantel clock and a stack of magazines on the sideboard. The clock was a wedding gift, big and heavy—big and heavy as time itself—with a loud sound, too. *TRPP Q SCHAOUS TRPP Q SCHAOUS.* All through the house you can hear it. The TV PEOPLE move it off the sideboard, down onto the floor. The wife's going to raise hell, I think. She hates it when things get randomly shifted about. If everything isn't in its proper place, she gets really sore. What's worse, with the clock there on the floor, I'm bound to trip over it in the middle of the night. I'm forever getting up to go to the toilet at two in the morning, bleary-eyed, and stumbling over something.

Next, the TV PEOPLE move the magazines to the table. All of them women's magazines. (I hardly ever read magazines; I read books—personally, I wouldn't mind if every last magazine in the world went out of business. *Elle* and *Marie Claire* and *Home Ideas*, magazines of that ilk. Neatly stacked on the sideboard. The wife doesn't like me touching her magazines—change the order of the stack, and I never hear the end of it—so I don't go near them. Never once flipped through them. But the TV PEOPLE couldn't care less: they move them right out of the way, they show no concern, they sweep the whole lot off the sideboard, they mix up the order. *Marie Claire* is on top of *Croissant*; *Home Ideas* is underneath *An-An*. Unforgivable. And worse, they're scattering the bookmarks onto the floor. They've lost her place, pages with important information. I have no idea what information or how important—might have been for work, might have been personal—but whatever, it was important to the wife, and she'll let me know about it. "What's the meaning of this? I go out for a nice time with friends, and when I come back the house is a shambles!" I can just hear it, line for line. Oh, great, I think, shaking my head.

Everything gets removed from the sideboard to make room for the television. The TV PEOPLE plug it into a wall socket, then switch it on. Then there is a tinkling noise, and the screen lights up. A moment later the picture floats into view. They change the channels by remote control. But all the channels are blank—probably, I think, because they haven't connected the set to an antenna. There has to be an antenna outlet somewhere in the apartment. I seem to remember the superintendent telling us where it was when we moved into this condominium. All you had to do was connect it. But I can't remember where it is. We don't own a television, so I've completely forgotten.

Yet somehow the TV PEOPLE don't seem bothered that they aren't picking up any broadcast. They make no sign of looking for the antenna outlet. Blank screen, no image—makes no difference to them. Having pushed the button and had the power come on, they've completed what they came to do.

The TV is brand-new. It's not in its box, but one look tells you it's new. The instruction manual and guarantee are in a plastic bag taped to the sides, the power cable shines, sleek as a freshly caught fish.

All three TV PEOPLE look at the blank screen from here and there around the room. One of them comes over next to me and verifies that you can see the TV screen from where I'm sitting. The TV is facing straight toward me, at an optimum viewing distance. They seem satisfied. One operation down, says their air of accomplishment. One of the TV PEOPLE (the one who'd come over next to me) places the remote control on the table.

The TV PEOPLE speak not a word. Their movements come off in perfect order, hence they don't need to speak. Each of the three executes his prescribed function with maximum efficiency. A professional job. Neat and clean. Their work is done in no time. As an afterthought, one of the TV PEOPLE picks the clock up from the floor and casts a quick glance around the room to see if there isn't a more appropriate place to put it, but he doesn't find any and sets it back down. *TRPP Q SCHAOUS TRPP Q SCHAOUS.* It goes on ticking weightily on the floor. Our apartment is rather small, and a lot of floor space tends to be taken up with my books and the wife's reference materials. I am bound to trip on that clock. I heave a sigh. No mistake, stub my toes for sure. You can bet on it.

All three TV PEOPLE wear dark-blue jackets. Of who-knows-what fabric, but slick. Under them, they wear jeans and tennis shoes. Clothes and shoes all proportionately reduced in size. I watch their activities for the longest time, until I start to think maybe it's *my* proportions that are off. Almost as if I were riding backward on a roller coaster, wearing strong prescription glasses. The view is dizzying, the scale all screwed up. I'm thrown off balance, my customary world is no longer absolute. That's the way the TV PEOPLE make you feel.

Up to the very last, the TV PEOPLE don't say a word. The three of them check the screen one more time, confirm that there are no problems, then switch it off by remote control. The glow contracts to a point and flickers off with a tinkling noise. The screen returns to its expressionless, gray, natural state. The world outside is getting dark. I hear someone calling out to someone else. Anonymous footsteps pass by down the hall, intentionally loud as ever. *KRRSPUMK DUWB KRRSPUMK DUWB*. A Sunday evening.

The TV PEOPLE give the room another whirlwind inspection, open the door, and leave. Once again, they pay no attention to me whatsoever. They act as if I don't exist.

From the time the TV PEOPLE came into the apartment to the moment they leave, I don't budge. Don't say a word. I remain motionless, stretched out on the sofa, surveying the whole operation. I know what you're going to say: that's unnatural. Total strangers—not one but three—walk unannounced right into your apartment, plunk down a TV set, and you just sit there staring at them, dumbfounded. Kind of odd, don't you think?

I know, I know. But for whatever reason, I don't speak up. I simply observe the proceedings. Probably because they ignore me so totally. And if you were in my position, I imagine you'd probably do the same. Not to excuse myself, but *you* have people right in front of you denying your very presence like that, then see if you don't doubt whether you actually exist. I look at my hands half expecting to see clear through them. I'm devastated, powerless, in a trance. My body, my mind are vanishing fast. I can't bring myself to move. It's all I can do to watch the three TV PEOPLE deposit their television in my apartment and leave. I can't open my mouth for fear of what my voice might sound like.

The TV PEOPLE exit and leave me alone. My sense of reality comes back to me. These hands are once again my hands. It's only then I notice that the dusk has been swallowed by darkness. I turn on the light. Then I close my eyes. Yes, that's a TV set sitting there. Meanwhile, the clock keeps ticking

away the minutes. *TRPP Q SCHAOUS TRPP Q SCH-
AOUS.*

Curiously, the wife makes no mention of the appearance of
the television set in the apartment. No reaction at all. Zero.
It's as if she doesn't even see it. Creepy. Because, as I said
before, she's extremely fussy about the order and arrangement of furniture and other things. If someone dares to
move anything in the apartment, even by a hair, she'll jump
on it in an instant. That's her ascendancy. She knits her
brows, then gets things back the way they were.

Not me. If an issue of *Home Ideas* gets put under an *An-
An*, or a ballpoint pen finds its way into the pencil stand, you
don't see me go to pieces. I don't even notice. This is her
problem; I'd wear myself out living like her. Sometimes she
flies into a rage. She tells me she can't abide my carelessness.
Yes, I say, and sometimes I can't stand carelessness about
universal gravitation and π and $E=mc^2$, either. I mean it. But
when I say things like this she clams up, taking them as a
personal insult. I never mean it that way; I just say what I
feel.

That night, when she comes home, first thing she does is
look around the apartment. I've readied a full explanation—how the TV PEOPLE came and mixed everything up.
It'll be difficult to convince her, but I intend to tell her the
whole truth.

She doesn't say a thing, just gives the place the once-over.
There's a TV on the sideboard, the magazines are out of
order on the table, the mantel clock is on the floor, and the
wife doesn't even comment. There's nothing for me to
explain.

"You get your own supper OK?" she asks me, undressing.

"No, I didn't eat," I tell her.

"Why not?"

"I wasn't really hungry," I say.

The wife pauses, half undressed, and thinks this over. She

gives me a long look. Should she press the subject or not? The clock breaks up the protracted, ponderous silence. *TRPP Q SCHAOUS TRPP Q SCHAOUS*. I pretend not to hear; I won't let it in my ears. But the sound is simply too heavy, too loud to shut out. She, too, seems to be listening to it. Then she shakes her head and says, "Shall I whip up something quick?"

"Well, maybe," I say. I don't really feel much like eating, but I won't turn down the offer.

The wife changes into around-the-house wear and goes to the kitchen to fix a *zosui* and *tamago-yaki* while filling me in on her friends. Who'd done what, who'd said what, who'd changed her hair style and looked so much younger, who'd broken up with her boyfriend. I know most of her friends, so I pour myself a beer and follow along, inserting attentive uh-huhs at proper intervals. Though in fact I hardly hear a thing she says. I'm thinking about the TV PEOPLE. That, and why she didn't remark on the sudden appearance of the television. No way she couldn't have noticed. Very odd. Wierd, even. Something is wrong here. But what to do about it?

The food is ready, so I sit at the dining-room table and eat. Rice, egg, salt plum. When I've finished, the wife clears away the dishes. I have another beer, and she has a beer, too. I glance at the sideboard, and there's the TV set, with the power off, the remote control unit sitting on the table. I get up from the table, reach for the remote control, and switch it on. The screen glows and I hear it tinkling. Still no picture. Only the same blank tube. I press the button to raise the volume, but all that does is increase the white-noise roar. I watch the snowstorm for twenty, thirty seconds, then switch it off. Light and sound vanish in an instant. Meanwhile, the wife has seated herself on the carpet and is flipping through *Elle*, oblivious to the fact that the TV has just turned on and off.

I replace the remote control on the table and sit down on the sofa again, thinking I'll go on reading that long García

Márquez novel. I always read after dinner. I might set the book down after thirty minutes, or I might read for two hours, but the thing is to read every day. Today, though, I can't get myself to read more than a page and a half. I can't concentrate; my thoughts keep returning to the TV set. I look up and see it, straight in front of me.

I wake at half past two in the morning to find the TV still there. I get out of bed half hoping the thing has disappeared. No such luck. I go to the toilet, then plop down on the sofa and put my feet up on the table. I take the remote control in hand and try turning on the TV. No new developments in that department either; only a rerun of the same glow and noise. Nothing else. I look at it a while, then switch it off.

I go back to bed and try to sleep. I'm dead tired, but sleep isn't coming. I shut my eyes and I see them. The TV PEOPLE carrying the TV set, the TV PEOPLE moving the clock out of the way, the TV PEOPLE transferring magazines to the table, the TV PEOPLE plugging the power cable into the wall socket, the TV PEOPLE checking the screen, the TV PEOPLE opening the door and silently exiting. They've stayed on in my head. They're in there walking around. I get back out of bed, go to the kitchen, and pour a double brandy into a coffee cup. I down the brandy and head over to the sofa for another session with Márquez. I open the pages, yet somehow the words won't sink in. The writing is opaque.

Very well, then, I throw García Márquez aside and pick up *Elle*. Reading *Elle* from time to time can't hurt anyone. But there isn't anything in *Elle* that catches my fancy. New hair styles and elegant white silk blouses and eateries that serve good beef stew and what to wear to the opera, articles like that. Do I care? I throw *Elle* aside. Which leaves me the television on the sideboard to look at.

I end up staying awake until dawn, not doing a thing. At six o'clock, I make myself some coffee. I don't have anything else to do, so I go ahead and fix ham sandwiches before the wife gets up.

"You're up awful early," she says drowsily.

"Mm," I mumble.

After a nearly wordless breakfast, we leave home together and go our separate ways to our respective offices. The wife works at a small publishing house. Edits a natural-food and life-style magazine. "Shiitake Mushrooms Prevent Gout," "The Future of Organic Farming," you know the kind of magazine. Never sells very well, but hardly costs anything to produce; kept afloat by a handful of zealots. Me, I work in the advertising department of an electrical appliance manufacturer. I dream up ads for toasters and washing machines and microwave ovens.

In my office building, I pass one of the TV PEOPLE on the stairs. If I'm not mistaken, it's one of the three who brought the TV the day before—probably the one who first opened the door, who didn't actually carry the set. Their singular lack of distinguishing features makes it next to impossible to tell them apart, so I can't swear to it, but I'd say I'm eight to nine out of ten on the mark. He's wearing the same blue jacket as the previous day, and he's not carrying anything in his hands. He's merely walking down the stairs. I'm walking up. I dislike elevators, so I generally take the stairs. My office is on the ninth floor, so this is no mean task. When I'm in a rush, I get all sweaty by the time I reach the top. Even so, getting sweaty has got to be better than taking the elevator, as far as I'm concerned. Everyone jokes about it: doesn't own a TV or a VCR, doesn't take elevators, must be a modern-day Luddite. Maybe a childhood trauma leading to arrested development. Let them think what they like. They're the ones who are screwed up, if you ask me.

In any case, there I am, climbing the stairs like always; I'm the only one on the stairs—almost nobody else uses them—

when between the fourth and fifth floors I pass one of the TV PEOPLE coming down. It happens so suddenly I don't know what to do. Maybe I should say something?

But I don't say anything. I don't know what to say, and he's unapproachable. He leaves no opening; he descends the stairs so functionally, at one set tempo, with such regulated precision. Plus, he utterly ignores my presence, same as the day before. I don't even enter his field of vision. He slips by before I can think what to do. In that instant, the field of gravity warps.

At work the day is solid with meetings from the morning on. Important meetings on sales campaigns for a new product line. Several employees read reports. Blackboards fill with figures, bar graphs proliferate on computer screens. Heated discussions. I participate, although my standing in the meetings is not that critical because I'm not directly involved with the project. So between meetings I keep puzzling over things. I only voice an opinion once. Isn't much of an opinion, either—something perfectly obvious to any observer—but I couldn't very well go without saying anything, after all. I may not be terribly ambitious when it comes to work, but so long as I'm receiving a salary, I have to demonstrate responsibility. I summarize the various opinions up to that point and even make a joke to lighten the atmosphere. Half covering for my daydreaming about the TV PEOPLE. Several people laugh. After that one utterance, however, I only pretend to review the materials; I'm thinking about the TV PEOPLE. If they talk up a name for the new microwave oven, I certainly am not aware of it. My mind is all TV PEOPLE. What the hell was the meaning of that TV set? And why haul the TV all the way to my apartment in the first place? Why hasn't the wife remarked on its appearance? Why have the TV PEOPLE made inroads into my company?

The meetings are endless. At noon there's a short break for lunch. Too short to go out and eat. Instead, everyone gets sandwiches and coffee. The conference room is a haze of cigarette smoke, so I eat at my own desk. While I'm eating, the Section Chief comes around. To be perfectly frank, I don't like the guy. For no reason I can put my finger on: there's nothing you can fault him on, no single target for attack. He has an air of breeding. Moreover, he's not stupid. He has good taste in neckties, he doesn't wave his own flag or lord it over his inferiors. He even looks out for me, invites me out for the occasional meal. But there's just something about the guy that doesn't sit well with me. Maybe it's his habit of coming into body contact with people he's talking to. Men or women, at some point in the course of the conversation he'll reach out a hand and touch. Not in any suggestive way, mind you. No, his manner is brisk, his bearing perfectly casual. I wouldn't be surprised if some people don't even notice, it's so natural. Still—I don't know why—it does bother me. So whenever I see him, almost instinctively I brace myself. Call it petty, it gets to me.

He leans over, placing a hand on my shoulder. "About your statement at the meeting just now. Very nice," says the Section Chief warmly. "Very simply put, very pivotal. I was impressed. Points well taken. The whole room buzzed at that statement of yours. The timing was perfect, too. Yessir, you keep 'em coming like that."

And he glides off. Probably to lunch. I thank him straight out, but the honest truth is I'm taken aback. I mean, I don't remember a thing of what I said at the meeting. Why does the Section Chief have to come all the way over to my desk to praise me for *that*? There have to be more brilliant *homo loquens* around. Strange. I keep eating my lunch, uncomprehending. Then I think about the wife. Wonder what she's up to right now. Out to lunch? Maybe I ought to give her a call, exchange a few words, anything. I dial the first three digits, have second thoughts, hang up. I have no reason to be calling her. My world may be crumbling, out of balance, but is that a reason to ring up her office? What can I say about all this anyway? Besides, I hate calling her at work. I set down the receiver, let out a sigh, and finish off my coffee. Then I toss the Styrofoam cup into the wastebasket.

At one of the afternoon meetings I see TV PEOPLE again. This time, their number has increased by two. Just like the previous day, they come traipsing across the conference room, carrying a Sony color TV. A model one size bigger. Uh-oh. Sony's the rival camp. If, for whatever reason, any competitor's product should get brought into our offices, there's hell to pay, barring when other manufacturers' products are brought in for test comparison, of course. But then we take pains to remove the company logo—just to make sure no outside eyes happen upon it. Little do the TV PEOPLE care: the Sony mark is emblazoned for all to see. They open the door and march right into the conference room, flashing it in our direction. Then they parade the thing around the room, scanning the place for somewhere to set it down, until at last, not finding any location, they carry it backward out the door. The others in the room show no reaction to the TV PEOPLE. And they can't have missed them. No, they've definitely seen them. And the proof is, they even got out of the way, clearing a path for the TV PEOPLE to carry their television through. Still, that's as far as it went: a reaction no more alarmed than when the nearby coffee shop delivered. They'd made it a ground rule not to acknowledge the presence of the TV PEOPLE. The others all knew they were there; they just acted as if they weren't.

None of it makes any sense. Does everybody know about the TV PEOPLE? Am I alone in the dark? Maybe the wife knew about the TV PEOPLE all along, too. Probably. I'll bet that's why she wasn't surprised by the television and didn't mention it. That's the only possible explanation. Yet this confuses me even more. Who or what, then, are the TV PEOPLE? And why are they always carrying around TV sets?

One colleague leaves his seat to go to the toilet, and I get up to follow. This is a guy who entered the company around the same time I did. We're on good terms. Sometimes we go out for a drink together after work. I don't do that with most people. I'm standing next to him at the urinals. He's the first to let out with a gripe.

"Oh, joy! Looks like we're in for more of the same, straight through to evening. I swear! Meetings, meetings, meetings, going to drag on forever."

"You can say that again," I say. We wash our hands. He compliments me on the morning meeting's statement. I thank him.

"Oh, by the way, those guys who came in with the TV just now..." I launch forth, then cut off.

He doesn't say anything. He turns off the faucet, pulls two paper towels from the dispenser, and wipes his hands. He doesn't even shoot a glance in my direction. How long can he keep drying his hands? Eventually, he crumples up his towels and thows them away. Maybe he didn't hear me. Or maybe he's pretending not to hear. I can't tell. But from the sudden strain in the atmosphere, I know enough not to ask. I shut up, wipe my hands, and walk down the corridor to the conference room. All the rest of the afternoon's meetings he avoids my eyes.

When I get home from work, the apartment is dark. Outside, dark clouds have swept in. It's beginning to rain. The apartment smells like rain. Night is coming on. No sign of the wife. I loosen my tie, smooth out the wrinkles, and hang it up. I brush off my suit. I toss my shirt into the washing machine. My hair smells like cigarette smoke, so I take a shower and shave. Story of my life: I go to endless meetings, get smoked to death, then the wife gets on my case about it. The very first thing she did after we were married was make me stop smoking. Four years ago, that was.

Out of the shower, I sit on the sofa with a beer, drying my hair with a towel. The TV PEOPLE's television is still sitting on the sideboard. I pick up the remote control from the table and push the on switch. Again and again I press, but nothing happens. The screen stays dark. I check the plug; it's in the socket all right. I unplug it, then plug it back in. Still no go. No matter how often I press the on switch, the screen does not glow. Just to be sure, I pry open the back cover of the remote-control unit, remove the batteries, and check them with my handy electrical contact tester. The batteries are fine. At this point, I give up, throw the remote control aside, and slosh down more beer.

Why should it upset me? Supposing the television did come on, what then? It would glow and crackle with white noise. Who cares, if that's all that'd come on?

I care. Last night it worked. And I haven't laid a finger on it since. Doesn't make sense.

I try the remote control one more time. I press slowly with my finger. But the result is the same. No response whatsoever. The screen is dead. Cold.

Dead cold.

I pull another beer out of the fridge and eat some potato salad from a plastic tub. It's past six o'clock. I read the whole evening paper. If anything, it's more boring than usual. Almost no article worth reading, nothing but inconsequential news items. But I keep reading, for lack of anything better to do. Until I finish the paper. What next? To avoid pursuing that thought any further, I dally over the newspaper. Hmm, how about answering letters? A cousin of mine has sent us a wedding invitation, which I have to turn down. The day of the wedding, the wife and I are going to be off on a trip. To Okinawa. We've been planning it for ages; we're both taking time off from work. We can't very well go changing our plans now. God only knows when we'll get the next chance to spend a long holiday together. And, to clinch it all, I'm not even that close to my cousin; haven't seen her in almost ten years. Still, I can't leave replying to the last minute. She has to know how many people are coming, how many settings to plan for the banquet. Oh, forget it. I can't bring myself to write, not now. My heart isn't in it.

I pick up the newspaper again and read the same articles over again. Maybe I ought to start preparing dinner. But the wife might be working late and come home having eaten. Which would mean wasting one portion. And if I am going to eat alone I can make do with leftovers; no reason to make something up special. If she hasn't eaten, then we can go out and eat together.

Odd, though. Whenever either of us knows he or she is going to be later than six, we always call in. That's the rule. Leave a message on the answering machine if necessary. That way, the other can coordinate: go ahead and eat alone, or set something out for the late arriver, or hit the sack. The nature of my work sometimes keeps me out late, and she often has meetings, or proofs to dispatch, before coming home. Neither of us has a regular nine-to-five job. When both of us are busy, we can go three days without a word to each other. Those are the breaks—just one of those things that nobody planned. Hence we always keep certain rules so as not to place unrealistic burdens on each other. If it looks like we're going to be late, we call in and let the other one know. I sometimes forget, but she, never once.

Still, there's no message on the answering machine.

I toss the newspaper, stretch out on the sofa, and shut my eyes.

I dream about a meeting. I'm standing up, delivering a statement I myself don't understand. I open my mouth and talk. If I don't, I'm a dead man. I have to keep talking. Have to keep coming out with endless blah-blah-blah. Everyone around me is dead. Dead and turned to stone. A roomful of stone statues. A wind is blowing. The windows are all broken; gusts of air are coming in. And the TV PEOPLE are here. Three of them. Like the first time. They're carrying a Sony color TV. And on the screen are the TV PEOPLE. I'm running out of words; little by little I can feel my fingertips growing stiffer. Gradually turning to stone.

I open my eyes to find the room aglow. The color of corridors at an aquarium. The television is on. Outside, everything is dark. The TV screen is flickering in the gloom, static crackling. I sit up on the sofa, and press at my temples with my fingertips. The flesh of my fingers is still soft; my mouth tastes like beer. I swallow. I'm dried out; the saliva catches in my throat. As always, the waking world pales after an all too real dream. But no, this is real. Nobody's turned to stone. What time is it getting to be? I look for the clock on the floor. *TRPP Q SCHAOUS TRPP Q SCHAOUS.* A little before eight.

Yet, just like in the dream, one of the TV PEOPLE is on the television screen. The same guy I passed on the stairs to the office. No mistake. The guy who first opened the door to the apartment. I'm one hundred percent sure. He stands there —against a bright, fluorescent white background, the tail end of a dream infiltrating my conscious reality—staring at me. I shut, then reopen my eyes, hoping he'll have slipped back to never-never land. But he doesn't disappear. Far from it. He gets bigger. His face fills the whole screen, getting closer and closer.

The next thing I know, he's stepping through the screen. Hands gripping the frame, lifting himself up and over, one foot after the other, like climbing out of a window, leaving a white TV screen glowing behind him.

He rubs his left hand in the palm of his right, slowly acclimating himself to the world outside the television. On and on, reduced right-hand fingers rubbing reduced left-hand fingers, no hurry. He has that all-the-time-in-the-world nonchalance. Like a veteran TV show host. Then he looks me in the face.

"We're making an airplane," says my TV PEOPLE visitant. His voice has no perspective to it. A curious, paper-thin voice.

He speaks, and the screen is all machinery. Very

professional fade-in. Just like on the news. First, there's an opening shot of a large factory interior, then it cuts to a close-up of the workspace, camera center. Two TV PEOPLE are hard at work on some machine, tightening bolts with wrenches, adjusting gauges. The picture of concentration. The machine, however, is unlike anything I've ever seen: an upright cylinder except that it narrows toward the top, with streamlined protrusions along its surface. Looks more like some kind of gigantic orange juicer than an airplane. No wings, no seats.

"Doesn't look like an airplane," I say. Doesn't sound like my voice either. Strangely brittle, as if strained of nutrients through a thick filter. Have I grown so old all of a sudden?

"That's probably because we haven't painted it yet," he says. "Tomorrow we'll have it the right color. Then you'll see it's an airplane."

"The color's not the problem. It's the shape. That's not an airplane."

"Well, if it's not an airplane, what is it?" he asks me. If he doesn't know, and I don't know, then what *is* it?

"So that's why it's got to be the color," the TV PEOPLE rep puts it to me gently. "Paint it the right color, and it'll be an airplane."

I don't feel like arguing. What difference does it make? Orange juicer or airplane—flying orange juicer?—what do I care? Still, where's the wife while all this is happening? Why doesn't she come home? I massage my temples again. The clock ticks on. *TRPP Q SCHAOUS TRPP Q SCHAOUS.* The remote control lies on the table, and next to it the stack of women's magazines. The telephone is silent, the room illuminated by the dim glow of the television.

The two TV PEOPLE on the screen keep working away. The image is much clearer than before. You can read the numbers on the dials, hear the faint rumble of machinery. *TAABZH-RAYBGG TAABZHRAYBGG ARP ARRP TAABZHRA-YBGG.* This bass line is punctuated periodically by a sharp metallic grating. *AREEEENBT AREEENBT.* And various other noises are interspersed through the remaining aural space; I can't hear anything clearly over them. Still, the two TV PEOPLE labor on for all they're worth. That, apparently, is the subject of this program. I go on watching the two of them as they work on and on. Their colleague outside the TV set also looks on in silence. At them. At that thing—for the life of me, it does not look like an airplane—that insane machine all black and grimy, floating in a field of white light.

The TV PEOPLE rep speaks up. "Shame about your wife."

I look him in the face. Maybe I didn't hear him right. Staring at him is like peering into the glowing tube itself.

"Shame about your wife," the TV PEOPLE rep repeats in exactly the same absent tone.

"How's that?" I ask.

"How's that? It's gone too far," says the TV PEOPLE rep in a voice like a plastic-card hotel key. Flat, uninflected, it slices into me as if through a thin slit. "It's gone too far: she's out there."

"It's gone too far: she's out there," I repeat in my head. Very plain, and without reality. I can't grasp the context. Cause has effect by the tail and is swallowing it whole. I get up and go to the kitchen. I open the refrigerator, take a deep breath, reach for a can of beer, and go back to the sofa. The TV PEOPLE rep stands in place in front of the television, right elbow resting on the set, and watches me extract the pull ring. I don't really want to drink beer at this moment; I just need to do something. I drink one sip, but the beer doesn't taste good. I hold the can in my hand dumbly until it becomes so heavy I have to set it down on the table.

Then I think about the TV PEOPLE rep's revelation, about the wife's failure to materialize. He's saying she's gone. That she isn't coming home. I can't bring myself to believe it's over. Sure, we're not the perfect couple. We've had our spats in four years; we have our little problems. But we always talk them out. There are things we've resolved and things we haven't. Most of what we couldn't resolve, we let ride. OK, so we have our ups and downs as a couple. I admit it. But is this cause for despair? C'mon, show me a couple who don't have problems. Besides, it's only a little past eight. There must be some reason she can't get to a phone. Any number of possible reasons. For instance... I can't think of a single one. I'm hopelessly confused.

I fall back deep into the sofa.

How on earth is that airplane—if it is an airplane— supposed to fly? What propels it? Where are the windows? Which is the front, which is the back?

I'm dead tired. Exhausted. I still have to write that letter, though, to beg off from my cousin's invitation. My work schedule does not afford me the pleasure of attending. Regrettable. Congratulations, all the same.

The two TV PEOPLE in the television continue building their airplane, oblivious of me. They toil away; they don't stop for anything. They have an infinite amount of work to get through before the machine is complete. No sooner have they finished one operation than they're busy with another. They have no assembly instructions, no plans, but they know precisely what to do and what comes next. The camera ably follows their deft motions. Clear-cut, easy-to-follow camera work. Highly credible, convincing images. No doubt other TV PEOPLE (Nos. 4 and 5?) are manning the camera and control panel.

Strange as it may sound, the more I watch the flawless form of the TV PEOPLE as they go about their work, the more the thing starts to look like an airplane. At least it'd no longer surprise me if it actually flew. What does it matter which is front or back? With all the exacting detail work they're putting in, it has to be an airplane. Even if it doesn't appear so—to them, it's an airplane. Just like the little guy said, "If it's not an airplane, then what is it?"

The TV PEOPLE rep hasn't so much as twitched in all this time. Right elbow still propped up on the TV set, he's watching me. I'm being watched. The TV PEOPLE factory crew keeps working. Busy, busy, busy. The clock ticks on. *TRPP Q SCHAOUS TRPP Q SCHAOUS.* The room has grown dark, stifling. Someone's footsteps echo down the hall.

Well, it suddenly occurs to me, maybe so. Maybe the wife *is* out there. She's gone somewhere far away. By whatever means of transport, she's gone somewhere far out of my reach. Maybe our relationship has suffered irreversible damage. Maybe it's a total loss. Only I haven't noticed. All sorts of thoughts unravel inside me, then the frayed ends come together again. "Maybe so," I say out loud. My voice echoes, hollow.

"Tomorrow, when we paint it, you'll see better," he resumes. "All it needs is a touch of color to make it an airplane."

I look at the palms of my hands. They have shrunk slightly. Ever so slightly. Power of suggestion? Maybe the lighting's playing tricks on me. Maybe my sense of perspective has been thrown off. Yet, my palms really do look shrivelled. Hey, now, wait just a minute! Let me speak. There's something I should say. I must say. I'll dry up and turn to stone if I don't. Like the others.

"The phone will ring soon," the TV PEOPLE rep says. Then, after a measured pause, he adds, "In another five minutes."

I look at the telephone; I think about the telephone cord. Endless lengths of phone cable linking one telephone to another. Maybe somewhere, at some terminal of that awesome megacircuit, is my wife. Far, far away, out of my reach. I can feel her pulse. Another five minutes, I tell myself. *Which way is front, which way is back?* I stand up and try to say something, but no sooner have I gotten to my feet than the words slip away.

First published, *Par Avion* magazine, June 1989
TRANSLATION BY ALFRED BIRNBAUM

Haruki Murakami (b. 1949), author of *A Wild Sheep Chase* (1982) and *Hard-Boiled Wonderland and The End of the World* (1985), is the most popular author of his generation. Himself a translator of numerous authors from F. Scott Fitzgerald to Truman Capote to John Irving to Raymond Carver, Murakami was perhaps the first to break with the "old school." His brisk, casual writing style and offhand humor breathed fresh air into the dark, brooding introspection and exquisitely labored sorrows of the traditional Japanese novel. Other works include the novel *Dance Dance Dance* (1989), short-story collections *A Slow Boat to China* (1983), *Dead Heat on the Merry-Go-Round* (1985) *Firefly, Burn the Barn, and Other Stories* (1984), and *Another Attack on a Bakery* (1986), and travel writings in *A Distant Drum* (1990). The translation of the title story from his latest collection TV PEOPLE (1990), included in this anthology, was first published in *The New Yorker*.

SPROING!

Eri Makino

Well, you *do* see what I mean, right? Say what? Oh, the beers? Hey, you didn't have to return them now. No rush. But listen, you come on in. It's cold out there. Did I *tell* you what happened yesterday? I *didn't*, did I? At the PTA meeting—no, that wasn't it—Parents' Day—no, wait, at the whatzitcalled—at the Parents' *Social*. What for? You know, like I *told* you, for the nursery school. Oh? Yours didn't? Buffet lunch in this department store banquet room. *And* they had beer! I'm practically bubbling, "Beer too, eh?" as I pour myself a few. Funny looks? Nah, not *me*. I'm the type people don't notice. You know, just a *kuroko*—a shadow behind the scenes. Well, well, beer left over? So there I am, helping myself to more. Just once, when I spill some, people start giving me the eye. Later, there's talk of singing *karaoke*. But you know, I can't stand that silliness. "Hate to run *but*, today, it's the husband's day off," I tell 'em and come straight home. He's not here. *Perfect!* I'll get working on my novel, but then my stomach starts to ache. And then my son comes home from school. On his own. The bus stops in front of this building, though, so it's not like it's a real big deal.

I'm working at the *wa–pro*—my word processor. And my son comes up and starts talking about what happened at nursery school. No, *not now*, I don't wanta hafta hear *that* when I'm at the word processor. Still, mother's duty and all. I listen, "Uh-huh uh-huh," with half an ear.

"Mommy, know what?" That's how he starts up, the kid. "Today I...at school I...I drawed a picture, of Jack 'n the Beanstalk."

"Really? Drew Jack and the Beanstalk, did ya?" *Tippetty tap tap*. That's the word processor.

"Jack's face! I drawed it."

"Uh-huh uh-huh." *Tappetty tap*.

"'N then, I drawed the body, square. 'N then, I drawed hands 'n I drawed feet."

"Drew it good, did ya?" *Tip tap*. What a *nuisance!* Me with my stomach all aching, too. Hurry up. Quit talking and go out and play somewhere.

"No I, uh, Jack's fingers, uh, I could only draw two 'n only three toes."

"Hmm, that so?" *Tap tip*.

"Mommy, know what? I..."

"What *is* it? *Enough* already! So you drew Jack and the Beanstalk. So *what?*"

"Mommy, know what? I...the blue badge person, she told me to stop drawing already, so I stopped. That's why, Mommy, I...I couldn't draw all of Jack's fingers 'n toes."

"What's your *problem?* You can draw them next time."

"But Mommy, know what? The blue badge person told me to stop, so my Jack 'n the Beanstalk..."

"I know, I know. You couldn't draw all the fingers and toes. Fine, okay, enough. Hurry and get changed. You're starting to *rile* me."

"Mommy, know what?"

Sure enough, my stomach is shot, and now my head's going too. I can't stand it. Then he goes and starts *sniveling*. No, really. *Always* ends up like this. Here I am, happily working at the *wa–pro* and I end up feeling *guilty* 'cause I'm too busy to listen to the kid.

"Listen, Mommy's not mad. Mommy's just saying you can draw it again tomorrow."

"But Mommy, know what? Um, I, the blue badge person told me to stop drawing already, so I...I put my picture of Jack 'n the Beanstalk...I went and left it on my desk..." By then he's *boo-hoo-hoo*ing away. "'N...now, my picture, I don't know where it went to!"

"It's all right. Teacher'll take care of it for you."

"But my picture, it'll end up somewhere. Teacher'll forget 'n it'll get lost!"

"Teacher'll keep it *safe* for you."

"But Mommy, I...does Teacher know I left it on my desk? Does Teacher put it away? Mommy mommy, I dunno what happened to it!"

"Look, how's *Mommy* supposed to know? Listen, Mommy's got a tummy ache, *okay?*"

By then it *really* hurts, so I take something for it. But 'stead of getting better, it only gets worse. I figure I better lay out the *futon* and lie down. *Really!* What did I expect? Taking medication during the day like an idiot! And then my son sits down, right by my pillow, sniveling away.

"But Mommy, I...what's gonna happen to my picture of Jack 'n the Beanstalk!" I feel like crying *myself*.

"Why don't ya ask Head Teacher? Head Teacher knows everything. So if Teacher don't know, just ask Head Teacher."

"But Mommy, if I ask Head Teacher sump'n like that, won't she get mad at me?" *Snivel snivel.*

"She won't get mad. That's Head Teacher's *job*. Mommy doesn't know everything about nursery school, so if there's something you don't know, you can ask Teacher or Head teacher. It's *okay.*"

"But if I asks 'em sump'n like that 'n they get mad, what'll I do?" *Snivel snivel.*

Gee, I'm *sorry*. Here I haven't even given you any tea. What would you like? English tea? Oolong tea? Say what? Hot? Okay, hot oolong tea. Anyway, no kidding, yesterday, I slept the whole day away. First time I've slept right through my husband's day off. And then, get *this*, this man—who up till now woulda yelled "Where's my dinner!"—just picks up the phone and orders Chinese food.

"Mommy says her tummy aches," the boy tells him. "That's what she said when I got home, too," our daughter chimes in. Then, who knows *why*, but the boy tells his father, "Daddy, don't worry, I, when I get bigger, I'm gonna get Mommy t'learn me how to cook." Beats *me*. Maybe that's why he phoned out, without so much as a word. That *really* surprised me. Then afterwards, he washed the dishes even. Tears came to my eyes, lemme tell you. It's got to be the first time he's *ever* done that in our entire married life. This is the same person who shouted "What am I supposed to do for dinner?" when I was sick in the hospital. Maybe the talk about divorce the other day did some good after all.

You, you're lucky. Your husband's a prince. Pulls in good money, doesn't play around or nothing. So how come I got married? Didn't I ever *tell* you? Wasn't like *I* wanted to get married, you know. Marriage—uh-uh, *no way*. I must've told you it was a *forced* marriage? C'mon, why would *I* do the forcing? It was me who got roped into it. You better *know* it. We were working at the same place. Uh-huh. How come? Well, *me*, I liked the place 'cause men and women got equal pay. Fact is, I entered the company telling everybody, "I'll be here till they make me president." How long'd I last? Eight months. They laughed in my face when I quit.

Oh? So you think I must've liked him since I went out with him, eh? *No way*. I just wanted to have a little fling. Hadn't had *any* fun till then, so figured I might as well have a good time. No, *really*, I'm the serious type. This guy, though, it's like he never even *spoke* to a girl before, he looked like such a dear sweet boy. Wasn't till afterwards I find out he's been playing the field. It's not fair. *This* is what happens when someone who's never fooled around screws up, but bad. Sleeping with him was *one* thing, but next thing you know, the whole office's buzzing about engagement rings and marriage and you can guess what. Like they stuck a "been-sleeping-with-him" badge on me.

So how come someone running around all over the place took it into his head to wanna get *married*? Must have been the right one for him, huh. *Me,* I didn't want to get married. Been *choosier* if I had. All I wanted was a little *fling,* so I took what I could get. Turned into one *big* mess, though. Every time I tried to get rid of him, I made things worse. Everyone figured us for lovebirds. *Pure* hell. I didn't want to get married. *He* did. I tried to run away. He wouldn't let me go. I kept my distance, made up all kinds of reasons like "I'm too busy." Me, *I'm* not the type to come right out and say *no,* but *forget* about talking roundabout to soften the blow. Saying *any*thing was the mistake! What's worse, though, he's the kind who yells just like *that.* Em*bar*rassing! Getting yelled at in front of everyone! Anyway, he even guarded the door after work, waited for me outside. So that's how I slid into this *swamp.* Not me, *no way*, wasn't *my* intention to get married. Knew exactly what would happen if I did. And, well, that's exactly what *did* happen. Maybe even worse.

Listen, I've got a story you wouldn't *believe*. It's confrontation time, right? He's saying, let's get married. I'm telling him sweet of you but no thanks. We're at his place. It's a showdown. I've been thinking, if I agree, then it's curtains for me. I've got to *end* this thing once and for all. Hey, I don't go for casual sex, after all. Which is also why cheating's out of the question for me.

Atmosphere's tense. And he's wearing such a *look*, you wouldn't believe. Then, he whips out this *knife* from somewhere.

"If you won't marry me, I'll kill you first and then I'll kill myself."

Boy, am *I* in a fix. This is what I get for my little fling. Talk about *disgrace!* The mere *thought* of dying over something like this! Like one of those crimes of passion. I think about my parents and friends. This would put the whole *family* to shame. Gotta get out of this mess. Get scared and I'm a goner. Gotta think straight here.

"Well, I'm not saying I'll never, ever get married, you know."

"Okay, then, when's it going to be?"

"Now, let's not get hasty here, but, say, sometime, maybe."

"That may be fine for you, but not me."

I'm buying time like this. Pretty soon, he's got to go to the bathroom. I'm looking cool as can be. But *inside*, I'm rattling like a bag of bones. He locks me in the apartment and heads to the bathroom. I can hear him going down the hall. You're telling *me*! The stinking apartment didn't have but a rooming-house toilet *down the hall!*

"Now!" I think. It's the second floor. I practically *leap* up onto the window sill and start kicking, *hard* as I can. A couple good kicks and the whole thing goes *flying*, frame and all. I jump to the ground. Pitch black, can't see a thing. No matter, I run and run. *Barefoot!* Scramble up a big old fence, jump down on the other side, dogs barking, I'm cutting through somebody's yard, even maybe knocked my way through a wall. Weirdest thing is, I didn't have *not one* scratch on me.

Finally I come to a bright street, look around and find a *sushi* place. I run inside.

"Please! There's some *weirdo* chasing me!"

The old guy there gets right into the act. Pulls down the shutter, puts some young guys on the lookout.

"There's a strange person wandering around out there."

"What do you want me to do? Call the police?" he asks. But I don't want *no* such thing.

"Oh no. I'd like to go home. Could you call me a taxi, please?" Just *listen* to me, like some *debutante*. I borrow a pair of slippers and get into the cab. Once home, that's it for me. I come down with a fever and hit the sack.

Next day, I don't even bother to call in sick. First time I ever done that. Head's completely out of it. Each time one of those police cars goes by *eee-ooo-eee-ooo* my heart just about stops. Wonder what happened to him after I split. Maybe they found his dead body somewhere. It'll get into the papers. I'll have to leave Japan. Gone and screwed up my whole *life*. What I get for doing such an idiotic thing. Have to bear the mental and physical scars for the rest of my days.

Ding dong!

"Anybody home?"

Can you *believe* it? There he is, all suited up, necktie and everything, up at my place with a what-was-that-all-about-last-night? look on his face.

"Hey, there's a man here to see you," my mother says. That *useless* mother of mine.

"I *don't* want to see him. Tell him to go *away*. Tell him I'm sick in bed and can't see him."

"Such a thing to say! After he came all this way to see you. What's the matter with you, sending him home?"

And *then*, Mother Dear goes and invites him in. 'Course, far as looks go, he's *not* bad. Impresses you as the serious type at first. And need we mention he's a graduate of *the* Gakushuin University? So much for my mother. She and he start acting like long-lost friends. I kid you not. She just couldn't *wait* to marry me off. Got to keep up appearances, after all. Didn't matter *who* the guy was.

"Honestly! Here this fine gentleman is paying you a get-well visit, stop being so rude and show your face," she tells me. Mother Dear gets me outa bed and I wind up having to see this guy. I *tell* you, this guy's like...like Jekyll and Hyde. *Flip flop.* In such good spirits now, you'd think yesterday didn't happen. He's so cheerful, *and* he's still going on about getting married. I'm flabbergasted. I mean, what can I say? My head's so mixed up, I just sort of blank out as I walk him to the train station.

Here I'm saying, "But I don't want to get married," and

here he keeps making plans.

"Okay, forget about marriage. At least meet my parents." So I do. And can you picture it? I'm getting the full *fiancée* treatment. Now I'm not the sort to make *waves*, so I sort of go along with it.

Figuring it'll *never* happen, I tell him, "Only if we get married in Hawaii and buy a condo." Then, just like *that*, he calls to say, "I've made reservations for Hawaii. Everything's set!" And I don't even *want* to get married. Then our parents are meeting each other, and my mother, Mother Dear, she's already preparing for the big day. And no one even *bothers* to ask *me* what I think of all this.

Pretty soon what with all this anxiety, I'm flat on my back in bed. And then,

Ding dong!

Oh-oh, not *again*. I get this funny feeling. The guy, he's gone and hired a moving van, hauled all his things from that *flophouse* of his and while he's at it, he's come for mine! Somebody *help* me! I feel like screaming, but who is there to help? Dad's fighting it out in business, *nowhere* to be seen, as usual. Which just leaves my *useless* Mother (Dear).

"Oh, *Mother*," the guy says, "hurry it up, please." So she flutters about, throwing my things together, the whole kit and kaboodle which he and the driver load into the van. We aren't even *married* yet and, before I know it, they are cramming *me* into the van too, carting me off like another piece of luggage. I mean, what *is* this? I got *rights*, you know! So then comes the Hawaiian wedding and the honeymoon. And like some kinda *bad* dream, married life begins. Right, like they always say. Everyone says I was the *perfect bride*. Wunnerful wunnerful. Nothing but *lies*. A girl shouldn't get married 'less she really wants to.

Might as well be a slave. Marriage is just one big slave trade, anyway. Lots of people who don't love each other go and get married, just so's they can make some sorta *life* together and call it *marriage*. Took me a while get that down.

Oh, hey, I'm *sorry*. I've kept you so long with this story. What? Changed your mind about going shopping? Well, if that's the case, no hurry, eh? Don't have to work today myself. A little *early*, maybe, but there's beer in the fridge. Kids won't be home for awhile. Wonder what *did* happen to the kid's Jack and the Beanstalk picture? Maybe I shoulda called in about it. Well, gave him a note for the teacher, anyway. Teacher's got it tough, too. You *said* it. Right now she's probably getting this "Head Teacher, guess what? Know what? I... Yesterday I drawed a picture of Jack and the Beanstalk, but know what? I drawed the body and the head okay, but know what? I couldn't drawed hands and feet..." The principal's probably getting a stomach ache. *Some*body, *do* something with this kid, she'll be thinking. Wait a sec, let me fetch the coldest ones. I can be pretty choosy. With beer, at least. Always gotta be cold. Oh, *c'mon,* once in a while won't hurt. Figure I'm on the road to alcoholism anyway. Say what? You've been drinking for 20 years? You're way ahead of me. Let's see, I been drinking since I was 18, so that makes 10 years plus. Okay, okay, so maybe I'm a little loose with my numbers. But hey, who's to worry.

Me? Gee, I don't know. Well, I like my kids. What? You can't *mean* it. You *hate* kids? You *always* hated them? Well, take me, I didn't much like them myself when I was young. But I'm *glad* I had 'em. Say what? *Painless* delivery? It's like, *the* worst, says this friend of mine. Labor pains are just like climax with the *good* part missing. By the last of it, anything goes. No more no more, I can't *take* it! I can't *take* it! For*get* the kid! Cut me *open*, pull it *out*, do *any*thing! But by then *boom!* out comes the baby. Yeah, feels like you just took one *enormous* crap.

"*Did* it!" you think. "Done born, *finally!*" That one moment, all the pain, the whole nine heavy months, everything hits. I got so *emotional*. Soon as I saw the baby's face, I burst into tears. Talk about *happy*. This is *my* baby. What I been carrying all this time. I was *lucky*, 'cause I had the baby

in a university hospital. With a whole bunch of nursing students there. Pure and kindhearted still. They're working
hard, massaging my back, holding my hand. And *me*, I'm trying to make it easy for them too. No, *really*, I'm telling jokes,
making them laugh. We're having a *great* time, having a ball,
like, when the pains come. So we start having chats between
the contractions. *Until* I can feel the baby's on its way.

"I think it's coming," I tell the doctor. But they're all in an
uproar right then. Two delivery tables are in use, so this
other woman and me, we have to wait on labor tables.

"No, you've got a while to go, from the looks of you,"
says the doctor.

The delivery attendant checks, just in case. "Doctor, I can
see the head already!"

So they have me change places with one of the women on
the delivery tables and within *five* minutes, the baby's born.
Honest, it's gotta be one of the most important chapters in a
person's life. I'm *so* emotional and excited, soon as I see the
baby's face I start to cry. *One* attendant makes sure to tell the
others in my room and soon everyone's crying, all the student
nurses and delivery attendants, like in some fairy tale. Honest, my oldest was *so* cute. Well, who *knows* what anybody
else thought, but I could *look* at her all day long. She was
just *so* cute, I couldn't hardly stand it. *And* I was still young
and healthy. Could do housework, child raising, work, and
still have energy to burn. Didn't even bother me that my husband brought his pals home all the time. I'm such a softie,
anyway. Anytime anyone tells me "It's a wife's duty...," "It's
a mother's duty...," "It's a daughter-in-law's duty..."—which
is what my mother-in-law says—I'd do it. Now I realize how
selfish my husband was, thinking only of himself. But I went
along with it. If even the *teensiest* thing wasn't how he liked
it, boy, did *he* yell! He was *always* yelling. He's a little better
now, but *really*, I was miserable for the *longest* time. There I
was doing my *darndest*, but if anything wasn't right, he and
the mother-in-law *sure* complained. Most of the time, they'd

blame the way I *did* things. *Really.* Me, such a *lovely* wife
and a *lovely* daughter-in-law. And a *good* mother, too. On
top of that, I was even studying. Wanted to think that tomorrow'd be a *little* better than today. Guess I honest-to-good-
ness *believed* it, too. *Some*day, better times, they *had* to
come,...a big bright happy future. *Really*, I was so young.

I had second thoughts about having another baby. You
know, whether I could go on working with two kids. Wasn't
as young as when I had the first. And work was going well
too. But the sad truth was, even though my husband *did*
make fun of my job—called it *women's* work—we wouldn'ta
had enough to eat without it.

"It's tough being an only child," my husband says and,
well, I guessed I agreed that it was.

"You can stop working as soon as it gets to be too much,"
he says, like it was nothing. Is the guy *dense?* Like money
grows on trees or something. I tell him, his golf trips and
whoop-dee-dos with his pals, they happen only 'cause of my
working. but he simply can*not* understand. Yeah, just a big
baby. His mother's a tough old bird and his father's impossible too. Like father, like son, *right?* Yells at the drop of a hat.
Only *later* does he start to feel bad and acts, I dunno, like a
big *old* baby. Then he's fighting with the mother all the time.
Every New Year's they have one *doozie* of a fight, and she
ends up saying, "That does it, I'm leaving." I'd really rather
not be around them as it's lousy for the children, but as long
as we're together, my husband is always dragging me along
to his folks. Figures if *I'm* filial to his parents, then I'm doing
his share, too. The very *idea.* Hates to dirty his own hands.
Doesn't matter how dirty *mine* get. That's just how he is.
Queer fish, eh?

Anyway, it was one *hell* of a year. For one thing, my
English tutoring—I'm doing pretty well if I get, say, two new
first-year junior high students. This time I get *eight* kids. It
was *insane.* The primary school kids I had were all coming
on graduation. For a while there, looked like I'd be left high

and dry. Thought I'd be *desperate*, so I made up these flyers and passed 'em out every day. Even had the neighbors in on the act, handing 'em out like it's their business. Still, housewives are housewives. No *offense*, but, *well*, it's true. You used to work yourself, so it's different with you, but *them*, they hand out one measly flyer and it's a big thing. I'd been thinking to hand out maybe two *thousand*. Was even planning to knock on doors. A real *drag* and that's the truth. The neighbors? Picture it, they'd as soon play a *leisurely* game of tennis and here they are lugging a huge bag around in the drizzling rain. They get tired after a half hour. Not the fun they thought it'd be. One woman even got all dolled up to hand 'em out. *That* and their know-it-all comments like, "This'll be fun" or "One house call and they'll sign up for sure." As if it were *that* easy. With flyers alone, you're doing great if you get one taker for every thousand you hand out. And knocking on doors, fifty house calls might snag you one student. And you know, it's not cool for a teacher to be drumming up business herself. Looks like you're *begging*, and the parents and students give you no respect. Best to hire yourself a pro, but *expensive*. Fifteen thousand yen per student signed, *plus* five percent of their monthly tuition. When I heard *that*, I knew I was in the wrong business.

I sure didn't expect so many new students! And then, of course, this is the year I go and get pregnant with my second. Soon as the second semester starts, I feel *awful*. Go to the hospital and you bet, I'm pregnant. "Give yourself a break before the next one," I'd been telling myself, but I get pregnant *just like that*. *One* time did it! What's worse, I'm verging on a miscarriage. The next-door neighbor gets the word, sees me fixing dinner, and breaks out crying. A regular rooming house, that condo. Walls like paper.

"Why should you have to fuss—your husband this, your husband that? Shouldn't *you* be relying on *him*?" the neighbor says. Hits like a *gong* right over my head. Here my husband's getting the full treatment and I wouldn't have dreamed of asking for a little tenderness myself. Pretty *dumb*, now that I think about it. All my friends' husbands, they're *so* kindhearted, every one of them. Yet, somehow, I'd figured them for the exceptions. And *now*, seems even my neighbors' husbands look after the children and fix dinner when their wives are sick. Oh, really? Well, aren't *you* the lucky one. *Wha—?* You mean he fixes meals on his days off? And does the shopping, too? C'mon, enough already.

Wasn't much later, my ovaries got all screwed up. Ended up in emergency. Thought I was built solid, but went and overdid it. Never rains till it pours, in buckets. *Really.* That's the time my husband yelled up a storm at the hospital.

Yelled when I had my first too. He's sure sweet with *other* people, though. When his pals bring their wives over, he's passing out cushions for the pregnant ones and all. Real nice to his pals. Even when we were just married, had his pals over practically every day, one or another staying overnight more often than not. No, *really*, if you add up all the guys who stayed over, comes to *quite* a number. And here's the bride, sleeping all alone, while he spends the night with his pals. I wondered if he was gay at first. Too bad, woulda made a *dandy* divorce case.

But back to going into the hospital. I was in my third month with the youngest. Had an operation, full anesthetic. They make a mistake the first time, had to operate a second time. How come? Well, I dragged myself into the hospital the day before a three-day weekend. Mother Dear was visiting. Heard I was in danger of miscarrying and was only *too happy* to drop by. Can't even visit her own daughter without a reason. You'da thought she was over for a good time. The woman, she doesn't give a *hoot* about my welfare. But, that's the kind of mother she is. I can't barely walk down that dark hospital hall, and what does she do, she settles her fanny in a chair and says, "Boy, am I pooped!" Sounds like my husband, *don't* it?

Me, her own *daughter*, so edgy now, I'm ready to *cry*.

Same as when I'm in the hospital and I say I'm in pain and, my husband says, "So what, can't be as bad as I feel."

"Bet it wouldn't matter much if I up and died would it?" I half dig at my mother, and she tells me, "But then I wouldn't have a place to go!" without so much as batting an eye. No joke. It's the *truth*. All the grief she's put me through, and then I have to go and get stuck with this husband. Is this fate or what?

So okay. It's the night before the long weekend and all the doctors and attendants are dying to get *out* of there. They're going, "Say we operate first thing next week" and making ready to leave. Fiddle around in somebody's insides, then up and go home, just like that. I figure, you can't just *leave* me like this, after poking around where it hurts. Come on, *do* something—*any*thing! Cut me open, anywhere you like. The doctors, they fiddle around a bit, but they don't see how my screwed up my ovaries are. All they say is there *might* be a problem with my uterus or something. They have this big discussion, and they give in. Emergency surgery it is. *Banzai!* I'm thinking. If they operate right away, things'll be okay. Intuition, I guess. Turns out, if they hadn't operated, I coulda gone into shock—maybe *died*—is what a nurse tells me later. They round up all the staff on the double.

"I'm right in the middle of eating some grilled liver"—the anesthesiologist. "Wouldn't ya know it. I just got home"—a nurse. "My wife's going to kill me. Already told her I'm on my way home"—the chief doctor.

"Oh I'm *so* sorry. Just when yall are about to go on holiday and all for little ol' *me* ," the patient smiles, all shy and ready to please. The picture of harmony in the operating room.

"I promise we'll sew you up beautifully," says the chief doctor.

"*My*, how *kind* of you. Thank you *very* much."

Intravenous feeding, catheter tubes, bedpans. I'm counting on my fingers the days till I'm released. Stitches come out, then one more week and I can go home.

"I made a big mistake at work, thanks to you," my husband says. That's right—turn around and blame it on me. Is this anything to say to a wife who flashes him a now-don't-you-worry-dear V-for-victory sign as she's being wheeled into the operating room? Well, guess that's doing good by him.

Bedpans, so of *course* I get constipated. My stomach's bloated. Which means no appetite. University hospital food stinks anyway.

"I'd love to have something nice to eat," I say to a husband who, 'cause of his work—or so he says—rarely visits. And *then* only to yell, "Stop being so selfish, you've had your operation, haven't you?" Just *once* my mother-in-law brings me *sushi* and gives me this *dirty* look.

Oh yeah, the *second* operation. Just one more week to go till I'm out. And I have to go and sneeze. *Ah-aah-aachoo!* A killer of a sneeze. Surprised myself, even. *That* did it. Hear this *swoosh* sound. What? Where? The incision? *Panic!* I grab my stomach and there's blood all over my hands. Every ounce of strength in my body just *goes*. They carry me out on a stretcher, to the operating room, again. Must be my lucky day, I think.

When they operate, I'm practically naked and it's winter too. What now? The heat's not on. That's right, the heater's busted. The anesthesiologist isn't the same old hand as last time, but some intern, learning as he goes along. I figure this is the end.

The anesthetic doesn't take. Not where it hurts in my stomach anyway. It's my feet that go numb. Pretty funny, huh. The doctors all go into a huddle.

"What'll it be? Sew 'er up as-is?" Meanwhile I'm *freezing* and the pain's even worse. Oh *please*, let's just get it o*ver* with. "We'll give you a little something to put you to sleep," they say and add something to my drip.

Then, next thing I know, I'm headed off to the great beyond. Didn't I *tell* you? Seems to me I told you this before.

But anyway, here's what happened.

I'm in this dark tunnel. Just trudging along in there. I can see a small light far ahead. Must be the way out. Keep walking closer and this bright light starts flooding everywhere. Don't remember much about it, 'cept that it was real nice. People dancing 'round in a circle like children, flowers blooming, wonderful just to be there. Pure *bliss*. Probably the happiest I ever felt in my entire life. I wanted to stay forever.

"Time to go home," someone says. Oh no, I don't want to go back. I want to stay here. I want to stay here forever. I don't want to leave. But return it is, that much I *know*. This time, I'm strapped onto this trolley thing and zoomed away high speed.

"Come in contact with the darkness of the tunnel and that part of your body will be lost," a voice threatens, so I scrunch myself up good and tight.

Suddenly the trolley brakes and I'm thrown into space. I look down and see myself, under lights, there on the operating table, looking like this amazingly tiny person.

"I don't wanna go back there!" As soon as I think this, *there* I am, back in my body. Feeling absolutely miserable. I don't want to forget this, I figure, so I tell the doctors the whole weird story. Too bad I can't remember everything now.

"Well, if it was such a great place, maybe I'll just send you *back* there, huh," the doctor says.

"If I go again, I'm never coming back."

Now, you got to *watch* yourself around a sick person. They can see right through you. It's the *truth*. They can see clear into a person's heart. So that's when I start thinking of leaving my husband. And that's when I see my mother-in-law thinking, "Just as well she dies along with that half-formed kid." Friends and neighbors come by. I can see, *plain* as day, who is worried about me, who was glad, who was disappointed I am getting well. My friendships sure changed course from then on. I was smiles-all-around up till I got sick. Used to be nice to everybody, doing all kinds of things for people. But when I realized that this life and this body is all I got, well, what's the point of sacrificing myself, and even my kids, for someone else's sake? I hadn't told you this yet—the *ugliest* part. My husband and mother-in-law told me to get rid of the baby. Mother-in-law said the same thing about my first one. Said, seeing as I was likely to lose it *any*way. My being a tutor's pretty rough on the body, besides, she said.

"The old lady says you're too free with your time," my husband tells me even. Had to contain myself after *that* one.

Later, well, it's one hell after another. I never *do* get my health back. Looking after two kids. Work's tough, too. The husband, he wouldn't *dream* of lending a hand. Wants it sweet and fresh-squeezed and nothing but. Let *others* have it not so good. All the *tasty* parts, he wants for himself. Oh well, same old story. And my youngest, he's not too strong—been to doctors, in and out of hospitals. Got to be I couldn't even find the time to think. Each day, a struggle just t'get through. Once a week, my mother-in-law'd come to visit, s'pposedly to look after the kids, but it's "Do this, do that"—nothing but *orders*. And good daughter-in-law that I am, I *do* it all. Listened to everything my husband said, too. Habit, I guess. You know what they say: tie a slave down long enough and they forget what freedom is. Well, that's how it was with me. Still, I held up somehow, making do by hook or by crook.

Then, last summer—you know *this* part—I discovered *Elvis*, right out of the blue. Never been busier at work, with most students studying for entrance exams, half of them for the university. It was *one hell of a* year. Wasn't feeling well *at all*, but here I was still scurrying 'round at top speed. "Keep this up and you'll burn yourself out," I told myself. "Burn myself out and what'll I have lived for?" All of a sudden, *every*thing lost its meaning. Life's still moving right along, but inside—*nothing*. Wasn't s'pposed to be this way. Wasn't this the best year ever for work? Come next year, the youngest goes to nursery school. Things'll get easier. You'll be able to do what you want. Oh, I *told* myself this over and over, but the emptiness just hung around. That's when it was, *Elvis*'s singing suddenly came through to me. *Really.* 'Course I liked him before, in junior high and high school. Liked him ever since, too, but lost his records somewhere along the way. And I'm not like my husband, with *time* on my hands to enjoy music—well, the truth is, I'd forgotten *all* about Elvis. Then, suddenly, Elvis's songs were *there*, slipping into the hollow places in my heart. Boy, was *that* a surprise. I liked Elvis before, but I never realized how *great* he was. With his singing, he shakes a person to the *bottom* of their soul. There I am, listening to his songs and collecting his videos, and I realize that the harder I look, the more my own life is losing its color. Or, no, my life has in fact always been like that—only I hadn't ever noticed. To me, wasn't no one *living* so much as *him* singing there in the videos. So full of *life*, it was a *miracle*. Too full of life to be *true.* You'd think, this is the only person in the whole *world* really living. He's so *full* of life. And that depressed me. 'Cause I saw how I had been *dying* away in life. I knew I was one *mess* of a sorry person. I'd been *lonesome* all this time and hadn't even noticed.

No, I'm not drunk. Okay, you're pretty happy, ya? *But*, could be you just think so. Bottom line is, people are *lonesome, lonely* things. They just cover it up somehow. Me, I hadn't even figured that one out.

What have I *done* with my life? I was thinking.

And then *he* sang:

> No *day goes by wasted—*
> *Each and every day's special—*
> *Each life's got its own special meaning.*

Way *I* figure it, that's Osaka dialect he's singing in. Now isn't that *some*thing! Memphis—the Osaka of America!

Really. From then on, I was *born* again. A *new* woman. Oh, you've seen it. I started writing like a soul *possessed.* To me, that was my reason for living. Maybe if I had a voice, I woulda been a singer. But I started writing as I can't carry a tune. No, I'm almost tone deaf. Isn't it *some*thing, though? Here I am tone deaf, and Elvis's songs get to me all the same? It's in*cred*ible. You know something? Elvis, the man, he helps alcoholics go straight. He saves physically and mentally handicapped children. *And* he helps me.

No kidding. I was able to talk back to my mother-in-law for the *first* time. And *that* did it—cut me off for life. What a relief! *Really*. My husband, he was pretty mad. That's right, he tells me, "I want a divorce." Actually came out and said it. Who'da thought that? And *me*, I just said, "Nope."

My daughter says, "Mom, I've never seen you get mad at Grandma before. First time you gave Dad what he deserves too." Even she's on my side. Up to then, I *hated* myself. My life was just sort of drifting here and there. Even now, I can't say I like myself *that* much. But I sure do like myself a *whole* lot better than before. I like myself a little more each day. Thanks to *Elvis*. If I'd kept on the way I was, I probably wouldn't even be in this world right now.

Sproing! The strings of fate just snapped.

Really. I didn't know it, but I had really high blood pressure. Two hundred over one-forty, they said. Can you *believe* it? Happened when they announced the results of the entrance exams. Went to see my students' scores, but all of a sudden, I felt just *terrible*. Called for an ambulance, then and there. You didn't know? And here we live in the *same* building.

"Teacher, it'd be a disgrace to have you die on us like that," my students told me. *Honest*. And I wouldn'ta known what I'd lived for either. Sure, when I think about it, I *do* like kids. Well, a *little*, anyway. I like my own, and I like my students too.

Ding dong!

Darn it! Went and forgot about the nursery school bus. Hey, I'm *sorry*. Here I've kept you so long, huh? Poor you

had to go and listen to the whole boring story. Say *what?*
You want me to listen to *yours* next time? But *you*, you've
got it made. You're happy enough with your husband and
kids, *right?* Got a *saint* for a mother-in-law too.

"Okay okay, forgive me. I went and forgot. Coming *right*
this minute. So, tell me, what happened? What about the picture of Jack and the Beanstalk? That *so?* Well, there you are!
Just like Mommy told you, huh? Teacher kept it for you."

Oh, okay, see you later. Drop by *any*time, you hear.

When I'm not busy with work, I mean. That time's no
good. Sure I'll lend you an ear. Okay, *gotcha*. When the kids
are away, eh? Kids can be *such* a bother. Okay, be seeing you.

First published, 1987
TRANSLATION BY MONA TELLIER

Eri Makino (b. 1953), a promising new author, writes with a frank-
ness and unsentimentality that goes against the weepiness charac-
teristic of older women writers. First published only four years ago
after her purchase of a word processor, Makino looks at the sham
of the Japanese male and speaks her mind. A rebel against the long-
standing convention of a separate "women's literature," she docu-
ments in *Turn-Down Tales* (1988) the entire rejection-slip process
of trying to publish in a Japan dominated by what she calls "men's
literature." This did not, however, stop her from winning the 4th
Waseda New Writer's Award for *Sproing!* (1987). With a sure ear
for the humor of her native Osaka dialect, also given free rein in
her novella *Entertainment* (1987), Makino's writing leaps gutsy
and full of life from the mouth of the average Japanese housewife—the average housewife who has found Elvis. Her latest novel
is *A Voice in the Dark* (1989).

CHRISTOPHER COLUMBUS DISCOVERS AMERICA

Gen'ichiro Takahashi

Sunday 16 September 1492

Heading west, we sailed day and night for perhaps thirty-nine leagues, though we added only thirty-six leagues. These days were somewhat overcast, with a little rain. Whence the Admiral declared that hereafter we would be blessed with such truly fine weather, fresh from morning on, should a nightingale but sing, we would have the perfect "April in Andalusia." It was then we began to spot bunches of extraordinarily green plants come floating up one after the next. The plants seemed to have come from land, so one and all thought we drew near some island. Yet the Admiral declared that we were not near any continent, that "the Continent is much further."

—Bartolomé de Las Casas,
The Voyages of Columbus

Actually, I always wanted to be Christopher Columbus.
To become Christopher Columbus!
To discover the Continent of America!

Spring 1972.

"Now, what does little _____ want to be when she grows up? A bride perhaps? A nurse?"

Full of smiles, the teacher posed the question to one little girl in the Fourth Group of the First Grade of Tateno Municipal Elementary School in Yokohama. The teacher had learned to do this at her alma mater, Tsukuba University. Ask them questions like these, they'd said.

"I want to be Christopher Columbus," answered the one little girl.

A brief silence.

"You must not say that."

That was the teacher's answer. Or, rather, Tsukuba University's answer. No, maybe not Tsukuba's. It might have been the answer of Takeshi Muramatsu, the professor under whom the teacher had written her graduation thesis, "The Jewish Question in Kafka." Hard to say where the answer came from.

"Good children do not grow up to be Christopher Columbus."

"O–kay."

The little girl decided to take it in stride. It would be a big stride. That's because she was a nice little girl.

Well, if I can't become Christopher Columbus all at once, I guess I could start with something simpler. After all, I'm only in the first grade. I could wait until high school.

So, the little girl said:

"Gee, then I'll settle on being _physically handicapped_. I mean, wouldn't it be great to have a _handicap_ in my _phys_."

The little girl really loved the sound of the words _physically handicapped_. Granted, she loved the sound of _Christopher Columbus_ much more.

Why sure, there was something ineffably sweet-yet-sour a-bout _physically handicapped_. It tasted of things to come, of hope.

Physically handicapped—the words welled up in the breast. Not unlike the classic "hep" college student getting off on words like *fuck*, though our revolutionary grade-schooler tuned in on words far more intense. Still nothing as flash as *Christopher Columbus*.

But this was not the sort of behavior a teacher could tolerate. *Physically handicapped,* for this rather passe teacher trainee, was also not the most awesome sound she'd ever heard.

"*That is a no-no!*"

"Teacher!" Having watched the whole play-by-play between the little teacher and the girl, Mookie, the First Grade Fourth Group's "Little Romancer," raised his hand.

"A while ago, I said I wanted to be an instructor at Yoyogi Seminar when I grow up, but that was a lie. Actually, I wanna be Christopher Columbus, too. And if that's no good, then *physically handicapped* would be okay. And the same goes for Hookie and Yuckie. Right, yah?"

Hookie and Yuckie both nodded like crazy.

"*That is a no-no.* Please think it over. What would it be like if everyone was Christopher Columbus or *physically handicapped*? That would really be a problem."

"No problem by me," said Seiko, the Class Rep. "Not any that I can see 'specially."

This is how little Seiko imagined the whole thing: Father would be Christopher Columbus and Mother would be *physically handicapped* and Big Brother would be Christopher Columbus and she, Seiko would be either Christopher Columbus *or physically handicapped*. What a fab family! A real Emperor's Prize derby-winner of a household. It had the makings of greatness.

"Teacher, you oughta become Christopher Columbus, too," said little Seiko.

"Either that or *physically handicapped*."

"Children, please be serious! Is that what you honestly think?"

"Yeah."

"Yeah."

"Yeah."

And as proof, all the kids who usually disagreed with little Seiko—Matchi and Toshi and Yotchan and Nahoko and Iyo and Akina and Yoshie—agreed on this point unanimously.

"Very well, then," said the teacher. "You just wait. I have to talk with the principal about this."

The teacher left.

And what do *you* think you would have to say to the principal?

Can't you see it? While you're strutting your drumsticks off to the principal's office, your First Grade Fourth Group kids have, in their fondest wishes, all set sail to discover the American Continent.

"Okay, then," said Mookie. "To America! Let's go!"

SIX WAYS TO BECOME CHRISTOPHER COLUMBUS AND DISCOVER AMERICA

Nine years pass.

The female, whom we might call the evolution of our revolutionary grade schooler, and I sit side-by-side on a bed. We have very little on.

Even so, I have no idea what I am supposed to do now. I can't figure out how to take the first step, what opportunity to grab.

"I want some money, okay?"

That's what the female says as I peel off her T-shirt and she kisses me.

"Really, I want some money!" She repeats herself as she tugs at her 27-inch Levi's on the bed. "This is capitalism. Don't you ever forget it," she adds for good measure while guiding my hand to where her breasts are supposed to be. Only I can't find them. I am confused.

"Hey, you don't go for boys, do you?"

"No."

"Well then..."

There is nothing to do but engage her in conversation, or *some*thing. That way, the least opportunity has but to present itself and I can do what you're supposed to do.

So, about the Continent of America.

Where was I now? I guess I must be stupid.

"There are six ways to become Christopher Columbus and discover America," I say.

"Really?"

"Uh-huh."

"Well, okay then, the *Six Ways to Become Christopher Columbus* will do instead of money."

The female removes her panties as if the act were sacred.

"All right. Fire away."

I try doing what I think you're supposed to do in a situation like this. But—what's going on?—she slaps me in the face.

"Prevert! *Do what you're* supposed *to do!*"

It seems I am supposed to tell her about the *Six Ways to Become Christopher Columbus.*

The first way is to *make a map for going to America, pack a lunch, and set out one bright clear afternoon.* Don't forget the compass and canteen. Wear sneakers. No special dress required.

First, make a map. A thorough, detailed map.

Let me explain what sort of map to make.

Say you start off from *here* (call it a coffee shop). The road goes straight for 30 yards. Then there's a cigarette stand on the corner, so naturally you have to turn right. Fine, you follow the gentle bend in the road toward the elementary school, ignoring the lame boy you might see running by. Yes, and also ignore the fact that there used to be an oak tree at the bus stop you just passed. But what about the young woman coming this way? Ignore her too. The American

Continent is more important to you at this point than any young woman. Reach the crossroads yet? Like it or not, you have to hang a left. Walk along the stone wall—you haven't got much choice—and you'll see a plaque with a name on it. Attention now. Not that there's any direct bearing on our present discovery of America, but that plaque should bear the name Shuntaro Tanikawa—you know, the poet. So you crossed a bridge, did you? Don't stop to look at the river now! There, you've found the VIVO vending machine. Fine. From here on, the going gets complicated, so be very careful. See that narrow alleyway between the PIPIN' HOT COOKIN' and the HEIWA SOGO BANK? Where it's too tight for a TOYOTA SKYLINE, but a HONDA CIVIC might squeeze through? So in, in you go. Thirteen yards on the left is a condom vending machine. Once you've gotten this far, look off at a 45° angle to your right. See the tiny Shinto shrine, complete with Inari fox statues and a fortune vending machine? Congratulations, you've made it. The Continent of America is right behind that.

Bet you're blown away.

See how easy it is to become Christopher Columbus?

No way, José. That'll never get off the shelf.

Our explanation up to now has only looked at the theoretical side of the question.

So let's move on to practical considerations. But first, jot down that map.

After that, all we've left to do is set out.

So here we go, map in hand!

Whereupon you get all in a frazzle (or maybe you don't) because the following just happens to occur to you.

From what "coffee shop" are we supposed to start out? Eh? Every coffee shop in the world can be called a "coffee shop," even specifically so. Of course, nobody bothered to check this out. Abstract "cafés" may appear in Raymond Queneau novels, but you can't drink *café au lait* in any of

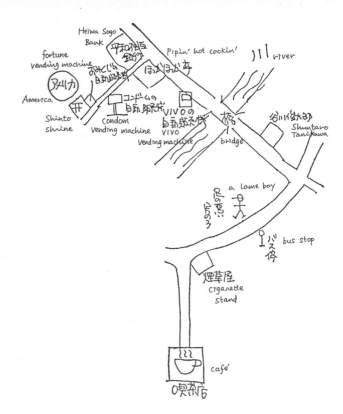

them, so what do you say we pass them up this time? Now if I could, I'd put in my vote for the ST. LAURENT ISHIKAWACHO SHOP (045-651-3808), where you can pretend to read *Madame Bovary* while looking at girls from the American School crossing their long beautiful legs as they struggle with strange-sounding Japanese constructions: "To-me-you-bring-a-cup-of-coffee-okay?"

The real world, however, is cruel.

So, map in hand, you set out from the ST. LAURENT ISHIKAWACHO SHOP, but before you reach any cigarette stand, you fall right into a *real* river. Sorry. The map is correct but the real world is wrong. It happens.

To continue, then, after much in-depth study of *Angle*

magazine, you set off from one of the most popular coffee shops for girls in Yokohama, the MOTOMACHI PARK NETTLE TREE ARBOR (045-623-2288). By the very same criteria, you could just as easily have opted for the EAST KANAGAWA STAR- DUST (045-441-1017), a ¥590 taxi ride away from Yokohama Station, and you know that the actress Kumiko Akiyoshi sometimes goes there. Still, the fact is, there's nothing around but seaside there, so you'd have to take another taxi to East Kanagawa Station to find a place that sells cigarettes.

Well, then, taking the MOTOMACHI PARK NETTLE TREE ARBOR as your starting point, you proceed 30 yards to discover that you can turn right at the public toilets. "So far so good," you find yourself muttering. They can turn the public toilet into a cigarette stand from tomorrow. You've cleared the first barrier. But where the bus stop is supposed to be is only a rough plastered wall with a plaque engraved with a poem by Willam Blake. Meanwhile, coming toward you are thundering herds of irrepressibly spirited matrons from the Motomachi Shopkeepers Association, all stuffed into skimpy tennis wear. For a second there, your spirits nearly nosedive.

Nonetheless, you quickly recover. In the city of Yokohama, with changeovers from a radical to conservative to reform to middle-of-the-road mayor, it's been decreed that buses stop not at bus stops but at poems. That's got to be it.

If it's earlier or later, you could see a lame boy or a young woman. Yes, yes.

You're getting the feel for this. Eventually you run into, not a crossroads, but a fork in the road. No matter.

To the right is that golf course the Seibu Group bought up. Okay, okay. So you fleetfoot it past not Shuntaro Tanikawa but the loan firm ACOM MOTOMACHI BRANCH. Why sure, this is the ACOM MOTOMACHI BRANCH which lends out Shuntaro Ṭanikawa at 73 percent interest per annum. That's it, that's it.

You gradually pick up the pace and walk straight into the, luckily, open front gate of the YOKOHAMA CHINATOWN

SCHOOL and out through the back gate. Somehow, it feels like a bridge you'd just crossed. That's it, that's it, that's it. Let's just keep it at that. What say we kept it at that.

The Continent of America is just a little further.

Then suddenly you grind to a halt.

You can't go another step forward.

Directly in front of you is—a mountain? an abuttment?—a huge obstacle jutting up at a 75° angle. A concrete piling common enough.

Care to climb over it? If you don't mind taking your life into your hands, that is.

Herein lies the difficulty of trying to discover the American Continent in *Yokohama*. There're hills everywhere, waterways everywhere, dead-ends all over the place.

Still, not to despair. On such a bright clear afternoon, why not take your time, have your lunch and continue on later? Isn't that why you packed your lunch?

Hey? Where d'you think you're going, *staggering* around like that?

Letting *it* get to you, are you? I've made the same mistake too, you know.

The police box right here on the left. I also believed there was the slightest possibility it was really the VIVO vending machine and tried inserting a hundred-yen coin. But instead of canned coffee, all I got was a canned cop.

Let me tell you about a friend who came closest to the mark.

He started out from the HOTEL NEW GRAND Coffee Shop. The hotel which MacArthur occupied in 1945. He—my friend—was a dedicated reader of Mitsuru Yoshida's *The End of the Battleship Yamato*, so he had his eye on the HOTEL NEW GRAND Coffee Shop. Of course, the real clincher came when he saw the last episode of *Starship Yamato* on TV.

CHANCELLOR DETHLER: From dusk to dawn, when all is naught, verily something will come again. Hallelujah, good-for-nothing scum of Terra!

After the TV show was over, he got up to go to the toilet. There, he leaned against the wall and sobbed out loud. For years now, he'd harbored close feelings for Dethler. But never had he imagined that Dethler read Roland Barthes! Poor Dethler! Poor Combatant Kodai!

So, near midnight, he made his departure from the HOTEL NEW GRAND Coffee Shop. Because he'd been in a hurry and hadn't had time to pack a lunch, he bought a PIPIN' HOT COOKIN' two-hundred-fifty-yen "seaweed special."

He walked 30 yards and bought two packs of Kents at the vending maching beside the front desk. And what do you think happened?

Isn't that a *young woman* stealing down from upstairs and isn't she shielding a *lame boy?* We're on a roll!

That was proof enough.

The Continent of America was right there inside the HOTEL NEW GRAND.

He raced upstairs.

Midway he ran into a drunk sitting on the stairs, singing *The Rain Has Cleared* to himself. He was so far gone, his voice broke into three parts—bass, tenor, and boy soprano.

"Isn't there supposed to be a bus stop around here?"

"Man, you drunk'r sump'n?" said the drunk. "Your talkin' to me's a bass stop. And the last run done be gone. You gonna have t'wait a while."

Proof enough. The American Continent must be nearby.

He was overcome with an inexpressibly profound sense of fulfillment.

Finally, the real world seemed to coincide with the map.

And on he went. That was the last ever seen of him. He vanished without a trace, there in the HOTEL NEW GRAND.

Three years later, I received a New Year's card from my friend. Postmarked Beijing, China:

Zdhravstvuitche Tovarich!
   Please be very careful when you use that map. What I took for America landed me in China. It was no fun, let me tell you. I'd like to see the guy who made that map. But what the hell, given my recent state, I figured I might as well search for America here. At least over here you can draw a salary to look for America. The Chinese call it "modernization." A kind of countermeasure against unemployment. Which is fine, but since there's no PIPIN' HOT COOKIN' and no HEIWA SOGO BANK here in China, I don't know where to turn. What's worse, there aren't even any bridges or rivers. If I complain, my Chinese comrades accuse me of "running dog-ism" and put me down as "hopelessly square!"
   "Make bridges where there are no bridges. Make rivers where there are no rivers. Make an American Continent, whatever it takes."
So say they. But I ask you, Tovarich, isn't that a cheap compromise? What and ho!
   PS: I got a Chinese girlfriend. Works as a stylist, sometimes models for *Fashion News*. Her grandfather is famous for having played mahjong with Mao Tse-tung. She's a good kid most of the time, but whenever I bring up Japan and suggest making the scene together, all she says is, "There are so many communists in that country, I'd be frightened to go"—and she starts to cry.
   Oh yes, about the coffee shop for the starting point, could it be the COFFEE SHOP ELENA next to the HOTEL PAVILION OF DREAMS? I just get that feeling. The PAVILION ÓF DREAMS runs ¥4,000 for

a "rest" and ¥7,000 for an "overnight," with a ¥2,000 surcharge for a Japanese-style room with *tatami* mats. Geographically speaking, I'd thought it was where Feliz College coeds and assistant profs went to make out, but apparently it's the girls from Yokohama Women's Business Academy who go there for nooners. Makes sense, don't you think?

Ring me in the event you set out from the ELENA and reach America. Call Direct Dial Beijing. But if you wind up in China instead, let's get together. Fridays and Saturdays, I'm knocking 'em back all day long.

So if, under the gentle sunlight of Beijing, you see a Japanese guy drinking Campari-sodas with the Rolling Stones blaring straight into his ear for lack of a Walkman DD, say hello. It'll be me. Take care.

Yours in friendship

Key West Club
Tienanmen Square, Beijing

The second way is to *say something clear*. The third way is to *say something unclear*.

On these subjects, I am something of an authority, if I do say so myself. I've been exposed to them practically every day since birth, and that's no exaggeration. My mother, for instance, who has kept at her meaningless utterances for some fifty-four years without fail and yet has never shown any sign of becoming Christopher Columbus, was talking about giving it all up next New Year's, but I talked her into waiting at least until she's eligible for social security.

"'Haste makes waste,' as the saying goes," says I.

"Don't they also say, 'Proof, not theory'?" retorts Mother.

This morning I find my young woman crouching on the

bed in delicate, white string panties and a windbreaker, trying to do an assortment of things.

She tries rolling dice in her head as fast as she can: six seconds sharp. A Nobel Prize–class accomplishment, she thinks.

A misthought. Persons with an IQ of 180 or above are said to be able to roll mental dice in four-and-a-half seconds. I learn from the fellow in the next bed in the psychiatric ward that there was a Nobel Prize–winning physiologist involved in these studies. This fellow could roll three dice in his head and have them all come up snake eyes. A fact which allowed all the other psychiatric patients to play craps in the fellow's head.

My young woman then extends her legs and gazes at *something of slight interest* off in space 10 centimeters from the tip of her toes.

This, too, proves pleasurable.

Apparently it gets her quite excited.

So I decide to throw in my one bit.

"Just now, was that something unclear I heard you say?"

"Uh-huh. Seems I did say something unclear. And to think that I'm the one who's always putting things so clearly. Surprised?"

"Umm."

"Sorry."

"Don't mention it."

That's when she decided to have some coffee. Anything else would have done just as well.

"Man, that's coffee."

"Uh-huh, bought it at the store. Oops! Said something unclear again. Today must be an off day for me."

The woman faces me with a big grin. It feels great to be told and telling unclear things.

Next, the woman and I sit down side-by-side on the floor and pour over a dumb dirty photobook and a dumb gruesome photobook I'd borrowed for her. Of course, anything else would have been perfectly all right.

"Filthy..."

"Mmm."

"Filthy..."

"Mmm."

"Filthy..."

"Mmm."

"Okay, let's look at the next."

The fun of looking at dumb genitalia has worn thin, so we move on to have fun looking at dumb wars and dumb accidents and dumb refugees and dumb...

"Horrible..."

"Mmm."

"Horrible..."

"Mmm."

"Horrible..."

"Mmm."

"Horrible..."

"Mmm."

"Okay, all done."

She shimmies to her feet. *Her eyes gleaming.* I wait for words to float forth from her lips.

Clear or unclear, one way or another, this would lead to becoming Christopher Columbus; it is all the same to me. Sometimes, though, there are moments that beat becoming Christopher Columbus.

And this, right now, is one of these.

She tells me:

"Let's eat."

The fourth way is the *Hanshin Tigers*. The fifth way is *William Shakespeare*. And the sixth way is *you-know-what*. If you want to know why, then you'd best ask him directly. I may not know myself, but maybe you can figure it out.

Walk three minutes from the north exit of Kannai Station.

Wait on the sidewalk across from Carriage House No. 10. At 11 P.M., which is closing time, you'll see employees put him and a plastic wash-bucket out on the pavement. They'll wrap him in a blanket to keep him from freezing. And they'll top him off with the Hanshin Tigers' baseball cap on his head.

"Go on home," the employees will say. Since 1974, Carriage House No. 10 has kept at him with the same message. During the intervening years, the upstairs bar has changed bartenders four times. The Hiroshima Carp have won three pennants, the Yakult Swallows once, the Chunichi Dragons once, and the Yomiuri Giants the rest of the baseball seasons.

"Go on home."

"I hate the phone ringing. Really hate it. So I'm always on edge when I'm home, worrying that the phone's going to ring."

Last night promised to give him a coat of snow.

"He'll catch his death," said my woman.

"Let's go rescue him," said my daughter.

We headed out. The fool needed rescuing. But there wasn't a taxi on the streets. The snow was so thick.

Snow kept coming down like crazy on the fire department patrol car that had skidded sideways in front of the Yokohama Harbor Post Office. Snow kept coming down like crazy on the fireman sitting idly on the steps smoking a cigarette.

"How goes it?" I asked the fireman.

"Like how? Like this," said the fireman under his breath. "Miserable snow."

Snow kept coming down like crazy even on his cigarette.

"It's all so white, a man can't tell what's his own cigarette."

By the time we got to Carriage House No. 10, he was virtually snowbound. His blanket was all covered in snow; the Hanshin Tigers' cap too. The only thing not covered with snow was under the overhang of the Hanshin Tigers.

"Jeepers!" exclaimed my woman.

"A snowman."

"Get up and go on home," I said to the man under the overhang. His eyelids twitched.

"Grandpa. You're a terrible sight," sympathized my daughter.

"Get it off of me. Whatever it is that weighs so much, get it off, quick," he groaned. Talking in his sleep, of course.

"It's real heavy."

"Good riddance."

We divide up the task of scooping the snow from off of him.

"It's off now, Grandpa."

"Still weighs a ton."

"Well, then. Brush, brush, how's that?"

"Still heavy."

"Dumbcluck!" Suddenly, my daughter blew her top.

"Stay buried in the snow for all we care!"

That opened his eyes.

Whereupon he saw the funniest thing.

Standing there in a white field of furiously falling white stuff, this large white thing, medium white thing and small white thing. Us.

"I wish you wouldn't hate me." He was on the verge of tears. "I'm sure I probably said *you-know-what.* again. But that's a problem for me too. I mean, I'm always fast asleep when I say *you-know-what.*, and any girl who hears me say it gets up and leaves. I never know what I said."

"You didn't say anything. So let's go on home."

"I wish you wouldn't hate me."

"We don't hate you. Let's go home."

"Sure. Only now, my eyelids won't open."

"Fool, it's only the snow on your eyelashes. We'll brush it off. There."

The first time he said *you-know-what.*, he was two years old. He was down with the mumps. His mother, who had him in bed with her, heard him say it.

His mother grieved deeply; in fact, it was said to have been the death of her.

"Boy, you better not sleep with girls. They'll only hate you for it. Also, remember to brush your teeth every day. It doesn't look good for an intellectual to have bleeding gums when he bites into an apple. Other finer points, I'm jotting down in a note for you; read it carefully. Oh yes, tomorrow's Tuesday; don't forget to put out the garbage. Okay, I'm going to die now."

Those were his mother's last words. But it was to no avail.

Because eventually, the day came for his first time with a girl. Call it fate, call it whatever.

This pretty much ought to be right.
Still, something wasn't happening.
Odd.
It was the girl's first time, too.
Down a bit lower. No, higher.
Ahem.
Hmm?
Like this?
Aaah!
Okay, then, let's call a time-out.

Too tense, maybe? Or possibly just some deeper disquietude from having read Yoshiyuki's *Until Dusk* the day before. Good novel, but useless at times like these.

Nothing a good night's sleep wouldn't clear up, though. The two of them fell asleep in each other's arms. All snug in the musky odor and wet heat, he dreamed the scenario that was to be his life in diorama. And the inescapable consequence of it was, he had to scream *you-know-what.*

He woke up.

The girl was sobbing as she gathered up the articles of clothing she'd neatly folded as she had undressed; she put them back on in reverse order. All except for the brassiere-then-panties. The last thing she'd taken off had been her panties, yet the first thing she put on was her push-up half-cup brassiere. Force of habit.

"You creep! You didn't have to say *you-know-what.*, did you?"

He planned to become a dramatist. First, he tried went the typical avant-garde playwright route. That didn't require any special intelligence.

Stage center: a roast chicken and a man in a Nazi uniform. A telephone keeps ringing. Man gives in, lifts receiver.

"Hello, *God* here, er, having a few drinks in Kabukicho, maybe you'd care to come join me if you've got time?"

Big deal!

What he really wanted were *brilliant shining words.* Weren't there more *flowering words*?

He traced back to the fifteenth century to find a vein rich with brilliant shining words. *The Shoyo Tsubouchi Translation of William Shakespeare.*

So much for modern drama. Here was everything you could ever want in beautiful, elegant words. He immediately committed any number of Master Shakespeare's lines to memory.

For instance:

Romeo and Juliet, Act 3, Scene 5. Romeo wakes in bed and lovingly asks Juliet:

> What time is it?

Midsummer Night's Dream, Act 2, Scene 3. Oberon angrily scolds Puck for giving a love potion to the wrong partners:

> Nitwit!

The Merry Wives of Windsor, Act 2, Scene 2. That all-too-famous line, which Queen Elizabeth yells at Falstaff as he passes Buckingham Palace in a Yoshimura custom-tuned Suzuki 1000GS on his way to the Indy 500:

I say, a bike!

King Lear, Act 3, Scene 2. Those immortal words spoken by the Fool to mad Lear as he wanders o'er the barren fields:

Just like a big wig, eh! The jerk needs a fix and starts waving his sword. Of all the gall, I swear, *bibimba bibimba!*

He set off. William Shakespeare and Hanshin Tigers and his seventh girlfriend, all piled into a Winnebago. Every one of the previous six girls had left crying the first morning after.

A fellow he got to know at a Yoshinoya BEEF BOWL offered him the Winnebago he'd been living in. The man had never read a book. Whenever he opened his mouth, all he could say was a sad and somber "Let me 'ave a go"—worthy of a true Shakespearean.

They left Yokohama and headed west.

A voyage to spread the glorious words of the fifteenth century. A voyage to discover America.

Nonetheless, as soon as people caught sight of them, *they scurried away like hens.*

"*That's proof enough,*" said he.

"America can't be far."

"America can wait; how far to the nearest SKYLARK? I'm sick of hamburgers."

"Wanna get down and soon," muttered the fellow in the driver's seat. "Wanna get down and bad."

As it turned out, the only ones who understood them were kindergarteners. The kids didn't know William Shakespeare from nothing, but in their powers of comprehension you could even say they had one up on our performing friends.

Bottom of the ninth. No outs, bases loaded.

Runner-on-third Ophelia leads farther and farther off base.

Ace relief pitcher Claudius sends a hawk-eye racing

around the field to Ophelia.

"*Li-li-li-li O-phe–li-a! Li-li-li-li O-phe–li-a!*"

The kindergarteners' cheering comes to a pitch.

Two swings, three swings of the bat, pinch hitter Hamlet sidles into the batter's box.

CLAUDIUS: "What's wit'ya, Hammy? Saw last night's game on the tube. All those pop-ups, kiddo; you'll never hit a slow curve at that rate!"

HAMLET: "Wuz happenin', Claud-o? These balls you been throwing lately, I hear they have a hard time reachin' the plate! Maybe ya oughta send 'em by parcel post—like by Yamato Home Delivery?"

"*Lez–go! Lez–go! Ham–let! Ham–let!*"

Claudius feints a throw, determined to hold Ophelia on third.

Little girls are screaming in the stands.

"*Watch-out watch-out O-phe–li-a! Don't stray too far off base! Bumble-boy Hamlet's grip's so loose, you'll wind up in a squeeze play! No-go watch-out O–phe–li–a! You're gonna get it!*"

Hamlet, caught in the squeeze, swings his bat through empty air. Between second and third, Ophelia gets the sting. The kindergarteners go wild, some even climbing up on stage, hysterical as Elizabethan theater-goers.

"*Knave!! Scoundrel!! Claudius-you-bag'o'piss!! Loaf!! Bungler!! Hamlet-you-idiot!!*"

HAMLET: "Lord! Lord! Why'd you call Ophelia out in the heat of the top of the third? And yet you've strung Claudius along until the bottom of the eleventh! Why didn't you get 'em to suspend the game?"

At night, they slept in the Winnebago. Inside the camper, it was a lot colder than outside. The fellow would sleep in the driver's seat. He'd conk out and, bingo, he'd be talking in his sleep.

"Wanna get down," the fellow would say under his

breath, cool and calm. "Wanna get down and bad."

Meanwhile, our dramatist and his woman slept in their built-in bunk bed. Top bunk and bottom bunk, apart.

"C'mon," voiced the woman, sadly, pleadingly. "C'mon c'mon c'mon c'mon c'mon c'mon c'mon c'mon c'mon." Ten times already.

But he did not answer. So she fell silent, too.

Far off, the fellow said it again.

"Wanna get down and soon."

Then, once more, darkness and silence.

He opened his eyes. Long before dawn. And yet, what was it in the air? Music? Hot and sweet-smelling, what was that?

"Wanna get down," said the fellow. "Wanna get down and bad."

And the woman said, softly, "Aren't you getting down now?"

That was the end of it. The fellow was sleeping with his woman. He decided to sleep on it. But by the dawn's early light, he was valiantly screaming. Incited by some irresistible force.

"What is it? Out with it!" Her pride hurt, the woman was beaming pure wrath and scorn down on the half-drowsing fellow. "I've had it! And here I thought you were an artist, you tight-ass! I'm leaving!"

We make it back to our place.

It has been a long, hard haul.

Outside, the snow keeps coming down like crazy.

Out there was cold, but here inside our place is warm. Out there was dark, but inside our place is bright.

Outside the window, one love hotel room light goes out.

"They're starting," say I.

"They're done," says my woman.

"They've found it," says my daughter.

"They ain't found nothin', ain't found nothin' t'all." Our dramatist Hanshin Tigers' fan mumbles to himself under the covers.

When—what do you know?—a different room light goes on.

"Company's arrived. Now the fun's going to start."

"They're checking out. Got to go to work early. The party's over."

"No, they found what they were looking for, like I said!!"

"What?" I ask. "Looking for what?"

"Books. Three books they bought at Yurindo and put in a paper bag. Which got separated from the bag and put somewhere they lost track of."

"Well, I don't know... In a love hotel? What's there to do with books?"

"Read."

"What for?"

"How should I know? I'm not the one reading."

When, all at once, every light in every window of the love hotel goes on.

"*Atchompriqué!*" My daughter's knees get weak from the shock.

"Say what?"

"I said, everybody's reading!"

"What for?"

"Whatever, that's they're business, isn't it? Dad, I hate you, nitpicking every little thing!"

"Don't hate me. I wish you wouldn't hate me."

At last, the fated hour hath arrived.

Time to hear out the root of misery.

"Sleep well, Hanshin Tigers. Sleep well, William Shakespeare. We'll be watching over you."

We station ourselves beside the sleeping man, our ears

cocked, that we might discern that grand epic single utterance of his.

Time elapses, until sleep claims us too. We're all so cozy.

Eventually, I have a dream next to the dreaming man— and it somehow seems to be his dream.

I'm out walking. All alone. But in the wrong place. "Dumb." I can just hear it.

Taken aback, I head home. When, halfway there, my mother is waiting for me. She's got all the time in the world, knitting away. She tells me, "Dumb. Real dumb." My mother's eyes, however, are laughing.

There's something I want to say. Something I have to say at all costs.

But before I can say it, he's screaming.

It's the scream of every lost soul on this earth who has died while searching for the Continent of America.

"あられちゃーん！！"

Here's how *The Voyages of Columbus* ends:

> *Verily it is God who makes for all good and all save sin is good. Thus, entertaining no thought that anything might occur but by the will of God, the Admiral in his wisdom, firm of faith, doubted not. Declared the Admiral, "This very voyage, as these records clearly show, must be deemed the wondrous working of miracles made manifest whence at sea. So it is that I, long the humble servant of Their Majesties, have withstood all detraction and criticism from those more notable than I, and rightly opposed the obstacles they have placed in the way of this voyage. I beseech of our Lord that this voyage shall be to the greater glory of Christiandom than heretofore ever realized." Having thus accomplished this first voyage to the Con-*

tinent of America and thereby having discovered it,
Christopher Columbus uttered these last words.
Thanks be to God.

First published, 1984
TRANSLATION BY ALFRED BIRNBAUM

Gen'ichiro Takahashi (b. 1951) is the *enfant terrible* of Japanese
"meta-fiction." After a bout of near-autism that followed his
dropping out of Yokohama University, he published *Sayonara to
the Gang* (1982), which deconstructed the language of pop media
hype and won him the Gunzo New Writer's Award. His second and
third novels, *Over the Rainbow* (1984) and *John Lennon vs the
Martians* (1985), further attacked the conventions of the story-on-
the-page, bringing zero-dimensional TV and cartoon characters
into a "real" world. The Mishima Prize-winning *Languid and
Sentimental Japanese Baseball* (1987), *Sundown in Penguin Town*
(1989), and his latest novel *The Secret of Planet 13* (1991) likewise
attest to his sensibility of excess and intellectual kitsch. Also known
as an essayist, sometime film scriptwriter, and translator of Jay
McInerney and others, Takahashi delights in confounding
expectations. To appreciate *Christopher Columbus Discovers
America*—which is excerpted from *Over the Rainbow*—fully, the
reader should take into account the fact that one of the largest
American naval bases in Japan is located in Yokohama.

MAZELIFE

Kyoji Kobayashi

K'S ROBOT

1.

For some reason, the intangible distressed K. Severe anxiety gripped him whenever he encountered it. K took pains to arrange every facet of his life so that all was perfectly clear. He assigned precise forms, time frames, and spatial demarcations to every thing and event.

But there were some things to which it was just about impossible to give a definite shape. Human emotions were probably the hardest for him to pin down. K's response to emotions approached raw terror.

At one time K had tried to rid himself of this fear of emotions by studying psychology. He thought that if he knew his enemy he might be less frightened of it.

For several months K took psychology classes at a university, reading Freud and Jung.

But as his studies progressed, K grew even more fearful of the unplumbed depths of the human psyche. The human interior, he learned, was more perverse than he had ever imagined, brimming with all kinds of unsuspected nastiness.

From that time, K's revulsion for anything having to do with the human condition doubled.

Several years passed like this, without incident. Then, one

day, by chance almost, K found himself in an all-out confrontation with the soul.

2.

It all started one autumn afternoon.

K was taking a stroll through his neighborhood.

K happened to look up at the marquee of the local movie theater. He saw the words *Autumn Sonata* written there. The poster near the entrance was rendered in soft tones, and the stills suggested a pleasant family story. K didn't know much about movies. From the title, he thought it was probably a love story or a romantic reverie. The director's name was Bergman.

He went in.

The movie was not what he expected. It was about a mother and daughter who desperately hated each other and who savaged each other hysterically from the first scene to the last.

K stared at the movie screen transfixed. He felt the blood draining from his face.

When it was over, K fled from the theater like a hunted creature.

He was in severe shock. His heart was pounding as if he had just awakened from a nightmare.

K's gaze careened wildly up and down the street, searching desperately for another movie, one that would make him feel better.

By coincidence, the move house right next door was showing a Woody Allen film. Everyone, even K, knew that Woody Allen was funny. Thinking he'd cheer himself up with a good laugh, K entered the theater with a light step.

A little knowledge is a dangerous thing. What K didn't know was that *just one* of Woody Allen's films was strongly influenced by the sinister Bergman. It was called *Interiors*. And there on the marquee above the movie theater K had just entered, the word *Interiors* glowered menacingly.

When he emerged from the theater two hours later, K was near madness. His face was chalky, drawn past white to a distinct and sickly blue. His eyes were vacant and his mouth hung slack and half-open. Staggering aimlessly, he stopped from time to time and just stood, staring blankly at the people who passed. On his face was an expression that registered the horror of being forced to endure one hundred and twenty minutes of the angst-ridden spite, the curses and keening, of a family of terminal neurotics—when all he'd wanted was a good laugh.

No more, resounded a voice from K's depths. I need help.

It was then that a big bright marquee with the words *Solaris* caught K's eye. Great, a science-fiction film. There wouldn't be any stuff about feelings and emotions in *that*. The promo blurb on the sign started: "A spaceship carrying an exploratory expedition arrives on the planet Solaris..." This time it was going to be okay for sure.

K was desperate. He plunged into the movie theater without further ado.

But, unfortunately for K, *Solaris* happened to be a deep, dark human drama by the famous sci-fi director Tarkovsky.

For two long hours, not a single adventure sequence, sexy girl, or space monster lit up the screen—there were only the character's anguished feelings...feelings...feelings...

K had no memory of returning home.

All he knew was that human beings terrified him. Everyone he saw was a monster churning with those sickening, turbulent feelings that K would never understand.

In the sky spun five half moons like crazy grins.

3.
The next day. Unable to recover from his trauma, K began to contemplate whether there wasn't some way to escape from human emotions entirely.

"I'll never know a day's peace as long as I have to face those dreadful things. I've got to do something. Hmmm. I could go to some deserted island. Then at least I'd escape from other people's feelings. Yeah. But that doesn't really solve the problem, does it? I'd still be left with my worst enemy—my *own* feelings. As long as I remain a human being, I can't escape from human emotions; and unless I escape from human emotions, I can't lead a peaceful life. That means...

"Hey, wait a minute.

"What would happen if I stopped being a human being altogether? If, for example, I were a robot.

"That's it!

"I'll become a robot! All a robot's actions are input into a central computer unit, and all it has to do is follow the computer's instructions. Not only will I be free from all emotions, but I won't have to worry or think about anything. What a relief! This is the discovery of the century!"

K immediately threw himself into his new project.

"All right, now calm down and think this through clearly. To become a robot, first I have to input patterns of action in response to various situations into my own head. Okay. To do that, I have to start with a detailed analysis of all the situations that could occur and decide how I should respond to each one. Right. Then I write them up into a program. That's the way to do it, I guess.

"Maybe I could try some program that already exists. They program members of religious cults, right? And they say you have to be socially programmed to be a successful executive at a big company. No. If I'm going do this, I want to do it my way, from start to finish. Anyway, I'll begin by trying to write the manual for just one situation."

And that's how K's robot project got underway.

4.

As a sort of test case, K decided to work on a program for the action of eating lunch out.

He started with an analysis of situation patterns.

1. Circumstances
   a. Leaving from home
   b. Already out of the house
   c. On a trip
2. Time available
   a. More than two hours
   b. More than an hour and one-half
   c. More than an hour
   d. More than thirty minutes
   e. More than fifteen minutes
   f. Less than fifteen minutes
3. Weather (K usually rode his bicycle to go out
   to lunch, so the weather was a very important
   factor)
   a. Good weather (which made him feel good
      and stimulated his appetite)
   b. Cloudy with a chance of rain
   c. Cloudy with no chance of rain
   d. Rain
   e. Rain or wind so strong as to make it hard to
      go outside at all (Most people would eat at
      home on days like this, of course, but some
      times when you least expected it K could be
      a perfectionist, and he wasn't satisfied until
      he considered every possible situation. Actu-
      ally, this could be a very dangerous person
      ality trait.)
   f. Extremes of heat or cold weather
   g. Other, unsettled weather, or natural or man-
      made disasters
4. Physical condition
   a. Excellent
   b. Excellent but not hungry
   c. Poor (digestive problems)
   d. Poor (problems other then digestive)

    e. Incapacitated (unable to leave the house
       under one's own power) (!)
  5. Budget
    a. More than ¥3,000
    b. More than ¥2,000
    c. More than ¥1,000
    d. More than ¥500
    e. Less than ¥500 (by far the most frequent
       case)
  6. Number of fellow diners
    a. 0 (that is, eating alone)
    b. 1
    c. 2
    d. 3
    e. more than 4
    f. Parties

Once he had analyzed the possible situations, K had to create concrete circumstances by matching each factor with every possible combination of all the others.

Before doing that, he calculated the total number of possibilities. Three times six times seven times five times six was eighteen thousand nine hundred. There were, in other words, eighteen thousand nine hundred possible responses to this situation.

So K started to write his program of responses to each of those eighteen thousand nine hundred situations. Obsessive by nature, K worked on his program with such concentration that he forgot to eat or sleep.

K progressed with amazing speed. He thought that if he could keep this pace up he would finish his program of all possible responses to all possible situations in two or three years.

But one day K awoke to a frightening truth. K was writing his detailed and utterly complete program in spiral notebooks, and by the time he had finished only about ten thousand response patterns, he had accumulated more than a hundred notebooks. By the time he was finished, he'd have more than two hundred. Two hundred notebooks to leaf through just to eat lunch—out.

And that was only the beginning. Other responses were more complicated. (According to K's calculations, there would be about seven hundred notebooks on eating dinner, one thousand four hundred on general locomotion, a whopping nine thousand seven hundred on daily life around the house, eighteen thousand nine hundred on making decisions, and the astronomical figure of one hundred twenty-three thousand six hundred programs on love.)

On the morning he finished the last program, K would suffocate under a mountain of spiral notebooks.

And to top it off, the possibility that K would complete all these programs in his lifetime was almost nil. A rough calculation suggested that it would take approximately two hundred seventy years and seven days (if he worked without sleep or rest) to write the complete set of programs of responses. It was enough to make your head spin.

Lost in thought, K bit his lip.

Isn't there anything I can do?

He bit his lip harder.

If I only wrote the important parts—no, that wouldn't work. An incomplete program was of no use at all. Well, maybe I should use some already prepared program. Nope. Even then, it would take a hundred years to learn to use it.

K bit his lip even harder.

But it didn't do any good.

And that's how K's robot project came to an ignominious end.

K'S GOD

1.

For some time after the sad end of the robot project, K was depressed. But then one day he suddenly started to think about why the project had failed.

"When you think about it, the cause of the failure was that I tried to write up a complete program on my own.

"A program for every possible human response is just too complex.

"There's a limit to my mental abilities.

"I should have thought more about that.

"Sure. The limits of the mind. As long as I'm human, I remain bound by them.

"Our mental limits are the cause of all the insoluble dilemmas of life.

"Wait a minute. Here I am, I want to transcend the human state, and I'm letting myself get held back by human limits. This is unbelievable.

"Well, not really, I guess. Since I'm a human being who wants to transcend his humanity, I guess the contradiction is inevitable, right?

"It's inescapable. When you think too hard about things, they always stop making sense. You've got to take it easy, real light and easy, one step at a time.

"But still, really, you'd have to be a God or something to put together a complete program for transcending humanity.

"This isn't going to be easy.

"A complete program.

"A complete person.

"Complete freedom from all anxiety.

"What if I designed the basic strategy of the program and then adapted it as I went along?

"No, that's no good. That's the same thing that all the great thinkers in history have done, from the beginning of time.

"Step one: Define the basic meaning of life.

"Step two: Apply step one to all the particulars of existence.

"Eventually, they all run out of time. Their philosophy is

subjected to superficial nit-picking by their disciples and becomes another 'ism' with all the rest.

"It's simply not worth the trouble.

"Maybe there's no choice but to bring a god into it. Gods, Buddhas, supernatural beings....Hey! a God!

"That might be it.

"I can ask a God to finish what I can't. What if my program, from the time I was born to the time of my death, were already finished in advance by God? That's a fresh angle.

"All I have to accept is that it's too hard to make my own program once my life has started, so a God writes a complete program for me before I'm born. It's like pro wrestling: it's a show, it's fun whether you lose or win. (And I don't care about winning or losing, anyway.) *It's just like being a robot.* Your free will ceases to exist. Though it might seem that you're acting of your own free will, it's all been built into your original program. You could say that even what I'm thinking right now is all part of my program.

"Yeah—fatalism.

"It's classic. How could I have missed it?"

K's cheeks glowed red with excitement. He lit a cigarette to calm himself. Intoning "God, God, God" with rising fervor and rocking back and forth in his chair with increasing enthusiasm, he finally flipped himself over and hit his head on the floor. But that didn't even slow him down. Rubbing his skull, he sat down again and continued with his thoughts.

"But there are hundreds of millions of people. Is it reasonable to suppose that a God can program the fate of every single one himself? (I mean, even programs for video games are pretty complicated.)

"Hmmm.

"Nope. It's impossible. Even God can't do that much. All he can do is point them in the right direction and hope for the best.

"Well, what about making a personal deal with a God?

"With Jehovah, for example. No, he's out. He's already given free will to human beings, what with Adam and Eve and all that. An irresponsible God: the people who follow him can only suffer. They can't become robots.

"There's Allah. I wonder if he understands Japanese? I guess so—after all, he's the god of a major world religion. But he's got so many followers, he probably wouldn't pay much attention to a new convert, and a Japanese convert at that.

"The Hindu Gods, masters of karma—they'd probably be good at programming. But where do I fit in the caste system? Outcaste, for sure. (And what if I was reincarnated as a cow?)

"The ancient Japanese Gods. Nah, I can't see how they'd be much use. They don't seem to have much interest in destiny. Passing tests, safe childbirth—that's more their line.

"The Buddhas. Definitely not. Too highbrow. No good for us low achievers.

"Zeus? He used to enjoy messing around with people's destinies. That was a long time ago, though. You have to wonder where he is now and what he's doing. He may not even be alive. (What happens to Gods when they're on the downslide? I wonder if they get part-time jobs as monsters or something. You never know—maybe Godzilla was a moonlighting God from somewhere.) Anyway, even if Zeus is alive and well, you sure don't hear much about him lately. He's got to be out of practice. Still, you'd think he could handle one person's fate—no, forget it. Zeus was partial to women, anyway. The men always got the short end of the stick. I can't see him helping me out.

"There are a lot of other Greek Gods. There must be one who's right for me.

"Let me see. Poseidon, lord of the sea. But what do I have to do with the sea?

"Hades, God of the underworld. He's not going to be

interested in my destiny as long as I'm alive.

"Hera, queen of the Gods. A very difficult lady.

"Apollo? If I had any artistic abilities, I might stand a chance.

"Aphrodite. No way she'd look at me.

"Hermes. I have absolutely no talent for business.

"Dionysus. Not a drinker.

"Ares. Not a soldier.

"Athena. Or a student.

"Ahhhh."

K let out a long sigh. It was a great idea, but no God really seemed to fit the bill.

Why?

K pondered his dilemma until at last it occurred to him.

"These gods are all too old.

"They're antiquated. Outdated.

"All of them have been around at least two or three thousand years. I mean, what've you got in common with someone ten years older, let alone three thousand? When you think about it objectively, of course they wouldn't be interested in helping me, even if they could. What I have to do is to find my *own* God somewhere. Or create one."

2.

So K set about creating his own God.

For starters, he headed for the university library to read up on how Gods were born.

It was a Saturday afternoon in October.

The autumn sky, without a single cloud, was transparent in its beauty. There was a light breeze, which made the day even more refreshing.

The fountain in front of the university library sparkled sweetly in the soft light of autumn.

It was a truly perfect day for the birth of a God.

K entered the library and headed for the reference room where he began to look up "Gods."

In less than an hour, dozens of tomes lay piled in front of K.

Two hours later, K had learned that over the centuries the human race had created a truly unfathomable number of gods. From ancient times, human beings had turned things near and far, visible and invisible, tangible and intangible, existent and nonexistent, thinkable and unthinkable—anyway, everything possible and impossible—into Gods.

There were sun Gods and moon Gods, star Gods, wind Gods, rain Gods, snow Gods, rumble Gods, whisper Gods, forest-fire Gods, ice Gods, mud Gods, mirage Gods, haze Gods, and mist Gods—and so forth, and so forth, et cetera. These were all natural phenomena that had become Gods.

Then there were lion Gods, tiger Gods, elephant Gods, zebra Gods, kangaroo Gods, lizard Gods, turtle Gods, whale Gods, shark Gods, giraffe Gods, badger Gods, spider Gods—and so forth, and so forth, et cetera. These were all animals that had become Gods.

Orchid Gods, peony Gods, chrysanthemum Gods, rose Gods, iris Gods, mangrove Gods, freesia Gods, digitalis Gods, arborvitae Gods, pine Gods, cypress Gods—and so forth, and so forth, et cetera. These were all plants that had become Gods.

Of course, Gods are made by people, so people were the most frequent models. These were male Gods, female Gods, hermaphrodite Gods, asexual Gods, incompetent Gods, all-powerful Gods, lustful Gods, phallic Gods (why did most male Gods have such big cocks?), yonic Gods, virgin Gods (male and female), boy Gods, girl Gods, infant Gods, elderly Gods, father Gods, mother Gods, ancestor Gods, hero Gods, ruler Gods, teacher Gods, cultural Gods, agricultural Gods, hunting Gods, fishing Gods, merchant Gods, sailor Gods, thief Gods, prowler Gods, murderer Gods (all Gods shared this trait to a greater or lesser degree), crazy Gods (likewise)—and so forth, and so forth, et cetera.

Then there were mountain Gods, sea Gods, sky Gods, and other Gods born from geographical features. There were Gods born from abstractions, such as the Gods of victory, Gods of beauty, Gods of death, Gods of poverty. And there were also Gods that were the pure product of the imagination—dragon Gods and half-beast, half-man Gods and things like that.

K was impressed. It seemed as if human beings were put on earth for the sole purpose of creating Gods.

Next K looked up the origins of the Gods. There seemed to be considerable dispute about this, and each book he read had a different theory. Giving up, he went to the encyclopedia, where he found three general theories set forth.

First, the animism theory of E.B. Tyler. According to Tyler, a second self, or soul, experienced at the moment of death, in dreams, and during mystic experiences, was transposed to nonhuman phenomena, leading to the birth of the idea of spirit, which is in turn the source of all Gods. The evolution of the concept of spirit leads to the postulation of a supreme God. Tyler says that the original inspirations for God were the vegetation, trees, and rivers of our world close at hand.

The second theory was the preanimistic theory of R.R. Mullet. Rejecting any complex notion like spirit, Mullet said the idea of God derived from a deep emotional response to a phenomenon perceived as powerful to a supernatural degree. In this case, the God's form was mystical and supernatural.

Third, P.W. Schmidt put forward the theory of urmonotheism. In complete contrast to the other two theories, Schmidt believed that the source of the general concept of deity was an original universal human belief in an all-knowing and supreme creator—God. All later developments were not evolutions but devolutions from this fundamental intuition.

After carefully examining these three theories, K chose the

first theory, animism, as his method for creating God.

If he was going to use the second, the preanimistic theory, K would have to base his God on some powerful supernatural phenomenon, and unfortunately, he rarely came across such things in Tokyo where he lived.

If he used the third, the urmonotheistic theory, he could create a God with nothing more than a pencil and paper, just as he pleased, since he was free to devolve the fundamental intuition of Godhead as he saw fit. But because this was his first time creating a God, he thought an all-knowing all-powerful deity might be a little too ambitious (not that it wasn't tempting). A project for the advanced student, clearly. K decided to give urmonotheism a shot once he had a little experience, but for now he'd set a more modest goal.

Compared to the other two theories, animism seemed a cinch. K was an expert at the dreams and mystic hallucinations that were its basic ingredients, and as for death, it was anywhere you looked—TV and newspapers and books. He needed a natural object that could serve as the base for the spirit, but all he had to do, after all, was pick anything he liked and assign it that role. That shouldn't be so hard. Once he'd got the basic shape of the God worked out, he could gradually improve it until he had made a supreme God, one for more advanced applications.

When K had settled on the basic plan, he left the library to get started on actually creating his God.

It was already dark. The wind that had blown during the day had stopped; there wasn't even a trace of a breeze. The beautiful fountain was turned off. But the still pool in its basin glimmered like a mirror, reflecting the lights of the night.

As if playing ring-around-the-rosy together in the heavens, five moons shone above him, illuminating and reflecting each other.

K left the campus and chose a quiet street for his way

home. The road had once been a waterway, but now it was a dirt path and lined on both sides with evergreens. From time to time the trees swayed, though there was no wind. Chrysanthemums were planted in beds between the trees and the road, and their spice was in the air.

K was filled with a strange excitement.

What fun it was to make a God! Compared to this, his robot project had been small-time. He didn't need the maze anymore. By creating his own God, he made the whole universe his maze. This was great. Terrific. I am eternally saved. Because I made God. I don't need destiny. I don't need a program. I will devote my life to nurturing the God I create. For the God that is eternally mine, and mine alone.

When he noticed his surroundings again, the huge elm tree that he often visited was towering above him. It looked down on him gently, as if offering its congratulations. Behind it shone the five moons. K stopped and looked up at the tree and the five moons.

And the spirit rose up in K.

"You are my God."

3.

In a frenzy of excitement, K set about the practical business of creating his God that very night.

He started with the task of identifying exactly what the necessary conditions for creating a God were. First he'd just brainstorm, listing every possible requirement he could think of, and then he'd eliminate the ones that weren't crucial.

This turned out to be a more critical step than he had thought.

Too many requirements might ruin the creation; too few and the God might not work right. If he overlooked some important factor, he'd create a defective God, and if he put the wrong thing in, he might create a God who wouldn't do what he wanted.

K worked with great care. Had he forgotten anything, made any mistakes? He worked slowly, checking each point again and again as he went along. As a result, it didn't go all that smoothly, and it was already early morning when he finished.

K finally arrived at six requirements for creating a God:

1. A God needs devotees who will worship it with their entire being.
2. A God needs a priest who will conduct its ceremonies of worship.
3. A God needs a shrine where it can be worshiped.
4. A God needs commandments for its devotees to obey.
5. A God needs a myth that gives it divine authority.
6. A God needs powers sufficient to satisfy its devotees.

When K had completed this list, he went to sleep, thoroughly satisfied. How long had it been since he had been so pleasantly tired?

And so the first day of creating God came to an end. K had built his God's skeleton.

4.

The next day, K set about meeting each of the six requirements he had identified.

First, devotees. This would be K's role. No problem with that.

Next, a priest. This wasn't so quickly settled.

At first K thought, What the heck?—he could just as well be both priest and devotee. But as he mulled it over, he began to worry that maybe the same person shouldn't try to be both things.

God is supreme existence. Devotees are the recipients of his power.

A priest is supposed to stand between God and ordinary people and connect them. He can't exist if he's separated from either one.

So what happens when this priest, who is an intermediary, is also a devotee? It's like a movie director making films for himself. As a director, he'd have to invent stuff to please the audience, and then as the audience, he'd have to try to enjoy the same stuff he'd just invented. Would that work? He'd either begin to detest himself or he'd go schizophrenic.

It wouldn't be good for the devotee, either. The devotee's adoration of his God mostly came from not understanding it. If the devotee was also a priest, he'd know what was going on behind the scenes and wouldn't be able to worship his God with the blind devotion required.

And the God would be in trouble, too. The absoluteness of the God depended on the absoluteness of the devotee. If the absoluteness of the devotee was compromised by his also being a priest, the absoluteness of the God would be kaput.

Hmmm.

K was lost in thought. If he couldn't solve this dilemma one way or another, his plan to create a God was likely to go down the tubes entirely.

Of course. The greatest dilemma of contemporary mankind was that it was forced to be its own priest and devotee at the same time.

Hmmm.

K puzzled over this problem for the entire afternoon.

Then, just as the sun was setting, K hit upon a brilliant plan.

Why not give the role of the priest to the huge elm tree itself?

The tree was a manifestation of the God, not the God itself. The God resided in the spirit of the tree and manifested its will through the phenomenon of the elm tree. The elm tree, as the phenomenon which received that spirit, as the intermediary priest, could communicate it to the people.

There was still something fishy about the whole thing, but K decided to call the problem solved. If he didn't, this was going to end up like the robot thing, which fell apart in the very first stage.

Number three, the shrine, was easy. A shrine is where the God is, so of course the area that he had been calling the maze was the shrine of his God.

Number four was commandments. These were, after all, a legal code, and you couldn't write a whole lawbook in a day. So K decided to just lay down the major rules and work out the details later.

1. Devotees must worship the moon every day. When they cannot see the moon, they must visualize its phases in their minds and then proceed to worship that vision.
2. Devotees must worship the Sun every day. When they cannot see the Sun, they must visualize its burning orb in their minds and then proceed to worship that vision.
3. Devotees must worship the great tree every day. When they cannot see the great tree, they must visualize the glorious great tree in their minds and then proceed to worship that vision.
4. Devotees must go through the maze every day. When they cannot go through the maze, they must visualize the shining shrine in their minds, and then go through that vision.
5. Devotees must chant the name of their great God every day, and they must vow never to worship other Gods, never to have congress with other Gods, never to recognize other Gods, and to be forever faithful to the one and only God.

When K had gotten this far in his commandments, he remembered that he hadn't named his God yet. But it was late. K went to bed.

And so the second day of creating God came to an end. K's God had acquired devotees, a priest, a shrine, and commandments.

5.

K spent most of the next morning riding around the tree on his bicycle.

The tree swayed gently in the morning breeze.

The soughing of the wind through its leaves was like the sound of waves caressing the shore.

The soft clear light of autumn robed the tree in its warmth.

K decided that his God was pleased with the progress he was making, and he took heart.

The day's agenda was finding a name for the God. K got started on it as soon as he got back from the cram school where he taught.

It went without saying that this was another crucial step, to which he'd have to devote the greatest care. He couldn't give his God some weird name. On the other hand, it wouldn't do to have the name be too predictable either. It had to be powerful yet elegant, have an aura of mystery while being utterly convincing.

K flipped through all kinds of books and searched through a dozen dictionaries trying to find the right name, but nothing really grabbed him. There were plenty of nifty names, but somehow they all lacked the punch he wanted.

As he pored over the possibilities, it occurred to K that in this situation, the best thing was to look for a sign from the God itself.

The autumn night was deep, and the streets were empty.

The night clouds trailed in strips that hid and revealed the moons, obscuring them only to let them slip out against the black sky once more.

As K looked up at the great tree in the pitch-black night, it seemed bigger and more imposing than by day.

The God looked down with authority on K.

It was magnificent indeed—in power, in wisdom, in size.

Gradually K felt an emotion akin to terror well up from the depths of his soul.

It was like a great black tide. It was like hope, and it was like despair.

It was like a moment that existed for all eternity. It was like the future, like the past.

It seemed to be a supreme power. It swept K away, tossed him about, battered him, and swallowed him whole.

K looked up at the tree for some time, as if in a trance. Without being aware of it, he closed his eyes and listened. Now he would hear the voice of God.

In the next moment, God's voice rang out with unbelievable clarity.

MOOO.

When K opened his eyes and looked up at the great tree, he saw a giant with the head of a bull bellowing lustily toward the heavens.

At that moment, all K's questions were answered.

This God was nothing other than the mixed-up manifestation of the ruler of the maze: the Minotaur.

And so the third day of creating God came to an end. K had discovered the God's name.

6.

The next day, K set about finishing up his God.

What remained was the myth and the powers. Since he now knew who his God was, he could work quickly, with no doubt or hesitation.

First the myth. Since he couldn't write the whole thing at once, he decided to start with the Minotaur's birth. Then he could add on to the story bit by bit. K licked his pencil.

Chapter One: Birth

The Minotaur, great tree God. His mother's name was Pasiphae. She was the wife of the King of Crete. His father's name is unknown. He was a bull.

The secret of the birth of the great tree God Minotaur begins with his mother Pasiphae.

Pasiphae was unnaturally proud of her own beauty. She thought she was the most beautiful creature in the world.

One day she made the mistake of saying that even Aphrodite's beauty could not compare with hers. And Aphrodite got wind of this. She was furious. She decided to put a curse on the bitch.

Burning with the desire for revenge, Aphrodite conjured up the most beautiful bull in the world and sent it to Pasiphae.

It was a wonderful white bull, so white that it shone, with eyes of fire. Its hooves gleamed as if polished, and its nose was red as coral.

Pasiphae fell head over heels in love.

But her beloved was a beast. It would never be permitted.

Love is blind. And on top of that, there was the power of Aphrodite's curse. She was done for. Night after night, Pasiphae's flesh burned with passionate longing.

Then, on a bright, moonlit night, the queen

succumbed to the flames of desire that consumed her from within. She summoned her favored retainer Daedalus and ordered him to construct a model of a cow with a secret hole.

Daedalus was the greatest inventor of his time. Later he escaped with his son Icarus from the very maze that he was to create.

When the model of the cow was completed, it was a marvel. It was so beautiful that no bull could help but fall in love with it.

Pasiphae was overjoyed.

The queen tore off her gorgeous robes until she stood completely naked. Falling on her knees, she got inside the cow costume with the secret hole.

And she leisurely strode to the pasture where the white bull was kept.

A year later, she gave birth to a child.

Of course it was not a human child. It was a monster with the head of a bull and the body of a man—the Minotaur.

Deeply shamed, King Minos ordered Daedalus to build a maze and lock Pasiphae and the Minotaur up in it.

That is how the Minotaur became the ruler of the maze and its undisputed master.

When K got this far, he stopped and sighed.

A maze. A half-man half-bull. Confusion. Sex with animals.

Wasn't this exactly what his life in the maze had been like up to now?

"The fact that I thought of this plan," thought K, "was a great inevitability."

Overcome with emotion, K bellowed, "Mooo."

Yes, yes! Under the protection of the Minotaur, a new life awaits me! he thought.

The final requirement for creating the Minotaur was that

he have power to benefit his devotees. Since this was the whole reason K had set out to create his God, it had been decided from the start.

In other words, salvation from human suffering. That was it. K sought nothing else.

7.

When K had finished his God, he hurried to the elm tree to announce his success.

The wind was strong that night.

Perfect full moons rode in the center of the sky, spinning round and round as if pleased with K's triumph.

The great tree was shaking violently. It seemed to be thanking K with its whole being, to be trembling with joy at having achieved deity.

K found his body vibrating with an otherworldly ecstasy, and he couldn't stop weeping.

Thus the fourth day of creating God came to an end. K's God acquired a myth and divine powers.

8.

For the next three days, K was filled with the bliss of having created his own homemade God.

But then it struck him that maybe he should try the God out to see if it worked.

Maybe K's God wouldn't be any use in a crisis.

K decided he wanted to test his God.

But all Gods take a terrible dislike to being tested. The Minotaur wouldn't like it either. It would be a shame if, fresh as he was, his God got cranky on him.

K decided to wait quietly for a chance to test his God.

Then, about a week later, an ideal chance to do so dropped into K's lap.

It all started when K ran into Kozue in town one day.

"Oh, it's you, K. I haven't seen you in ages. Are you still

the most unpopular teacher at the school?"

She smiled charmingly at K as she said it. They hadn't seen each other for about half a year.

"It's been a long time."

Kozue had changed remarkably. She had let her hair grow out, and she dressed in the trendiest clothes. But the biggest change was in her eyes. They were illuminated by a strange glow that had never been there before. It was a look of a new wisdom—and at the same time the look of someone possessed.

"You make me feel like an old man," said K, looking her up and down.

"What are you talking about—you're still young. Drop the routine. It doesn't work. If you're free today, why not come along with me? I'll show you a good time."

Aroused by the change that had come over Kozue, K readily agreed.

"So, what are we going to do? Do you want to eat something?"

"We can always eat later. I'm not even hungry."

Kozue raised her arm, hailed a cab, and slid quickly in.

K got in too and the taxi sped off at a fast clip, out of the maze in no time at all. K was a little uneasy, but he decided not to worry about it: God was on his side.

Ten minutes later, the cab stopped in front of a department store.

"Okay, we're here."

Kozue marched into the store, watching K fumble to pay the taxi driver out of the corner of her eye. K was a little let down when he realized that the "good time" wasn't exactly what he had in mind, but he followed Kozue into the department store.

Kozue wove her way through the maze of intersecting aisles without the slightest hesitation. With the lightness of a butterfly, flitting along its invisible migratory path. K had no sense of direction, and he kept getting lost, which made him uncomfortable and anxious.

"I'll bet you never come to places like this," Kozue teased K over her shoulder as he tried desperately to keep up with her.

K couldn't tell the truth—that it had been three years—so he just made some vague noises.

"You could learn a thing or two here, you know. About what women really like."

And Kozue smiled.

They crossed one elevated walkway after another, rising from floor to floor, riding escalator after escalator, until they arrived at the floor that sold famous brand-name women's accessories.

It was bathed in a glow like the soft light of late summer, designed to create an atmosphere of languid elegance.

The aisles were wide, and the flow of people had obviously been calculated to the nth degree. There were no crowds, no clots of jostling shoppers. Everything flowed gracefully, effortlessly.

Kozue stepped into the languid current. Her brisk trot was magically transformed into the *de rigueur* languid slouch. And he noticed suddenly that her eyes took on a new light. Her gaze was lolling and unfocused, like that of a junkie.

"You know, I only really feel alive when I'm here. Every single thing here is waiting for me to appear, and none of them will ever disappoint me. Isn't that great? Here, I'm the queen, I'm Mother Mary, I'm the Savior," incanted Kozue, as if in religious ecstasy.

K was silent, baffled as to how he should reply.

Kozue went on, as if she were talking in a dream. "Do you know why they need me here? Because without me, all of the things here are nothing but useless trash. They only come to life when I buy them. Here, I'm their creator. I can be a God here. That's why they all call out to me so desperately. 'Look at me!' 'Buy me!' 'I'm useful.' 'I'm pretty!' You don't believe me, do you? But it's true. I can hear their voices. Their sweet, tempting voices. Many call, but few are chosen;

only one or two will know the joy of being bought by me today. When I finish my shopping and have to go home, they all cry out together. They scream for me. That really makes me sad. But there's only so much I can do right now. I can't save them all. So I tell them that I promise to save them the next time I come, and then I leave. Do you understand what I'm talking about? Oh, look!"

Suddenly Kozue's eyes snapped sharply back into focus.

"It's perfume. Don't you think it's marvelous?"

Inside the showcase an impressive lineup of crystal bottles bore the proud labels Chanel, Guerlain, Van Crif, Coti, Houbigant, Helena Rubenstein, Elizabeth Arden, Richard Hudnut.

"K, can't you hear them? They're calling me, all of them."

Ignoring the puzzled K, Kozue called the salesgirl and had her take out the samples. She started sniffing and testing them. Finally she found one she liked and she asked the salesgirl the price.

"K," purred Kozue, "can I ask you a favor? This poor little bottle of perfume has been waiting for me in a corner of the showcase for such a long time. It's saying that it had given up hope that I would ever come. It's very happy that I'm finally here. It says it's finally found its rescuer. K. You know what I'm saying, don't you? Please. Help me and the perfume out. If you do, I'll do anything you want to prove my gratitude. All right? Please, K? Pleeease."

K couldn't figure out how serious Kozue was about all this, but he liked that "I'll do anything" part, so he agreed.

When the salesgirl told him the price, his knees almost buckled. That tiny crystal perfume bottle, two inches high, cost almost one month's salary.

"I don't have that much money on me."

"Well, use a credit card," replied Kozue coolly.

"What I'm trying to tell you is that I don't even have that much money in my bank account."

"You don't even have this much in the bank?" Kozue

flashed a look of utter dismay. "You're really hopeless." She let out a dramatic sigh. "What kind of man can't even buy a lady a little present she wants? Aren't you ashamed?"

Kozue's eyes flashed with a crazed resentment.

K was spooked.

"Well, you could always buy it on credit. In twenty-four installments. Then you'd only have to pay a little more than ¥10,000 a month. All right? Sign up for credit. Please."

"I can't buy it on credit, either."

Kozue shrieked.

"It's more than I can afford."

"But I'm *asking* you. Come on, pleeease. If you buy it for me I'll do whatever you say. All right—the miniature bottle is okay. Even you can buy that, right?"

Just then a wonderful plan for testing his God sprang into K's head.

"All right, I'll buy it. But on one condition. I want you to show me your God."

"My God? I haven't got any God!"

"Yes you do. What about the voices you hear?"

"Oh, the voices. Sure, fine. I'll make sure you hear them. But first buy the perfume."

K smiled gleefully.

One God will not allow the presence of another God. And K's commandments forbade him from having congress with any other God. If K heard the voices, his God wouldn't take it lying down. He would appear before K like a husband who had caught his wife in her lover's arms and drive the interloper away. And K would have been able to test the God's love for him, and his power, without any risk.

With the greatest reverence, K bought Kozue her miniature bottle of perfume.

9.

Thirty minutes later, K sat across from Kozue in the cafe

of the department store.

The bewitched, trancelike glaze had disappeared from Kozue's eyes. Her knowing look had returned.

"I'm sorry. For acting so spoiled. When I hear the voices, I simply can't resist."

"Do you always buy the things that call to you even when you're alone?"

"Of course. Fur coats and dresses and jewels. I buy anything. But sometimes they're too expensive and I have to take them back. I buy everything on credit, so I lose track, you know? I have enormous bills. I mean, I'm in credit hell, really."

"What is your monthly payment?"

"Hmmm. Well, I guess it's about ¥200,000. No, maybe more. During the bonus season sometimes I have to pay about ¥500,000 at a crack."

K was taken aback.

"I'm amazed you can pay it all. Does your family help?"

"Don't be ridiculous. If they knew about this, they'd kill me. That's why I'm looking for a sugar daddy so desperately. But you know, there aren't many rich, generous types out there. I really feel like I'm working my fingers to the bone, and for what?"

Kozue smiled in an untroubled, even sexy way, and gracefully lifted her legs and crossed them in the opposite direction.

"When did you first start hearing the voices?"

"About a year ago. I don't know why or how it started, really. I mean, I just had nothing to do and so I went to department stores every day. And then after about a week, when I was looking at a dress in a show window, I heard a voice."

"What did it say?"

"It said, 'This dress would look really nice on you.'"

"Is that all?"

K was a little disappointed.

"That's all."

"And it's gone on ever since?"

"Ever since."

"Have you ever resisted the voices?"

"Why should I have to resist them? The voices always tell me what to buy, and they've made me smarter, too. When I really need some money, I come here and the voices tell me some way to get it. I can't live without the voices any more. That's why I come here every day, to hear them."

"Really."

K lit a cigarette. The most important part was next.

"So, what do I have to do to hear the voices?"

"Hmmm. I got a little carried away back there when I said I'd help you, I guess."

"Hey, I paid in advance, you know."

"I know. That's why I'm giving it serious thought. Just be quiet a minute."

Kozue closed her eyes and kept still. After several moments, she suddenly announced in strange voice, "Okay. It's all settled."

"What is?"

"I was talking to the voices inside me. I told them that there's this guy who wants to talk to them and asked them if they would. And they said it was okay, they would. But there's a condition."

"A condition."

"Starting today, you have to go to the department store every day until you hear the voices."

"How long will it take?"

Kozue fell into a trance again, like a medium communicating with the dead.

"What do they say?" asked K in a whisper. Kozue slowly opened her languid eyes.

"They say they don't know. But if you come here every day, it won't take long, they say."

K was relieved.

"And I have some good news for you. I'm going to sleep with you, for buying me the perfume."

"Is that what the voices say?"

"No, I say so." And as she did, Kozue's eyes shone like those of Pasiphae, draped in her marvelous cow skin.

10.

K's visits to the department store started the next day.

Whenever he could spare a few moments, he headed for the store. He stayed there as long as he could.

K tried everything to provoke the voices.

He had the salespeople bring out all kinds of samples. But he didn't buy anything. He stuffed his wallet full of cash. But he didn't spend it.

Unfortunately, the voices didn't go for the bait. Once or twice it even occurred to K that the voices might be nothing more than Kozue's delusions. But he hastily banished such doubts. If he admitted Kozue's voices were delusions, he'd have to admit his God was a delusion, too. The voices existed, no question about it. And when the voices appeared to him, K's God would appear, too.

The end of the first week of his visits to the department store arrived.

K went downtown as soon as he got up and entered the store just as it was opening. He wasn't teaching that day, and K felt great.

K started at the cosmetics counter.

A girl of about fifteen or sixteen was asking a salesclerk a question. She was very pretty, and K enjoyed watching her. She looked the clerk right in the eye as she spoke, nodding as the clerk began to explain something.

Then, the girl's hand stretched out casually, deftly enclosed a lipstick on the counter, and slid it into her shopping bag.

The clerk never noticed, and went on speaking. The girl then thanked her and walked in the direction she had been shown.

For a brief moment, K wasn't sure what he'd seen. Gradually it dawned on him that he had witnessed a shoplifting. The girl had already disappeared into the crowd. There was nothing he could do.

Then, five minutes later in the bargain department, a well-dressed middle-aged woman dropped a blouse she had been holding up into her shopping bag. Before he could blink, not three seconds later, she had slipped another blouse into the same bag.

K looked around for someone he could report the woman to. As he scanned the room, he saw a young secretary-type popping a sweater into her bag. The girl noticed K watching her with his mouth open; she grinned cheerfully and walked away.

K couldn't believe his eyes.

What was going on? He had to be dreaming.

Suddenly a blank space opened in K's mind.

And then he heard a voice that seemed to burrow in through the opening.

"Don't worry about it, honey. You go on and take whatever you want."

K came out of his trance. Great. Now his God would come.

K listened.

He didn't hear anything.

K looked around.

He didn't see anything.

K closed his eyes and chanted his God's name.

But all he saw was the blackness behind his eyelids.

11.

The scene that then unfolded before K's eyes next was too weird for words.

A serious-looking young guy pulled a stadium jacket off a mannequin, put it on, and walked off briskly. A little girl in a sailor suit stuck a Snoopy doll under her arm and disappeared with it. A stout gentleman stuffed a pair of flowered women's panties into his coat pocket. A girl decked out in the *Jean-Jean* look tucked a Scheafer fountain pen into her bra. A shabby office-worker-type slipped an Akina Nakamori tape into his trousers pocket.

And through all of this, the voice kept whispering insistently to K.

"Don't worry about it, honey. You go on and take whatever you want."

When he looked down, K noticed he was gripping a little glass knickknack in the shape of a cat.

"Don't worry about it, honey. You go on and take whatever you want. These things are all here just for you."

Flustered, K put the glass cat down.

"Hey, honey, what the matter? Maybe you don't like the glass cat. Then take the fish—it's nice. Look. Finest Venetian glass. Go ahead—pick it up. These things are all here just for you, really."

"I'm not going to shoplift."

"Why not? Everyone's doing it."

"I don't want to get caught!"

"Ha, ha, ha, ha. You're the old-fashioned type, aren't you. Well, how about this then: Why don't you buy it? You're such a clever little fellow."

"Okay, all right, I will."

K mumbled as if he were possessed.

By the time he realized what was he doing again, K found that he was carrying a shopping bag. Shit, he thought, and dug out his wallet. Just as he had feared, almost empty.

Shit, he thought again. What was *with* his God?

12.

The insistent voice continued to whisper in K's head.

"Honey, don't you want anything else? Get everything you want."

"Shut up, will you?"

"Now stop being so nasty. How about this kitchen table?"

"I don't want it. The one I have now is fine."

K was waiting for his God to arrive.

But there was no sign of him.

"Is that so? You really *like* that crappy kitchen table you have? Nobody eats on that kind of old-fashioned junk these days. If you eat on this table every day, you'll feel different. And if you feel different, your life will change. That new life that you've been wanting so badly will be yours for the asking."

"Anyway, I'm almost out of money. You should know that better than anyone."

"Oh my, my. So that's what you're worried about? It's all right—you don't have to have money. You have a cash card, right? All you have to do is go down to the first floor and take some money out at the cash machine. But a credit card would really be better. Yes, that's much better. The credit office is on the fourth floor; go sign up there. If you have a credit card you can buy what you want whenever you feel like it. Yes—you go and get a credit card."

"I don't want to."

K took the escalator up to the next floor.

"Why are you so mean, honey? If you have a credit card, you can buy whatever you need. You can have a whole new life, just by signing your name. Then you won't need your miserable little God."

"It's ridiculous to think that you can buy a new life by buying things."

"You're the one who's ridiculous, honey. I'm not trying to sell you things you don't need. Look at what you've bought so far. They're all things that, unconsciously, you've been wanting every day. I want to give you a real life. You're afraid to look real life in the face. That's why you've built that silly maze and shut yourself up in it, then invented a God that will solve all your problems. You're just like a little boy. Without your maze, your God—without your mama's apron to hide behind—you can't do anything. If you keep on like that, you'll never have a real life."

"A real life?"

"Yes. What I want to give you is a real life. You congratulate yourself and are oh-so-pleased that you look down on *things*, but a life is made up of things. Be brave: listen to what things have to say."

K was in the stationery section.

"Hey there! Please! Buy me! I'm a great fountain pen. Here, pick me up. I feel better than any fountain pen you've ever used. And I'm only ¥20,000. That's all, just ¥20,000!"

"I don't need a fountain pen. I don't want to write anything."

"That's exactly why you need me. If you have me, you'll feel like writing every day. The reason you haven't written anything so far is that you were never lucky enough to find a fountain pen like me. I'm only ¥20,000. That's all, just ¥20,000!"

"Too bad. I'm broke."

"There are credit cards. I'm only ¥20,000. That's all, just ¥20,000."

"Anyway, I don't feel like buying a fountain pen."

K left the stationery department.

"Sir! Sir! Buy me! I'm a drafting set! Everybody says I'm very easy to use!"

"I don't do any drafting, so you may as well give up."

"Who cares? I'm a lot sturdier and better made than that fountain pen over there, so why not give me a try? ¥55,000 for the set. I'll last a lifetime. ¥55,000 for the set. ¥55,000 for the set!"

"Ahem. Can I say something here? I'm a ballpoint. Not the usual ballpoint, though. I'm manufactured with the new super-duper double-XX feature that makes it incredibly easy to write with me. And I last two and one-half times longer than other ballpoint pens. I'm well designed—I mean, I won a design award, right? So, okay, just try me once. I'm a little more expensive than the old type—¥150. But I'll give you a full ¥150 value. I'll give you a full ¥150 value!"

"Hi, there, fella. Buy me! I'm beautiful. A beautiful globe. Your life will change if you have me. Come on, buy me—please? All this knowledge, for only ¥27,000! Knowledge for ¥27,000! Knowledge for ¥27,000!"

"If you want knowledge, I'm your guy. I'm a globe of the *moon*. ¥15,000. From the instant you hang me in your room, you'll feel so trendy, so sophisticated. I promise."

K's God was still nowhere to be found.

"Just ¥15,000. You won't be sorry."

"Honey, the life you're living now is not a real life. You're like some kind of hermit. You've got to face reality. You've got to take the first step to a real life. The cash machine is on the first floor. The credit department is on the fourth floor. This globe of the moon is wonderful, isn't it? You want it, don't you? You have to get what you want. To get a real life."

"I come in all sorts of different sizes. If you hang a whole set in your room it will look terrific—really stunning."

"Hanging a set of moon globes of different sizes, huh?"

"Yes, exactly. Right there in your own room you'll feel like you're floating through space. If you get them all, from the smallest to the largest, it's only ¥78,000.

"¥78,000?"

"Hurry up, honey, The cash machine is on the first floor. The credit department is on the fourth floor."

When K realized where he was, he was on the down escalator headed for the first floor. What on earth am I doing? he thought.

K got mad at himself and rode the escalator back to the seventh floor. How many times would he have to be fooled before he learned?

The seventh floor was a war zone.

"Buy me!"…"I've got the latest features!"…"¥850"…"As a design accessory for your room"…"Men's grooming"…"Very convenient, and only ¥5,000"…"A credit card is a great bargain"…"Today Parker ballpoints are"…"Buy me, oh please!"…"New model"…"For your health"…"How you plan your schedule"…"You'll feel like a great writer"…"Buy me, mister!"…"Buy!"…"Buy!"…"Buy!"

When K looked behind him, the elevator and the escalator had disappeared. The entire floor was overflowing with a sea of things, things, things…

"Oh, God!" K screamed without thinking. And that's when it happened.

MOOOO.

A loud bellow echoed over the sea of things.

Everything went black and grew deathly quiet.

Then K heard heavy footsteps approaching, with rumbling thuds.

Yes, there it was: a giant man with a bull's head, the Minotaur, appeared before K as his God.

K thought he was saved.

13.

But, the next moment, the unbelievable occurred.

The Minotaur roared: *Drink mooore! Eat mooore! Take mooore women! Buy mooore things! Spend mooore money! Satisfy me! Gratify me!*

14.

In that instant, the architecture of K's mazelife collapsed.

The Minotaur demanded that K break all the rules that he had made for himself up to now and devote himself solely to the pursuit of pleasure.

The Minotaur demanded that K go to fancy restaurants every day and eat so much that he thought he would burst.

As a result, K swelled up into a blimp.

The Minotaur demanded that K drink until he was plastered. As a result, K had a permanent hangover.

The Minotaur demanded that whenever K came across a girl he would proposition her with a "How about a little fuck?" Not even his students were safe. As a result, K's reputation at the school dropped precipitously and there was no chance that his contract would be renewed for the next semester.

When he went to a department store, the Minotaur demanded that K buy everything in sight. If he didn't have enough money on him, he would get some from a cash machine, and if he still didn't have enough, he would be forced to buy it on credit. As a result, K's apartment was packed to overflowing with stuff.

But the Minotaur was still not satisfied. It continued to bellow: *Drink mooore! Eat mooore! Take mooore women! Buy mooore things! Spend mooore money! Gratify me! Satisfy me!*

K's economic condition declined drastically. His savings were gone in three days. His credit bills were up to ¥100,000 a month in no time. And they kept increasing at a terrifying pace. He borrowed the money he needed from loan sharks, even though he had no prospects for repaying it.

It wasn't only his economic condition that declined. K's health was ruined. His stomach hurt, and the slightest exercise left him puffing. He couldn't sleep, and his face was as pale as a corpse. It was only a matter of time before K's body would give up the ghost.

But the Minotaur showed no sign of pardoning him.

The Minotaur loved unhealthiness more than health, disorder more than order, rape more than lovemaking. It loved the vulgar more than the refined, anguish more than reflection, and destruction more than creation.

Everyone thought that K had lost his mind. K wished he had. How much happier he would be if he were crazy. But the Minotaur wouldn't permit even that. The Minotaur demanded that K observe his self-destruction with icy coolness. Nothing delighted the Minotaur more than K's suffering, and in this alone the God seemed truly satisfied.

K went on like this with no end in sight.

Then one night K sighed.

What a stupid thing I did, he sighed. I wanted to create a God and I summoned a demon. And a foul-minded maze-demon at that. How could I forget that the Minotaur was born of evil, and his maze was a forest of error?

K felt sick and went to throw up in the bathroom sink.

From the skylight over the bath he saw crescent moons, dancing a polka scornfully at the zenith of the night sky.

K took several deep breaths to calm down.

At this point, I have to go for broke, even if it means annihilation. I have to break my chains and run for it. *With* the Minotaur. Yes. I don't know if the Minotaur is a God or a demon, but I created him and I breathed life into him. It's my duty to run with the Minotaur—no, it's my destiny.

Destiny! Isn't this exactly what I have been waiting for? I was drowning in a sea of possibilities unable to grab hold of any solid thing. I was struggling with all my might to get away from all those possibilities. I was a prisoner of the demon "possibilities." I don't need possibilities any more. All I need is to follow my destiny. Isn't that why I laid out the maze, tried to build my robot, and created my God? When I think about it now, they were all miscalculations, but now at last I've really found my destiny. And it's the most noble and supreme destiny in this world—annihilation.

K looked up at the moon through the skylight and was so shocked that he nearly collapsed.

Where five moons had danced in the heavens, K saw, for the first time in his life, a single crescent moon, shining divinely like the single, remaining possibility it was.

First published, 1985
TRANSLATION BY JEFFREY HUNTER

Kyoji Kobayashi (b. 1957) first received attention as a writer while still in graduate school at Tokyo University, where he was an active member of the University Haiku Society. *Telephone Man* (1984), his first novella, ably demonstrated his avowed aim to infuse prose fiction with haiku aesthetics, winning him the 3rd Kaien New Writer's Award, while another novella, *The Tale of a Novel* (1986), was nominated for the coveted Akutagawa Prize. Kobayashi has also written a serialized newspaper column on haiku, since collected under the title *A Practical Course in Haiku for Young People* (1988), and edited the PEN Club's critical anthology *What is Haiku?* (1989). Kobayashi is no staid classicist, however; his genius is to address the alienation of the "information age" in a youthful yet emotionally distanced style somewhere between paragraphed prose and line-by-line haiku. Kobayashi's latest novel is *The Fall of Zeus Garden* (1989).

The second half the novella *Mazelife* (1985), excerpted here, takes up after an introductory survey of the protagonist K's circumscribed sphere of activities—which K calls his "maze"—a nexus of predetermined pathways by which he goes about his daily routine.

MOMOTARO IN A CAPSULE
Masahiko Shimada

TRIANGLE

From the time he was twelve, Kurushima idolized the brave, beautiful phalluses of primitive sculpture. Phalluses like oversized nightsticks: heavy, gleaming, black, hard, glaring provocatively heavenward, brimming with a fearless laughter, as if they had a special connection with some omnipotent god. "Wish I had a cock like that," was the thought that found natural expression in his dreams.

The Kurushima-of-his-dreams had an ideal penis, manmade of a light alloy, which he would strap onto his own organ in the toilet every morning before he went out. This was a one-touch operation, like capping a bottle. The device had great flexibility; even attached, it in no way hindered his normal functions. Moreover, it was doubly useful since he could take it off and swing it around and use it as a weapon. He had only to wear it and self-confidence was his.

People have to take responsibility for their own genitals. That area, which shies from strangers' glances, may be a breeding ground for the sorrows and sufferings of the self. Whenever Kurushima eyed his, he grew depressed. This was his conclusion:

"My genitals were made for masturbation. Masturbation, my genitals, and my room form a fatal triangle."

Kurushima employed several techniques to protect his genitals. When he stood, he struck a particular pose. He would stuff his hands in his pockets and cross his legs. When this posture did not work, he would plant his hands in his groin, forming a wall around his genitals, a variation of standing at Attention. Or if he were sitting, he would shield his genitals by lifting his knees or by planting his arms like posts to barricade his inner thighs.

In his own words: "To protect one's genitals is to protect oneself. One's genitals are the guardians of one's identity." An earth-shattering thesis. He also said this: "The penis, like the tongue, nose, eyes, and ears, is a sensory organ. Its sensations are the keenest." And: "A penis has an outside and an inside. Men of action develop the outside. Men of thought develop the inside."

Kurushima's housing-development–variety penis was appropriate to the introspective man. His introspection was near-autistic.

Kurushima idolized the outside world. But he needed some momentum to propel him beyond the narrow slit of his aluminum-grated window. He passed the time reading books, listening to cassettes in his room. And once a day, as if he had suddenly remembered to do so, he would flip through the pages of his scrapbook. Dozens of naked women. Whom shall we do today? Yesterday was the girl from New York with a 36-inch bust. Today, let's diddle that former pop singer for old times' sake.

Not a bad life, but...

Momotaro the "Peach Boy" burst from his peel and developed respectable genitals. But then he had to go kill ogres. That was a drag, tiresome. There was a cute girl in the village. He would lure her up into the hills, push her over, and... But if he couldn't do that, he was fine holed up in the house, masturbating. Not a bad life, but...

Kurushima-Momotaro was perplexed. "Got to do something... But if I screw up, I'll look awful—who knows how many times worse." If he did something and failed, the girl in the village wouldn't give him the time of day. But if he succeeded, he'd have his city girl, and he wouldn't even need his right hand.

Kurushima, with this singular world view, liked the phrase "Recluse in Action." He often thought: "That's the sort of person I'd like to be." But by only thinking about it, he was no more than "Recluse in Introspection." Extremely run-of-the-mill. He thought: "Here I am shut up in this housing-development capsule, and there's nothing I can do about it. But someday, I'll do something. Someday... Meanwhile I'll lie low and wait for my chance." So he sat and watched through the crack of his sunless aluminum-grated window and waited for that unreliable item called "opportunity."

Kurushima rolled into college like a rube on a package tour, not glancing to either side, glued to the guidebook, following the course. Kurushima was the model tour-package tourist, but he could have used a sidekick. Supposing he went in for the normal teamwork... Momotaro did have his dog, monkey, and pheasant for sidekicks, and without them the ogres would have made a plaything of him, an errand boy, using him to death. Alone, he would have been nothing.

EXPANSION AND CONTRACTION

Kurushima had a childhood friend, Komochi, and the two of them would sometimes meet in town and talk about the old days. This childhood friend was also in college. But if Kurushima was at best a student, his friend was at worst a student. In other words, no matter how you stretched it, Kurushima was just a student, while his friend merely assumed the guise of a student. Upon entering college, this Komochi stopped lying low and began to blossom into a reasonable human being. Since then, the gap between Komochi and Kurushima grew a few inches wider each year.

A few days before, Kurushima had been in a bookstore with the latest volume of a philosophy series in his hand, admiring the beauty of its jacket, when out of the corner of his eye he saw Komochi pass by. He placed the book back on the shelf and tailed him. Komochi stopped in the new-books corner and was scanning the contents page of a book entitled *The Æsthetics of Interpersonal Relations*. Kurushima circled behind to surprise him with an upper-arm grip, but Komochi spun around and shouted, "Gotcha, *Cruci-man!*"

"Wrong," said Kurushima. "Nobody nails me with that anymore. My name is Kurushima."

"Nah, you're still the same painful *Cruci-man*. Ha, ha, ha!"

Kurushima forced a smile. But it wasn't long before the smile wore thin.

"What you been up to?" Komochi said, instantly framing an image of Kurushima as hopeless as ever. So what Komochi went on to say was, "*I'm* OK, staying on top of things."

"How about a coffee? I'm buying. We've got some catching up to do," Kurushima said.

Komochi slipped *The Æsthetics of Interpersonal Relations* back onto the shelf, hitched up his pants, and said, "Coming?"

"Weren't you going to buy that?"

"There's nothing written in it that isn't common sense. Nothing new. If my name sold books, *I* could've written it," he said, full of confidence.

Come to think of it, ever since elementary school Komochi had been a genius in dealing with people. Everybody loved him. On the other hand, nobody really loved him. It was as if he were skipping rhythmically over the pavement stones that were his friends; Kurushima was a cracked pavement stone that would always bring him to a halt. Otherwise he might sprain his ankle.

Kurushima thought of Komochi as a true friend, even as someone he owed a great deal to. Komochi had tutored him in masturbation. When Kurushima was thirteen, Komochi showed up one day with a paper bag full of pornographic magazines. Opening one up, he demonstrated for his pupil Kurushima the technique of actively appreciating the arts.

Kurushima felt the thrill of a child at the circus, his whole body about to pop out through his eyes. That was his primal experience, and to some extent, it defined his character.

Out of the vast number of naked women he'd pored over, one had stolen Kurushima's heart. She became his older sister, his mother, his wife. She had a doll's name, Shinobu Yoimachi.

She became a spread in a magazine when she was eighteen, so by now she would be twenty-six. She'd gone straight from the street to big-screen porn—with an image of innocence and purity. In her third film she was recast with a sassy bit part, then not much later retired to home life. Shinobu was frozen with a smile on her face. Kurushima had never seen her with any other expression. She may have been smiling in a desperate effort to divert people's eyes from her naked body. Still, it was not a friendly smile; it was a paradoxical smile, one that held her entire attraction for Kurushima.

Shinobu possessed smooth, volcani-form breasts with smoldering orange nipples. She was lying on a red bed, legs entwined, protecting her genitals with her hand. This was the pose of a woman caressing her own body, about to tell a story. The caption read: "After dropping out of a Tokyo high school, she was a delinquent for a time, some of it as the Madonna of a motorcycle gang. Shinobu Yoimachi, a Cinderella found in a pub where she worked as a part-time waitress—she captures your heart and won't let go."

Kurushima loved her for the longest time. He still loved her; her smile, forever eighteen, was flecked and grainy. Komochi, who had supplied Shinobu, was their Cupid, their dark-skinned, hairy, lovable, impudent angel.

"Anything interesting happen lately?" Komochi asked, lighting a cigarette. "Met anybody interesting?"

"Mildly. One of those New Lefties, I forget which faction. Man, he's filthy and he's flighty. He goes to the print shop every day and picks up leaflets to distribute. He has to be careful when he walks down the street, so he carries some kind of stick. Always wearing sunglasses and saying stuff like, 'I can't let my identity slip,' acting like a spy or an exile being chased by assassins. A little Trotsky. He's living in a dream world, but I still like him."

"New freshmen are all assholes," Komochi said. "They're like machines—the legacy of the examination system. After being machines all their lives, they can finally become human beings in college. But it takes them a while—like guys being so tense their first chance at sex that they can't get it up, or like women who cramp up and can't get their juices going. They're not human beings and they're not machines and they're useless. Some return to the land of the living faster than others; if you say to them, 'Hey, try this,' they'll try it. You get these hayseeds up from the farm, lonely and helpless. They want to do something but can't bring themselves to do it. They're looking for friends—somebody, anybody, even New Lefties. Maybe your friend is like that. You meet somebody, you think they're nice enough, and they turn out to be Lefties. You end up passing out leaflets because you think you owe them something."

"What's wrong with that? That's what youth is about, isn't it?"

"Ha, ha, ha! 'Youth'—the word reeks of semen!" Komochi squinted, tossing off a laugh. And with that laugh the conversation ground to a halt. True to form, he'd quickly pinpointed Kurushima's awkward stance and pulled the discussion out from under him. He was always that way with Kurushima.

Kurushima fell silent.

A lull ensued. Then suddenly, Komochi spoke up. "Next month I'm leaving the country."

"An overseas trip? A sex tour?" asked Kurushima. He glanced up at Komochi, who clicked his tongue and let out an extra big breath.

"I'm going to Egypt. Two years with the Japanese Embassy." Komochi's silent drum was pounding away.

"Really? Wow!" In that instant, Komochi swelled by a turn, and Kurushima shrank by a turn. "What an asshole," Kurushima thought as he shifted his hands to shield his genitals. "This hot shot figures he can swallow me whole."

"If I spend two years in Cairo, I'll meet a lot Egyptian politicians and literati. From here on, it's going to be important to have friends in Third World literary circles, heh heh heh... It's dizzying the way the world is moving. Get caught unprepared, and you'll be dragged along by the system. *We* have to be the ones moving the system. Connections in the Third World'll bring the system to your door. Think about it." Komochi's entire being had become a mouth about to suck Kurushima in. Komochi, a snake.

"It's not going to be easy—the work or the life there," said Kurushima, the frog.

"But if you can't make a few sacrifices, you're no good for anything anyway."

"Ha, ha. Well, okay, fine. You'll do great."

"From now until the beginning of next month, it's going to be farewell parties nonstop. I'm supposed to meet this guy Inonaka for a few drinks in a couple of nights. You want to come?"

"That's okay. I'll pass."

"Aw, c'mon. Inonaka wouldn't harm a hair on man or beast, and he's got a lot in common with you. I think you'll get along."

"I...I hate guys like him," Kurushima resisted Komochi with all his might. Silently, Kurushima grumbled: "Run off to Egypt or who cares where. I'm staying here in Japan. If anything happens, I'll see it with these eyes. You never know, next month there could be a revolution."

Though probably not. The map of Japan wouldn't be redrawn anytime soon.

INONAKA

As it turned out, Kurushima shrank by another turn.

"So much for my friendship with Komochi," he thought and immediately resigned himself to his fate. Meanwhile, Komochi, for his part, also decided to cut things off with Kurushima. Which is why he thought to introduce Kurushima to Inonaka: as a farewell present.

The meeting place was just outside the wicket at the train station, where the flow of people was so fast that anyone standing was in the way. The walking too-big-for-a-coin-locker farewell present didn't show up on time.

"I'm going to go get cigarettes," said Komochi, who disappeared, leaving the two sight-unseen strangers to find each other. Kurushima felt foolish standing there without the least clue how to recognize Inonaka. Not that it bothered him. He stood there like an obstacle. At least ten guys passed by who could have been Inonaka; none were. Then came the fifteenth or sixteenth, a guy with sunglasses and long hair, who walked back and forth in front of Kurushima. Twice. "This can't be him. I don't want this to be him," thought Kurushima. It wasn't him. Kurushima felt buoyant with relief, but then the man addressed him in a low voice: "Aren't you Kurushima of the XX-faction?"

The words sounded strange. Kurushima reflexively cupped his genitals with both hands for protection. He wanted to deny the charge, but his vocal chords clutched for air.

"I want you to come over here for a minute," the guy said.

Newspaper headlines sprang into Kurushima's head: "Gang Violence! Innocent Student Victimized!" His body grew iron-hard and heavy, refusing to move. Eyes, cheeks, ears, mouth, shoulders, all drew into tight triangles; his penis drew its head back into its skin, like a turtle. Why was the man laughing?

Komochi then appeared behind him, grinning. With the return of his ally, Kurushima's triangles rounded off slightly.

"Inonaka, meet Kurushima."

"What?" Kurushima needed about five seconds to absorb this information.

"Sorry if I scared you." Inonaka the actor removed his sunglasses and bowed. "You had to rush things, didn't you, Komochi. Shithead." Kurushima looked at Inonaka from the waist down, hands thrust deep into his pockets. Then their eyes met. Both quickly looked away again, as if they had just seen their own mother's worn-out cunt.

"Let's eat," said Komochi, the matchmaking official, his toothy grin still floating in place.

The three of them went into the Mexican restaurant on the top floor of a building. They ate tacos and drank tequila. Their tongues were burning from the chili sauce, which made them want more tequila. Kurushima and Inonaka liked the music and atmosphere of the place; they affected a pseudo-Latin mood. They started to run their tongues to beat the heat. At first, Komochi, the genius of interpersonal relations, soloed the main themes of the conversation with the other two merely adding dissonant notes. But gradually they built up an active, harmonious accompaniment. They realized they were both residents of the same rut. Like Kurushima, Inonaka had been cell-cultured in a capsule of a massive housing development They had many things in common: the gaze of a somehow dull-witted person; an exceedingly commonplace face; less-than-rhythmical, unsettled movements; a voice suited to exclamations like "What the—?!" and "Cripes!" The matchmaker proved the odd man out.

"I've been playing viola for a year. The viola is close to the human voice. In the orchestra, it stays in the background. It doesn't stand out. The violin has this piercing whine and the cello sounds out of sorts; they play the losers. There's something awkward about them. But the orchestra couldn't hang together without the viola; it would be too thin, flat. That's why I like it. Besides, there aren't many people who play it, so even if you're no good, you get treated like you're important. You can always blame mistakes in a performance on the violins or cellos," said Inonaka gleefully. "If I ever said anything like this around the orchestra, I'd be in trouble..."

"If you play a musical instrument, you must be some kind of artist," Kurushima said, nodding.

"Nah, you couldn't call me an artist. It's something I do because I don't have anything else to do. A tennis racket's too thin, so I prefer the viola. It's a little thicker. Anybody can play the viola. You follow the exercises and practice your scales. You write in the fingering numbers on your score and press the strings by the numbers. You play anything?"

"No. I just listen. Mostly classical stuff. I like Mahler. I feel secure in the stubborn repetition of themes."

Inonaka nodded three times. Komochi, having polished off all the food and drink, sat idly by.

"You want more tequila? Waiter, more tequila!" Komochi shouted with gusto. The evening was supposed to have been a send-off for Komochi, but had turned into a get-to-know-you for Inonaka and Kurushima. He was left adrift.

"So the two autistics hit it off."

"Autistics? What are you talking about?" asked Inonaka, after thinking it over.

"I remember cutting class with you in high school and going off to eat noodles in some stand-up joint. You couldn't make up your mind, but finally decided to get your big butt in gear. You ate a bowl of plain *soba* and a bowl of *udon*. You were so thrilled. You said, 'I've never done anything like this before.' If that isn't autistic, I don't know what is. Heh heh." Once more, that grin. "Now Kurushima here, being Kurushima, used to see a shrink regularly."

"Did not." Kurushima lifted his glass and fired up his tongue. "I only went once, when I had insomnia around exam time. I just went to see if it would do any good."

"They made you draw pictures, didn't they? Weren't you schizophrenic?"

"What are you talking about? There was nothing wrong with me. I'm perfectly normal," said Kurushima, his hands digging toward his groin to cup his genitals.

"You're pretty weird, the two of you," Komochi said. Both Kurushima and Inonaka wore the faces of patients listening to medical examination results. Doctor Komochi was all teeth.

"I'm weird, weird, weird," thought Kurushima, repeating the name of his disease to himself.

Then suddenly his expression changed and he said, "Weird? I'm tired of people who see things in two dimensions. I hate it. Right or left, sane or crazy, elite or drop-out, gloomy or cheerful. I utterly reject such simplistic dialectics."

"You're drunk." Komochi spoke in a voice that sounded like he'd been sober for ten years.

Kurushima's and Inonaka's eyes met. They nodded in agreement. "We're not this or that. We don't fit into neat categories," Kurushima said.

"You mean you're half-baked."

"No. It's more complicated than that. I'm...Kurushima," he blurted out.

"Don't kid yourself. You're either trash or you're crazy. Which is it?" Komochi said, pounding his belly and laughing.

"Guess I'm going to have to take steps," thought Kurushima.

REBELLIOUS PHASE

Komochi flew off to Egypt, leaving Kurushima and Inonaka in Japan, which he called the "land of Potemkin villages and papier-maché people." The two were to meet again in that giant terrarium of bad taste, Tokyo. In the middle of this artificial city was the district of Asakusa, an involved stage set with its temples, amusement park, betting parlors, movie theaters, and countless shops, amusements, shacks, and garbage dumps. On closer inspection, you could find the Rising Sun, military uniforms, Japanese swords, Buddhist altars, *zori*, shoes, prayer beads, frying pans, puffed-rice sweets, leather jackets, *kimono*, and masks; on the street there were cigarette butts, scraps of paper, spit, vomit, footsteps, car horns, police sirens, pigeons cooing, the sound of flapping wings, children's tantrums, shopgirls' voices, the cheap cymbals of mechanical toy monkeys, background music drowning into noise, the smells of *yakitori*, stews, *imagawayaki* cakes, coffee, incense, drunks, pigeon shit. Asakusa contains these ingredients as a minimum. Active recluses? Even Kurushima and Inonaka ought to blend right into Asakusa. There aren't many things that don't belong in mulligan stew.

The pair emerged from the subway station, bumped around a bit, and ended up in Hatsune Lane, stopping where the first mama-san called out to them, "Hi, guys, come in and have a drink. This place is on the up-and-up." They went into the shack of a bar and sat on the wooden bench.

They were their usual stiff selves. They poured each other a beer and drank a silent toast. The mama-san, on the verge of retirement from womanhood, elbowed into their silence. "Good to have you. Not too many customers like you come here. Mostly day laborers..."

Inonaka put on an understanding face and nodded like a psychiatrist as the woman started in about her grandchildren. The pair were stuck keeping her monologue going with "uh-huhs" and "I sees."

"Always asking for more allowance...I buy them shoes for their birthdays...This shop never earned me more than cigarette money...Plenty of customers forget to pay their tabs...Get a day's work and blow it on their Yoshiwara whores...But it's my only pleasure in life...My oldest grandchild is in eighth grade...But he's gone rotten, rides around on a motorbike without a license."

"Junior high school and riding a motorbike. Cool," said Kurushima, coloring his gaze with interest.

"He's in a Rebellious Phase. I tell him to be careful or he'll get in an accident, maybe hurt somebody, and all he says is, 'I know, I know.'"

"A Rebellious Phase...," murmured Kurushima, as if in

fond remembrance. "What was my Rebellious Phase like?" he thought to himself, recalling the girls in those pictures, Shinobu Yoimachi, his ideal, the girl he worshipped. "Come to think of it, as an actress, she always played rebellious parts."

"I bet you two don't come from around here. Not from Asakusa."

"You can tell, huh? Yeah, we just came over to hang out."

"Thought so. You look like good boys. From a good part of town."

Kurushima and Inonaka looked at each other.

"Good boys, eh?" said Inonaka, thrusting his hands deep into his pockets and crossing his legs.

Kurushima and Inonaka were two sorry youths deprived of their Rebellious Phase by an unknown something. In the sixth grade or so, a time when children become strangely discriminating in their ways, just before their Rebellious Phase, the two experienced a strange lull instead.

Most children got along well with their parents and teachers; in some sense, they were almost grafted onto them. These children would soon pay full fare on the bus, which gave them the illusion that adults were their peers. This was the flip-side to their precociousness.

But their illusions came crumbling down when the walls of control were laid bare. "The society of control runs on rules. Those who can't obey the rules are obliged to leave." That kind of cold, bureaucratic treatment only instilled the attitude that "You're not fool enough to take the sensible route, are you?" which led, like a standard opening move in a game of *go*, to the Rebellious Phase.

Kurushima and Inonaka, however, had grown up sheltered in their housing-development capsules, never directly encountering any cold walls. For them, the walls of control were covered in velvet, beckoning them to come rub their cheeks against the soft surface obediently. They'd been utterly fooled by smiling parents and teachers, and confined, de facto, to their cells.

Once a good boy, always a good boy, they thought. For if they turned into bad boys, they'd have to bear the responsibility. Until they figured out this thing called responsibility, they preferred to be good boys. Good boys got their perks. As a result, they grew up with bodies incapable of rebellion. They tried, but they couldn't flex any arm muscle. Their genitals recoiled into tight little balls. At times, the anxiety made Kurushima choke: "What if these aren't my genitals? What if I was castrated and this harmless penis for-masturbation-only was sewn on?"

"Kurushima, did you ever have a Rebellious Phase?" asked Inonaka, his chin propped on his hand, eyes staring into space. Kurushima twisted his lips, and with his finger against his neck, scratched like a dog using its hind leg.

"I thought I did. I once ripped off a can of corned beef from a supermarket. That was exciting. I thought I conquered the world. I ate it raw, like a star on TV. It was great. That must have been my Rebellious Phase...but I became a good boy again quickly. I told my parents all about it. I bragged to them about stealing. They didn't get mad. They just shut me up with 'Don't do anything to make your parents unhappy.'"

"And that was it?"

"Yeah. Really, I wanted to rebel. But everything around me was like a cushion. There was no way to rebel. The cushion absorbed all my energy. And that was it."

"So you were quiet as a lamb."

"That's right, a lamb. What's good for the system, unfortunately. But I still want to do *something*, before they make a company man out of me."

"A company man? Is that what you're going to be?"

"No. But if I keep going like this, I won't have any choice. I don't want to be *just* a company man. I want to take advantage of every situation, sieze the day, carpe diem, you know. I don't want to be a company man without having lived."

"Cool." Inonaka let his unfocusing eyes wander over the

daikon radishes and dried mackerel and aloe leaves that were scattered on the counter. The mama-san poured herself a cup of cold *sake*.

"The way I see it, we were robbed of our Rebellious Phase. We've never rebelled anywhere serious. Blame the Rising Sun." The words slurred out as if Kurushima had sand in his mouth. Then he scratched his neck again like a dog.

"So you want to do something?" Inonaka asked in an overturned voice.

"You've got to do something too. If we go on like this, all our hopes or dreams will go down the tube. We'll get old and look back and there won't be a thing worth remembering. Fucking depressing. We better do something right."

"What are you working up to?"

"Well, we got to start realistically, got to start small and build up."

"Build up? Sounds like cram school," Inonaka said with a forced smile, his eyes as bloodshot as if he'd been crying.

Meanwhile Kurushima ruminated over the sand in his mouth, his expression intensifying like a firecracker about to go off. Now and again, painful restrained moans escape his lips.

"Inonaka, I've got an idea. Mama, the check! Let's go. We'll have a ceremony. Don't worry. Just come along." Suddenly, Kurushima was no longer living Hamlet's soliloquy. He could hear fanfare trumpeting in his head.

Leaving the shacks, the two weaved through the mass of Asakusa. Inonaka tried to say something, but by now he was a mere onlooker. Kurushima kept moaning, more and more from some kind of pleasure.

"We need this for the ceremony. Let's buy it," said Kurushima, grabbing a Japanese flag from the front of a shop just as the shutter was coming down.

"Hey, what are you doing, buying something like that? Knock it off. Why...?" Inonaka started.

"Don't worry. I'm not going to abuse it. And I'm not

going to fly it from my front door." Kurushima folded up the flag and put it in his pocket like a handkerchief. He took off half-stumbling down another street and quickly surveyed the scene like a sentry. Spotting a hardware store about to close, he dove in, crying, "Lucky! Lucky!" He emerged clutching a pair of scissors.

"What are you going to cut?"

"Just wait and see. Let's go to the Asakusa Temple. It's easier to have a ceremony when no one's around." Kurushima had all the confidence of a Don Quixote, waving his arms as he advanced. Inonaka was Sancho Panza, quavering in pursuit.

The two entered the temple grounds, and the ceremony began. Kurushima pulled the flag from his pocket and unfolded it. He pursed his lips together in a straight line, cast a glance at Inonaka's now sharply trained eyes and gathered up the center of the flag. Then, scissors in hand, he took the red-dyed spot and—

"These scissors are lousy. They're cheap paper scissors."

"What the fuck are you doing?" asked Sancho Panza, his eyes knitted in a tight triangle.

A distorted red circle was cut out of the flag. The Rising Sun had become two separate pieces. Kurushima put the white part with the hole on his head and stuck the red circle in his pants, so as to protect his groin. "What do you think? Holistic anarchism and blushing-red birthMarx, or maybe burning-red pox Marx. Well anyway, something like that. Clever, no?" Kurushima struck a pose. "With this, we'll earn our stripes. Our Rebellious Phase has started. Of course, we're not rebelling against our parents or professors. We're rebelling against the State. We will expel the ogres from Ogre's Island!"

In Japan, with its highly developed Ogre's Island infrastructure, anti-establishment Momotaros had been all but annihilated. They had to do something to halt the extermination. They couldn't just laugh it away.

"What's the principle behind this rebellion?" asked Inonaka.

"We don't need a principle. This is a rebellion without a cause," Kurushima declared. He was tired of talking.

Inonaka was not satisfied.

"It's hard to explain the cause for a rebellion without a cause," Kurushima said, "but there is a reason. Only words are inadequate. Society underestimates the value of rebellion. Niceness is now the rage, and rebels are considered throwbacks to the past. Being nice means being obedient. Which is wrong. *Nice and rebellious* is best."

Kurushima's face was composed of many triangles, each triangle well-balanced and neatly positioned. It didn't strike people as ill-formed; it was boring to behold. His was the face of someone nice and obedient. And nice folk detest violence. So, too, do their genitals...

But at least, Kurushima wasn't obedient. His nipples told you that. Those vestigial organs were the only beautiful, masculine thing about him. The two little erections smiled fearlessly with a latent will to rebel.

"What we have to do is reclaim the Rebellious Phase that was stolen from us," he said. "People incapable of rebelling are cogs in someone else's wheel. That's what education does—it's an exercise in gearing down. And if we keep going like this, we'll start slipping between the gears. Everybody knows this. Nobody does anything about it, *really*. Sure, they complain, but in the end they're all good little boys who turn into good little company men. Not even worth being smug about. It's too normal. We have to put up a fight. We have to find out what makes us different. After that, if we like, we can still turn into company men. But if we're lucky, we could be heroes and leave them behind in the haze."

ARTIFICIAL GENITALS

After the ceremony, the two discussed their plan of action. First, to rebel required tools. In the past, the tools were hel-

mets, steel pipes, Molotov cocktails. Today those tools were
good only for digging your grave. Neither Kurushima nor
Inonaka knew the first thing about the use of violence
besides. For them, raised in a faux-pastoral environment, violence was alien. It was something that happened on television.

Their genitals were of no use. Their spongy tissues would
have to develop further to violate women. Their members
didn't get hard enough to ram it in. The only possible sexual
encounter for them would be if some kind young woman
took pity on them.

Possessed of bodies that reflexively rejected violence, they
could rebel but feebly. Hence they came to the very sensible
decision to start at the bottom. They would acclimate themselves to violence slowly, train their bodies for rebellion rigorously. They were guarded, knowing that something rash,
like throwing stones at a police station, would end their
Rebellious Phase in a concentration camp.

Inonaka quit the orchestra and joined a hard-rock band,
bringing with him that precious second phallus of his—the
viola. Hard rock is the music of sex drive, a means of con-
verting the wanna-do-it impulse into sound. Playing classical
music, he'd had trouble with *pianissimo* passages, but hard
rock was pure *fortissimo* sex. To hell with beautiful tone
color. Power was everything—three times more intense than
Stravinsky, twelve times more emotive than Mozart. Violent,
primitive, naked. Hadn't rock always stood for rebellion?
Inonaka would take this libidinal music, blend in some agit-
prop, and create a tool of rebellion against the State. To that
end, he'd practice making raw sounds with his viola. The
viola—second-string orchestral instrument—would rebel
with him. Revved up with courage the likes of which he
hadn't felt since the day he skipped school for that cheap
noodle stand, he dyed his hair red.

Kurushima, for his part, took his earnings from tutor-

ing—he'd saved the entire amount since he'd had nothing to
spend it on—and procured a complete set of tools for his
rebellion. He encased his head, which kneaded logic like clay,
in a red helmet and made his street debut as a latter-day
biker. He had never before even mounted one of those 50-cc
scooters favored by housewives. All he had done was walk,
all-too-safely, all-too-nondescript, hands buried in his pockets, warding off all possible threats to his genitals—pocket-
books, paper bags, umbrellas, lit cigarettes, lustful hands. By
the look of him, he was exhaustion on two legs, invariably
plodding homeward through threatening crowds. Now his
body from the waist down found itself astride a 250-cc sex
machine, a giant roaring ramrod on two wheels with lights to
banish the darkness.

With bloodshot eyes, the two made plans for their future.
Inonaka would drag out his rock band and Kurushima would
lead his young bikers, merging them together into a major
demonstration. They would stage a Tantrum Against the
State rock concert. After each song, smart and dumb alike
could take turns screaming into the microphone. They'd
shout anything they wanted: "Disband the University!"
"Mass Temporary Insanity!" "The Liberal Democratic
Party's Educational Reform Sucks!" They would rail and
wail and flail against the State. Someone had to lash out
against contemporary Japan.

The mere vision of himself leading this Tantrum Against
the State brought a tingle to Kurushima's nipples, hot breath
on the back of his neck. He would train for that day. He
would master his 250-cc chrome cock. He would go to the
driving school, five minutes' walk from his apartment, every
day until his artificial genitals were one with his own flesh.
He had to be able to change gears smoothly, to drive across a
narrow span without falling over, to skid his artificial genitals
in a figure-eight. Kurushima was ecstatic. Whenever he had a
free moment, he'd spread out a map and sketch in the route
of the demonstration in red.

One month after the cutout Rising Sun ceremony in
Asakusa, Kurushima got his license and hit the street for the
first time, fitted out with one of the brave, beautiful phalluses
he'd idolized since the age of twelve.

Kurushima put on his blood-red helmet, pulled the strap
tight, and kicked over the engine. It didn't start. He pulled
out the choke and tried again. The engine hesitated. On the
third try, it caught. The sex thruster grew hot, full of energy,
strong, hard. He turned the throttle a little more, producing a
full-throated growl. Not bad for a used bike. Gleaming black
body and provocatively up-thrust exhaust pipe. A fine
machine. The cock-on-wheels emerged from the apartment
courtyard to the public thoroughfare.

Kurushima wasn't sure what expression to wear while riding. The wind tickled his face, so no expression could be
fixed in place. The muscles in his cheeks twitched and mold-
ed a wry grin. Who's on this bike? he asked, pressing his face
to the rearview mirror, "This is me," Kurushima answered,
"me on wheels."

At his first traffic signal, Kurushima stretched his leg
down to the ground. Grunting, he glowered at the green
hatchback next to him. His eyes met the gaze of a woman
who looked like a mannequin in a shop window. Kurushima
grew anxious. The woman turned to the driver and spoke.
Then there were two damp smiles in the shop window.
"Smile back," Kurushima said to himself. "I'm the one riding. This is my prick."

The man and woman in the green box were about
Kurushima's age or younger. Whatever they were talking
about in their little box, whatever they touched between
them, whatever they were up to, what difference did it make?

The signal turned green. Kurushima wiped the smile from
his face and sped ahead, shooting a hot farewell of exhaust
fumes over the encapsulated pair, who in fact resembled the
Kurushima of a month ago.

Twenty minutes riding and his lower half still hadn't gotten used to the bike. He'd have to ride until it did. A petty bourgeois with the lower half of a hero didn't make any more sense than a hero with the lower half of a petty bourgeois. Astride his motorcycle, Kurushima was the former; dismounted, the latter. Not until he could use the machine at will would the hero of his fabulous imagination become the hero on the street.

Kurushima relaxed when he saw the road to the housing development he lived in. A comforting fatigue spread through his body. Yet the very next instant, his nerves grew taut again. A toy soldier was blocking his way. A uniformed man in a white turtle-shaped helmet raising his right arm Nazi-style and directing Kurushima to stop.

"There's a stop sign there. Didn't you see it?"

"What? A sign? I guess I didn't see it."

"Your license, please."

"It was just a careless mistake. I'm sorry." Kurushima scratched his neck like a dog.

"That's what everybody says. Every one you don't see is business for us. Heh, heh, heh."

The toy soldier's insult motivated him to train yet more earnestly. Every day, except when it rained, for about an hour after dinner, he faithfully staged his mock protest. On holidays, he ventured farther afield and made picnics of his demonstrations. He would learn the techniques by drilling, like studying for multiple-choice exams. Already there were signs that his artificial genitals were becoming part of his body. He became a master of "Marilyn Monroe riding," getting through traffic jams by wiggling his butt.

The biker also undertook to retool his imagination. He spent the next two weeks immersed in books. He spent time in the library. In his room or on the train, his hands were never without a book. He read and read, whatever his hands came upon. The latest philosophical works, anthropology, linguistics, Celine, biker diaries, comics, first-aid manuals, all of these blended together exquisitely in Kurushima's soft gray matter.

He loved to race down narrow alleyways. He took the route he'd mapped out for the Tantrum Against the State, adding small detours where shouting out slogans would be most effective. At times like these, Kurushima felt his whole being transformed into an ejaculating penis. His nipples cried out in ecstasy.

He painted his trademark in day-glo paint on his blood-red helmet and gleaming black bike. He didn't belong to any real, organized motorcycle gang. He was a lone lancer fighting his own struggle. His trademark told the story: a penis and a pen.

One Saturday evening, lapping up the narrow back streets, Kurushima spied a pack of toy soldiers gathering force at an intersection. It looked like action. So he turned off the engine of his artificial phallus, lit a cigarette, and made himself a spectator to the circus he felt sure was about to begin.

The toy soldiers, who were armed, were deep in discussion, speaking to their colleagues by walkie-talkie. Traffic was light, but people were milling about. This was an active nightlife district. There was alcohol in almost everyone, so it would take very little to set off a blaze of excitement. Also, satisfied and dissatisfied people were mixed in equal proportions. Middle-of-the-roaders, the type who like to watch, were few. Kurushima was one of the few.

Presently, from a distance, there resounded a loud gnashing of teeth. A gang of hyenas, riding bodies of steel, roared up in a burst of grease into the glaring lamplight. All that held them back were the toy soldiers masquerading proudly as the defenders of justice. It was a grand spectacle in the making, right in the middle of a public street.

The toy soldiers took firm grip of their nightsticks, ready to begin swinging. The hyenas loomed closer. Some had no helmets. Wearing sneakers with heels worn down, they spread their legs provocatively and thrust their jaws upward. Some bared their flesh and laughed. As the gang entered the intersection, the entire area was enveloped in noise, as if the hyenas had spotted fresh carnage. The moment they closed in, the toy soldiers started swinging, sending the horde scattering in all directions.

"Assholes!" the bikers cried, spitting out their textbook curses.

Most of the spectators appeared to side with the toy soldiers. Kurushima, of course, sided with neither.

Two hyenas grazed by him. One fallen hyena, in a last gasp of defiance, yelled out: "Remember this!"

The New Left had faded into the woodwork like the old Red Guard, wearing business suits of asphalt gray. As a result, the police lost their contentiousness and really had become like toy soldiers. They squared off against the motorcycle gangs only for the sake of appearance. There was a tacit understanding between them, for the bikers and the ogres of Ogre's Island had cut a deal. The prevailing order would not be threatened. This was the lesson Kurushima learned from the Saturday night circus.

Kurushima got himself all worked up. "How the hell am I ever going to carry my heroics off?" Compared with the bikers, he was an extremely "good boy," suffering from good boys' desires not to do anything too radical. If he joined a biker gang, there was a chance he could organize them into action. But would they have anything to do with a strange bird like him? With that, Kurushima became the good boy again. "Maybe I can't do anything," he muttered, "after all."

HALF TONES

The next time Kurushima and Inonaka met, it was in Asakusa again. There was no other part of town that kept its rudder down, no matter which way the wind blew. They ate stew in the same plywood shack of the mama-san with the rebellious grandson. Today she was interrogating a customer whose credit had worn thin.

Inonaka lowered his eyes and thrust his hands deep into his pockets. "The viola is a flop," he started. "It just doesn't go with rock. The music is so rigid, the viola can't break in. All I do is hold it under my arm while I pretend I know how to sing. I'm pretty bad. But worse, the band and I don't have a thing in common. They buy the party line. This Tantrum Against the State concert didn't interest them at all. 'Bor—ing' was their only response."

Inonaka parted his hair with his fingers. As if he were in great pain, his brow furrowed and he turned pale. "And I wish I never dyed my hair. I'm scared the color won't ever come out..."

"Hey, don't give up, man."

"How about you? You look like a changed being."

"Really? Well, to tell the truth, the bike terrifies me. Several times I almost wiped out. Once I snagged my mirror passing a car, and the driver started screaming. Then this cop showed up... Sometimes I think the bike is going to kill me. But then, sometimes it's fantastic. I feel like a *kamikaze* pilot, wanting to ride forever... Still most of the time, the whole biker scene sucks."

"Huh?" Inonaka's face registered total incomprehension.

"Motorcycle gangs do dumb stuff like gouge their bodies with barbed wire. The scars are supposed to be medals of honor. It's supposed to mean that riding is life. But all that tough born-to-die stuff is passé. I don't care if riding's one of the few things you actually can risk your life at these days. Thing is, for a bunch of guys risking their lives, they sure give up fast. Most of them retire from active duty at seventeen. 'Can't keep doing this bullshit forever,' they say. They treat it like a fad... Oh, forget it." Kurushima stopped for breath and downed his beer. "Mama, more beer and stew, please."

Kurushima started up again. "Got to do something with

these motorcycle gangs. Maybe start some 'art movement' or rally them behind some anti-nationalist banner. They've got to change, get out of their mindlessness. Their militaristic hierarchy is such a crock. The younger bikers have to be so submissive, it's pathetic. And this thing they have about home turf—they're so loyal to where they came from, they're like farmers. I mean, grass roots is one thing, but this is tribalism. If they want to fight, they shouldn't waste their energy. They should ram it up the State. Just think—if they joined together, they could be screaming stuff like 'Smash Disciplinarian Education!'"

The mama-san was silent. The plywood boards creaked when the wind blew.

"Aren't many bars like this left anymore," Inonaka offered.

Mama pretended to be thinking. Then she said, "Guess you're right. I've been doing business here for twenty-five years. Boy, have things changed. Japan's gotten so rich, everything's so prim and proper. When were you two born, anyway?"

"Nineteen sixty-something."

"Nineteen sixty-something? What's that by the Japanese calendar?"

"Showa thirty-something."

"That so? Yeah, people had life then. The students who came in here, their eyes were shining. They were thinking about how to change the world."

"Shining eyes, eh, mama-san. How about ours?" asked Kurushima, fearing the worst. The proprietress looked at their faces or, rather, at the glasses in their hands.

"All young eyes shine," she said, picking up the bottle and filling their glasses. "More beer, guys?"

Their eyes did appear to sparkle. But on closer look, you could see they were just watery. Watery eyes are siblings to yawns. And the father of yawns is...dissatisfaction.

"Not to change the subject, but I've been listening to a lot of Shostakovich lately. He's really great," said Inonaka, apropos of nothing.

"I wouldn't know."

"The 'Song of the Dead' from his 14th Symphony—I listen to it every day now. Brings tears to my eyes. Like the guy's playing games with tonality. There's this one melody line that flows so smoothly, and then at the end, just when he should return to the main theme, everything's off by a half tone. Trips me up every time. It's the wierdest feeling. That's what I like about it. That feeling of something that's not resolved."

"Wouldn't it be fun to be one of those half tones and play games with tonality. Tonality's got to be like the system. And the half tones play games with the system. Not bad," Kurushima mused, "I could be sharp and you could be flat."

"Even if we were half tones, we couldn't escape tonality, though. You could put it the other way and say the system was playing games with us half tones. Ha ha ha."

Inonaka's eyes watered up all the more, his laughing face unbearable.

Kurushima laughed, too. But at some point, the essence of his laughter was lost, and his face turning into a laughing death mask. "We've still got to do something," he said.

"Aaah," was Inonaka's castrated reply.

CASTRATION

Kurushima sat down to dinner with his parents for the first time in a long while. Afterwards, while his mother washed the dishes and his father scanned the evening paper, he watched a quiz show on television. An ordinary living room at 7:45 P.M.

"And now for the next question," said the announcer on the tube. His assistant read the question.

He got as far as "Since 1980, all national universities have—" when someone pushed the button.

"We're still in mid-question, but go ahead, contestant A," the announcer said.

"Conducted standardized entrance exams," said contestant A.

Buzzaanhh! Contestant A, who parted his hair just to the right of center, made a great show of slumping back into his seat.

"Too bad! There's still more to the question."

"...all national universities have held standardized entrance exams. What form are the answers?" asked the assistant.

"Multiple-choice," responded the living-room contestant Kurushima. "And I'm sick of hearing about it."

"Say, Shinichi, you just took that test," said his father.

"It was just a reflex test."

Kurushima was a master at filling in the small white bubbles on the answer sheet. Blackening the ovals quickly without going outside the lines was an art. A no. 2 pencil was best and it was fun to perform the simple, rhythmical action. *Scritch scratch scritch.* If only he could find a profession that would build on this talent, but all he could think of was the "censor" who blackened out genitals in pornographic photographs and films.

Kurushima stood up and looked at the tabletop.

"What happened to the tea?"

"I thought you didn't want any more, so I took it away," said his mother, an ordinary, conservative, housing-development housewife. She was the black hole of the household.

"I was still drinking it."

"How's college? Are you going to classes?" asked his father, who, being unaccustomed to speaking with his son, relied on these worn-out phrases.

"No way. But I'll get the credits."

"Just make sure you get the credits. If you have a job all lined up and then don't graduate, well, that would be..."

"You think I don't know that ten times over?" said

Kurushima, who wasn't much good at talking with his father either.

"You going out on your bike again tonight?"

"Yeah. If I don't run it at least once a day, the engine gets weird."

"Why are you so crazy about that bike lately? Shouldn't you be thinking about finding a job for after graduation?" his father expostulated dully.

"Getting a job is prostitution. Before that, I have to have my Rebellious Phase. You just sit back and watch and keep your mouth shut," Kurushima said, bolting from the table toward his room.

"Why don't you play tennis or something, instead of riding that bike all the time?" said his mother, straining to sound young.

"If I played tennis, I couldn't rebel against the State."

"Keep letting out hot air like that, and nobody'll like you. Girls won't like you."

"You think I care?"

"You think that a Rebellious Phase at this late date will amount to anything?" his father countered.

"Back when most guys go through their Rebellious Phase, I was so tame, wasn't I? You didn't have a thing to worry about. I can't go through my whole life being a total wimp," Kurushima said, clicking his tongue before going to hole up in his room.

He stared at the fluorescent ceiling light. A baby's crying pierced the housing-development courtyard. White walls, lace curtains, aluminum-grated window, bed. His cell. Like in a hospital.

Kurushima had his eyes set on working for a first-rate company as a final destination, but he was also struggling to break away from the package tour, waltzing to crawl out of the womb the State had made for him. "I'll get born, I'll show them. Of my own will, from this womb...rip the umbilical cord free..."

He checked his breathing. From the diaphragm. Exhaling through his nose. The rhythm of his breaths grew faster. His pulse stepped up in pitch. It pounded out a stammering SOS. "Got to do something." Kurushima's body became an acute triangle of suffering. His testicles were shrinking into his body.

He walked over to the bookshelf and took down the scrapbook where his 35-24-36 lover of ten years ago, Shinobu Yoimachi, lived. Kurushima dropped his pants and started to have sex with the naked girl on the desk. Her volcani-form breasts, her eternal triangular smile. "How's that? Good? Hurt a little more!" Kurushima rolled in the mess of his thoughts. He didn't know what he was thinking, but he was thinking. He pulled on his dick studiously, violently. It turned red from the friction. He changed his grip and pulled harder. "Tits, nipples, navel, cunt, cunt, cunt, countless cunts..." and then a white sputter. Those innumerable, poor, unsatisfied gametes, thrown away in tissue paper.

He closed the scrapbook. He didn't like having her around naked when business was done. He put her back on the shelf and wiped the sweat from his face. He lay down on the bed, thinking how he'd always been dissatisfied. "Everyone around me's so 'well-adjusted,' they're getting by just fine. But people who get along fine always end up stabbing someone else in the back. Young people in Korea, young people in England, they know the importance of violent action. Why don't young people in Japan? They're all just jerking off."

"The young people of Japan" was what Kurushima thought of as he looked at his crotch, then at his right hand. And then "the old people of Japan," who are really a bunch of assholes. Saving up all the money and power, tying up all the young people in the bonds of administration, forcing them onto the fascist bandwagon, not giving a damn that the wagon is headed full-speed for the concentration camp. Hell, somebody better stop it.

Kurushima pulled his helmet out from under the bed, his

key from the desk drawer, and headed for the front door.

"See you later."

"Remember, today's Saturday. Watch out for those motor-cycle gangs. If you get hurt, it'll upset your mother." Kurushima's father didn't turn to face him as he spoke. Kurushima paid no attention anyway.

The engine was in top form. The night air was uncommonly clear. There were more stars than usual. Maybe two days before full moon, but the unclouded orb tonight was sexy. "I ride—for myself, for Shinobu, for the moon." Kurushima breathed deep.

"*Ampo Funsai!* Smash the U.S.-Japan Mutual Security Treaty!" Kurushima shouted as he cut through the wind at 45 miles per hour. There was nothing anachronistic about that slogan; it was beautiful, lyrical Japanese. For an instant, Kurushima imagined the Emperor mouthing the slogan. That face, that voice—"*Ampo Funsai!*"

Tomorrow was Sunday. He and Inonaka could go somewhere far away. They could hold a demonstration, just the two of them. A demonstration in a terrarium is better than a desktop revolution. "We could play Shostakovich's 'Song for the Dead,' wear placards protesting disciplinarian education, drive slowly down the left lane. In the daytime, we could eat *onigiri* riceballs and drink pop. In the evening we could toast our victory with beer."

Kurushima hit the main drag. There were few cars and few people about. All of a sudden, a horde of motorcycles careened into view, the bikers holding something in their hands. "Pathetic, simple-minded fools." He wasn't afraid. "If I could get this crowd to join tomorrow's demonstration, it'd be the answer to my dreams. The Tantrum Against the State. I'm cool. Let me into your group."

Kurushima snaked his way near. They even had women in the gang. "Hey," he called out, the Kurushima-mark on his helmet glinting in the dark. Just then, a guy in red pants broke from the center of the group and rode up to him. The biker held high the staff of baptism by violence. Kurushima braked his bike full force with his whole body and crouched his upper half forward, trying to evade the first blow. In the next instant, a dull heavy thud came down on his helmet. Kurushima's steel sex machine wrenched out from under his clumsy stuntman's fall. He hit the street. The metal cock shot yards ahead as if it had a will of its own, then keeled over. He heard a woman's voice, clearly. A cry of pain or a shout of joy? He couldn't tell. "Shinobu? Is that you?"

He felt no pain, but couldn't get up. He wished he'd gone to the toilet before. What if the ambulance didn't have a toilet? His pants felt warm and damp. "Now I've pissed in my pants. No, maybe it's blood. It better be blood." The band of hyenas raced around him, like a boxer circling the body of his floored opponent, then roared off, leaving him in a cloud of exhaust. *One, two, three, four, five*...Kurushima tried to summon the strength to stand...*six, seven, eight*...Kurushima felt dizzy. A street lamp doing the count, pale light, full of love...*nine, ten*. No go. Kurushima had been KO'd. The street-lamp referees turned suddenly cold. "Is my rod still in one piece?" Five yards away, his 250-cc sex machine lay on the ground. The rearview mirror was lying alone on the side. "Tomorrow's demo has been cancelled." Here he was lying on the mat. Where was his fight trainer? "Mom will be furious. But first she'll cry. I hate that. Maybe there's some way I can to hide this accident." Kurushima reached his hand down around his knees. Blood. Sticky. And red, probably.

"Hey," a suffering Kurushima cried out from his cross.

"Listen to me...you government dogs...Shinobu..." He'd die if he kept silent. He needed to throw a tantrum, desperately. "Ahhh, got to piss, got to piss, why didn't I go to the toilet."

REPETITION

Shinobu Yoimachi stood in the kitchen, apron around her waist.

"I like my eggs over easy, with the yolk still runny and the white firm," said Kurushima, drinking his wake-up tomato juice.

"Coming home late again tonight, dear?" asked good wife Shinobu.

"Let's see, today I'm giving a speech at Sukiyabashi. Then I'll be leading a demonstration against disciplinarian education. And the rearview mirror of my motorcycle is broken, so I'll have to have it fixed."

Shinobu sprinkled salt and pepper on the eggs and brought them to the table. Meanwhile, she'd become naked. Kurushima nuzzled her volcani-form breasts, took her hot burnt-orange nipples in his mouth and sucked.

"You're always thinking of yourself," she said, "always caught up in your political shows. Try and think of me once in a while."

"Say, look who's here."

Inonaka had come to visit him in his hospital room. "You were really sound asleep. I thought you were dead," Inonaka greeted him. Inonaka's face assumed a complex, inimitable expression, trembling as if he were about to cry, trying to smile and pretending to look deep, all at the same time. Kurushima could only smile to cover his embarrassment.

"You really had a disaster."

"Sure bloodied my knee. But I'm getting out of here."

"The police looking for the biker who got you?"

"I think so. Mom's dealing with it. I don't care. I'm just the victim of a bunch of jerk-offs with more balls than brains. Maybe I should get out of this country. Japan is such a pigsty. It makes me sick."

"Where would you go? Japan's not so bad. You can still lead a demonstration here. The Soviet Union's a nightmare. Try holding a demonstration in Moscow, it wouldn't last thirty seconds. And that's only if you hightailed it out of there. Ordinary citizens just ignore the demonstrators, and the authorities put them in mental asylums."

"Well, I'm either crazy or I'm trash. Didn't Komochi say so? Told me I should make up my mind."

"If it's one or the other, then you're crazy. Crazy people can still be helped. Think about it: saviors are really out of their skulls."

"I'm not crazy enough to be really crazy," Kurushima said, scratching his neck like a dog.

Kurushima had the will to rebel, but he'd been turned into a dog—through surgery called "education." Dogs strain at the leash, trying to rebel, but as soon as they remember they're dogs, it's over. If they obey their master, they never miss a meal. But if they forget they're dogs and bare their teeth, the master says: "You're a dog. If you don't behave, I'll beat you so you remember."

"I think you should fall in love," Inonaka began. "Drown yourself in happiness, a nice girl with big tits. Fall in love, and the masters and the State fade away. Or maybe they come over to your side.

"Maybe revolution *should* be in the mind. As long as you can tell the system to fuck off, you're fine. If every petit bourgeois told the system to fuck off, the whole thing would be turned on its head. Start a family, start a revolution that way. Find a woman to mother you, and get your strokes the gentle way. It'd keep your cock in shape, too. Can't have you withering away in the middle of everything." Inonaka nodded to himself as he said this.

"Nah, I can't do that. I'm bound to keep on stammering about the bureaucracy. Even if I had a house and family, I'd have to throw tantrums. That's the way I am. Domestic bliss is great, but big tits aren't everything, you know. I'm not some hyena who howls every Saturday night or a dog scared of his master. I'm Kurushima. *Crucify* me if you like. I got to keep stammering on. I'm Kurushima, man. Kurushima."

"OK, Kurushima, man. If there were no Kurushima, it'd be all over for Japan. But still, even if you're Kurushima, why not do it with a girl with big tits?"

"Shinobu Yoimachi's got thirty-five inches."

"What? You got a girl! Thirty-five inches, huh? Hey, you'll have to introduce me."

"Sure thing. Her nipples are really strange and beautiful. Like mine. And she's got a nice smile. When I see her smile, my nipples ache."

First published, 1983
TRANSLATION BY TERRY GALLAGHER

Masahiko Shimada (b. 1961) is perhaps the most consciously "literary" of the authors in this collection. During his fourth year of studies in Russian and East European Literatures at Tokyo University of Foreign Languages, Shimada published the novella *A Tender Divertimento for Leftists* (1983) which was named runner-up for the 89th Akutagawa Prize. The following year he received the Noma New Writer's Award for *Music for a Somnambulant Kingdom* (1984). A prolific writer, he includes among his work the novellas *Cry of the Refugee Vacationers* (1986), *Requiem for a Conscious Machine* (1985), a short-story collection *Donna Anna* (1986), and the socio-pathological study on AIDS entitled *Unidentified Shadow* (1987). His most recent novels are *Dream Messenger* (1989) and *Rococo-ville* (1990). Recently, Shimada founded his own theatrical group. Published when Shimada was still in college, *Momotaro in a Capsule* (1983) was described by one Japanese critic as a "parody for which there is no original."

JAPAN'S JUNGLEST DAY
Michio Hisauchi

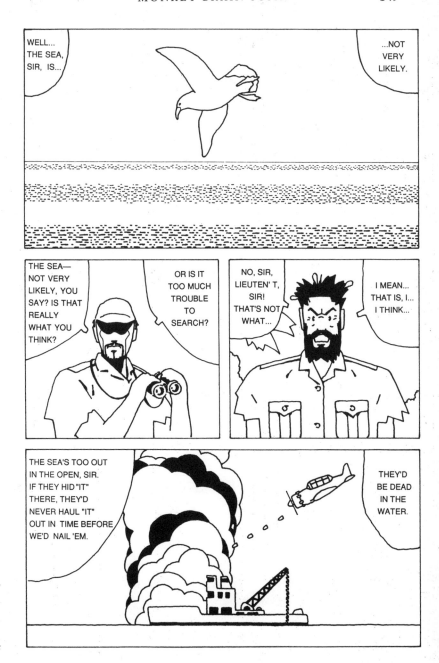

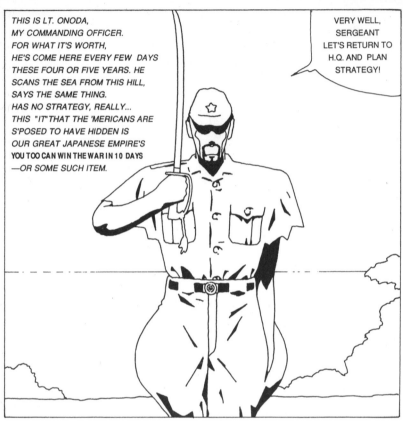

THIS IS LT. ONODA,
MY COMMANDING OFFICER.
FOR WHAT IT'S WORTH,
HE'S COME HERE EVERY FEW DAYS
THESE FOUR OR FIVE YEARS. HE
SCANS THE SEA FROM THIS HILL,
SAYS THE SAME THING.
HAS NO STRATEGY, REALLY...
THIS "IT" THAT THE 'MERICANS ARE
S'POSED TO HAVE HIDDEN IS
OUR GREAT JAPANESE EMPIRE'S
YOU TOO CAN WIN THE WAR IN 10 DAYS
—OR SOME SUCH ITEM.

VERY WELL,
SERGEANT
LET'S RETURN TO
H.Q. AND PLAN
STRATEGY!

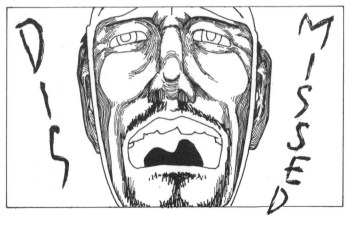

ACCORDING TO
THE LIEUTEN'T,
'MERICAN SPIES
STOLE "IT"
FROM JAPAN
AND HID
"IT" HERE
ON THIS
ISLAND...
WHICH, OF
COURSE,
IS NONSENSE.

I MERELY PLAY ALONG WITH THE LIEUTEN'T... HE MAY BE CRAZY, BUT I'M STILL A SERGEANT AND HE'S STILL MY SUPERIOR, SO I LET IT RIDE.

LIEUTEN'T, SIR, LUNCH IS READY.

ALL THE SAME, I DON'T REALLY UNDERSTAND HIS PROBLEM .... ONCE, WHEN THE LIEUTEN'T STOLE FOOD FROM ISLAND NATIVES, I SUMMONED UP MY COURAGE AND CHALLENGED HIM.

LIEUTEN'T, SIR, INASMUCH AS WE'RE S'POSED TO BE LIBERATING THE SUFFERING PEOPLE OF GREATER ASIA FROM ALLIED OPPRESSION...

I CAN'T SEE HOW... THAT IS, I MEAN... WE SOLDIERS OF THE JAPANESE EMPIRE SHOULD NOT...I MEAN... THAT WAS THE NATIVES' FOOD...

DO YOU REALLY BELIEVE THAT?

SOMEHOW, I DON'T KNOW WHY, BUT HE SEEMED SO CLEAR-HEADED WHEN HE SAID THAT— I COULDN'T HELP BUT RESPECT HIM.

EVEN SO, HE WAS STILL THE SAME LOONEY LOOKING FOR HIS 'MERICAN SPIES.

SO TELL ME, HOW'S THE LEF'TENANT DOING?

Y'KNOW, SAME AS EVER.

THE ONLY ONE I COULD EVER TALK WITH —ABOUT FAMILY, SAY— OR JOKE WITH WAS THE MEDIC.

WELL, GUESS THAT'S GOOD.

HE'S PROBABLY HAPPIER SINCE HE WENT OFF THE DEEP END.

SO IT GOES... IT'S HARD TO STAY SANE IN TIMES LIKE THESE.

STILL, Y'KNOW, DOC...

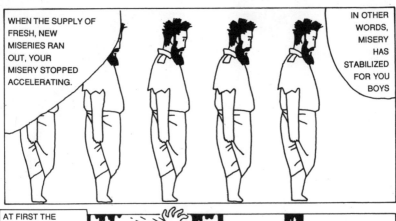

WHEN THE SUPPLY OF FRESH, NEW MISERIES RAN OUT, YOUR MISERY STOPPED ACCELERATING.

IN OTHER WORDS, MISERY HAS STABILIZED FOR YOU BOYS

AT FIRST THE WOUNDED, WHO WERE USED TO VISIONS OF FRONT LINE HELL, WERE TERRIFIED TO COME SEE US, MEDICS.

FUGGIT, GOTTA CUT.

BUT THEN THEY BECAME LIKE CIVILIANS GOING TO THEIR DENTIST WITH A TOOTHACHE!

SO YOU'RE SAYING THAT AT PRESENT I AM WITHOUT PALPABLE MISERY?

IT'S NOT THAT YOU ARE WITHOUT MISERY...

ONLY THAT YOU CAN'T RECOGNIZE IT AS MISERY.

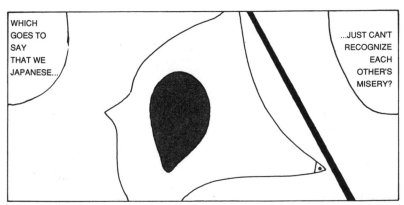

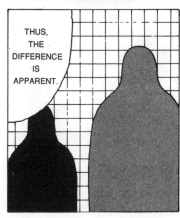

WELL, EVEN SUPPOSING JAPAN HAD IT BETTER OFF, WHO'S TO SAY WHETHER THERE IS HAPPINESS IN JAPAN AND THERE IS MISERY HERE —OR WHAT?

MAYBE IT'S BOTH— MAYBE IT'S ALL JUST IRRECONCILABLE RELATIVE DIFFERENCES.

SO, SAY WE WERE TO RETURN TO A HAPPY JAPAN, WOULD THIS MEAN THAT, JUST AS WE CANNOT RECOGNIZE OUR PRESENT MISERY, WE CANNOT RECOGNIZE HAPPINESS EITHER?

A-HA! LIKE I WAS SAYING, WE CAN TELL WHEN WE'RE ACCELERATING TOWARD EITHER MISERY OR HAPPINESS...

HOWEVER, AT REST IN A STEADY STATE OF MISERY OR HAPPINESS, WE CAN'T TELL IF WE'RE HAPPY OR MISERABLE.

SO TRY AS WE MIGHT, WE CAN NEVER KNOW OUR OWN ABSOLUTE MISERY? IS THAT WHAT YOU'RE SAYING?

THAT'S RIGHT. THERE'S NO WAY.

AND LUCKY THERE'S NOT EITHER— FOR IN FACT, YOU BOYS HAVE MORE MISERY THAN JUST THIS WAR IN THE PACIFIC.

THE SAME GOES FOR THE FOLKS BACK IN JAPAN... FOR THE 'MERICANS... FOR THE RUSKIES... FOR EVERY LIVING THING ON THIS EARTH AND IN THE WHOLE COSMOS.

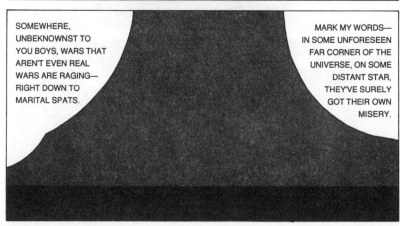

SOMEWHERE, UNBEKNOWNST TO YOU BOYS, WARS THAT AREN'T EVEN REAL WARS ARE RAGING— RIGHT DOWN TO MARITAL SPATS.

MARK MY WORDS— IN SOME UNFORESEEN FAR CORNER OF THE UNIVERSE, ON SOME DISTANT STAR, THEY'VE SURELY GOT THEIR OWN MISERY.

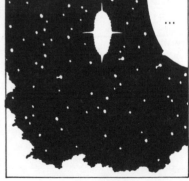

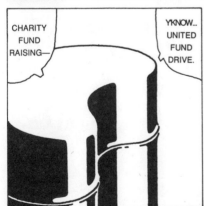

BE THANKFUL IT WAS ME WHO SAW YOU... IF IT WAS ANYBODY ELSE, YOU'D BE IN DEEP SHIT!

I SWEAR...

...

I DON'T KNOW WHY, BUT THE LIEUTEN'T REALLY SEEMS TO THINK YOU'RE A MESS KIT, DOC.

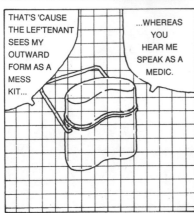

THAT'S 'CAUSE THE LEF'TENANT SEES MY OUTWARD FORM AS A MESS KIT...

...WHEREAS YOU HEAR ME SPEAK AS A MEDIC.

HMM...

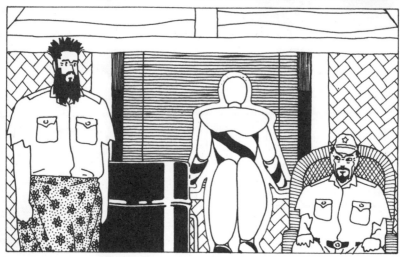

THERE'S SOMETHING I'D LIKE TO ASK YOU, ALIEN.

YOU CAME HERE ON A MISSION OF MISERY, DIDN'T YOU?

YES, THAT'S RIGHT.

EVERYONE IS IN AWFUL STRAITS.

ONLY WE'RE NOT MISERABLE— SURE, WE MIGHT HAVE BEEN MISERABLE WHEN WE GOT HERE...

BUT NOW, WE'RE NOT MISERABLE AT ALL.

DAMN FOOL, THE GUY'S A 'MERICAN SPY!

WHAT THIS MEANS IS THAT HE'S COME HERE TO ADD ANOTHER VECTOR TO OUR MISERY.

UH-HUH, ANOTHER VECTOR...

WHAT'S A VECTOR?

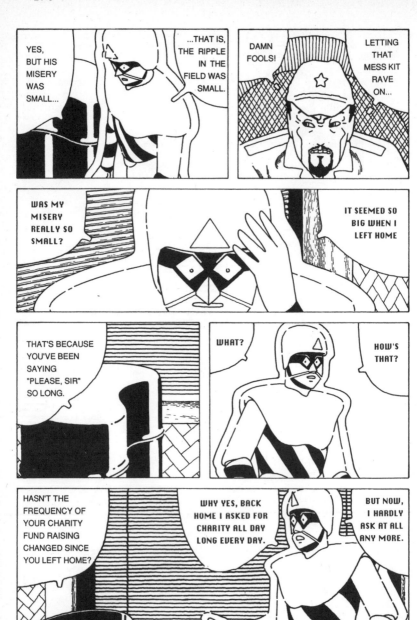

IN OTHER WORDS, OUR FRIEND HERE HAS SOLD OFF HIS MISERY LITTLE BY LITTLE...

HMPH

DARE YOU SAY MY MISERY... IF NOT THAT OF THOSE KIDS...

...GREW STEADILY LIGHTER AND LIGHTER?

WELL, FIRST OF ALL, YOU'RE NOT ONE OF THOSE KIDS, RIGHT?

AND YOUR MISERY IS DISTINCT FROM THEIRS.

IT'S THE MISERY OF AN ADULT SEEING ORPHANS.

HOW MUCH MORE OF THIS CAN I TAKE?!

THAT'S NOT TRUE— I SPENT YEARS LIVING WITH THOSE KIDS.

I KNOW THEIR MISERY BETTER THAN ANYONE.

I'M SURE YOU DO—ONLY YOU WERE FEELING THE OVERALL FIELD OF THEIR MISERY...

YOU DIDN'T ACTUALLY KNOW THE MISERY OF EACH SINGLE CHILD.

I'VE COME HALF WAY ACROSS THE UNIVERSE TO THIS NOWHERE!

WHO'D COME OUT HERE TO THE BOONIES FOR FUN?!

ALL I'M SAYING IS YOUR MISERY IS NOT THE KIDS' MISERY— NOT THAT YOUR MISERY IS INSIGNIFICANT.

YOU ALL MAY HAVE SHARED THE SAME MISERY FIELD, BUT EACH ONE OF YOU THEREIN HAD A UNIQUE MISERY.

WHICH ONLY PROVES THAT FIELDS COME TOGETHER TO FORM BIG FIELDS. WHICH THEN FORM VERY BIG FIELDS.

DIDN'T YOU FEEL GREAT MISERY ON LEAVING YOUR PLANET?

YES, NOW THAT YOU MENTION IT, I NEVER FELT SO MISERABLE— HOW DID YOU KNOW?

WHAT YOU FELT WAS NOT JUST THE ORPHANS' MISERY, BUT THE MISERY OF EVERYONE ON THE PLANET.

YOU ESCAPED THROUGH A WARP IN THE PLANETARY MISERY FIELD.

TRUE, THOSE KIDS WEREN'T THE ONLY MISERABLE ONES BACK HOME.

THAT'S WHY I THOUGHT TO LOOK TO THE COSMOS FOR HELP.

YET THE VERY IDEA THAT SOME-THING WOULD COME OF ASKING AROUND THE UNIVERSE FOR CHARITY...

PROBABLY EVEN PUT YOUR MIND AT EASE

HE MAY NOT HAVE HAD ANY STRONG CONVICTION THAT THE COSMOS WOULD CONTRIBUTE... STILL, ON THE OTHER HAND, OUR ALIEN FRIEND'S DEPARTURE FROM THAT PLANET OF MISERY WAS IN FACT A LAUNCH TOWARD HAPPINESS...

...IF IN FORM ONLY. HE GREW HAPPIER AND HAPPIER, THIS YIELDED TO AN INERTIAL MISERY...

...STRONG ENOUGH TO HOLD HIM TO THIS MISERABLE PLANET.

BAH!

CALL IT THE PANGS OF BETTER INSTINCT.

!

YOU MEAN TO SAY THAT I LEFT AT THE EXPENSE OF MY CONSCIENCE, OF MY INNER VOICE?

...I, WHO, MORE THAN ANYONE, WANTED ONLY HAPPINESS FOR THOSE KIDS?

YOU TOOK THAT INERTIAL MISERY NOT AS PANGS OF CONSCIENCE BUT AS THE KIDS' MISERY...

...WHICH GAVE YOU THE CONVICTION TO GO OUT ASKING FOR CHARITY.

AND WITH THAT ENERGY, YOU LEFT THE PULL OF YOUR PLANET'S MISERY.

A... AGH!

SO WHAT WOULD HAPPEN IF THE ALIEN RETURNED TO HIS PLANET?

HE WOULD FREE-FALL BACK TOWARD THE PLANET'S MISERY... UNDER THE PLANET'S POWER TO MAKE MISERABLE ALL OBJECTS WITHIN RANGE...

...WITH NO RESISTANCE AT ALL.

AND IN HIS FALL INTO MISERY, HIS INERTIAL MISERY WOULD DISAPPEAR.

OR RATHER, THE GRAVITATIONAL MISERY OF THE PLANET WOULD CANCEL OUT THE INERTIAL MISERY OF HIS ACCELERATION TOWARD MISERY.

THE DISCOMFORT OF KNOWING HE HIMSELF MUST BE-COME MISERABLE WOULD BE NULLIFIED BY THE EASE OF BEING WITH ORPHANS AGAIN...

...AND HE'D NEVER SUSPECT A THING.

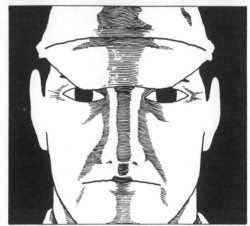

AARG

LIEUTEN'T SIR...

??

MAKE FOOLS OF THE IMPERIAL ARMY, WILL YOU?!

STOP IT LEF'TENANT!

YOU TOO NOW?!

A MESS KIT WOULD ORDER AN OFFICER?!

I'M NOT A MESS KIT, AND YOU'VE GOT TO STOP SEEING ME AS A MESS KIT.

IT'S TOO LATE, LEF'TENANT, YOU'RE COMING BACK TO YOUR SENSES. YOUR STEADY-STATE MISERY IS FADING.

THUD

YOU ARE NO LONGER AT HOME IN THAT ILLUSORY MISERY CALLED "WAR."

BUT FEAR NOT, YOUR REAL-WORLD MISERY WILL ONE DAY STABILIZE.

...

N..NO.... IT WASN'T ME... IT WASN'T MY CHOICE, MY OWN DOING...

THERE WAS JUST NO... NO OTHER WAY AT THE TIME...

LIEUTEN–'T!

LIEUTEN'T!

DOC, AS A MEDIC, WHAT DO THINK CAUSED THE LIEUTEN'T TO FLIP HIS NUT?

...

BY THE TIME YOU FOUND YOUR WAY HERE FROM YOUR OLD UNIT, THE WAR WAS ALREADY OVER.

HMM... I SUSPECTED AS MUCH.

DID JAPAN WIN?

DON'T BE SO COY— YOU KNOW JAPAN HAD NO CHANCE OF WINNING!

YEAH...

WHEN YOU GOT HERE, THERE WAS ONLY ME AND THE LEF'TENANT BECAUSE HE'D SURRENDERED EVERYONE TO THE AMERICAN ARMY.

AND HE DIDN'T EVEN BELONG TO THIS UNIT— HE WAS SENT TO RELAY COMMANDS FROM H.Q.

MEMORANDUM

CALL TO GLORY
AMERICAN FORCES ARE EXPECTED TO ATTACK BORI-BORI ISLAND ON OR ABOUT AUGUST 12. TROOPS OF SQUADRON III ARE TO MOUNT FULL COUNTERATTACK TO THE LAST MAN. MAY THE FLOWERS PERISH BEAUTIFULLY.

AUTUMN RECREATION

OF COURSE, HE WAS UNDER ORDERS TO DEFEND THE PLACE TO THE DEATH.

HE IGNORNED ORDERS AND SURRENDERED HIS TROOPS?

HE KNEW JAPAN WOULD LOSE, BUT THEN EVERYONE IN JAPAN SEEMED TO KNOW.

HE CAME TO TELL US NOT TO DIE LIKE DOGS, "CALL TO GLORY" OR NO.

AND THE UNIT LEADER HERE DIDN'T SAY ANYTHING?

THE UNIT LEADER, A COLONEL NANJO, HAD KNOWN THE LEF'TENANT SINCE CHILDHOOD. CLOSE FAMILIES... SCHOOLMATES...

ALL RIGHT, EVEN IF THEY WERE BUDDIES...THIS WAS DEADLY SERIOUS. ARE YOU TELLING ME THIS COLONEL AGREED WITH HIM?

NO, HE WAS FURIOUS WHEN HE HEARD WHAT THE LEF'TENANT HAD TO SAY.

DON'T EVEN MENTION IT AGAIN— AND I'LL SAY I DIDN'T HEAR YOU!

SAYING THAT, THE COLONEL ORDERED A FULL ATTACK AT DAWN.

BUT THE LEF'TENANT DIDN'T LET UP...

HE JUST HAD TO SEE THE MEN RETURN TO THEIR FAMILIES.

"YOU GO HOME TO YOUR WIFE, TOO."

"DON'T MAKE FUYUKO ANY SADDER THAN SHE ALREADY IS," HE SAID

HE'D KNOWN THE COLONEL'S WIFE FOR SOME TIME NOW...

SECRETLY HE WAS IN LOVE WITH HER...

...WHICH THE COLONEL SENSED AND MADE HIM ANGRIER STILL! HE JUMPED ON HIS OLD FRIEND'S WORDS:

ANY SCUM WHO'D FOOL AROUND WITH THE WIFE OF A SOLDIER HE'S COME TO RELIEVE OF HIS DUTY HAS NO RIGHT TO SPEAK OF HOME AND FAMILY TO DECENT SOLDIERS!

HE TURNED ON HIS WRATH.

PERHAPS THE LEF'TENANT FOUND THE COLONEL'S WORDS OFFENSIVE— CASTING MORE SHAME ON FUYUKO THAN ON THE FEELINGS HE'D HARBORED SO DEARLY...

...OR PERHAPS THE LEF'TENANT SAW FROM THE COLONEL'S FURY THAT HE'D HAVE TO CUT HIS FRIEND DOWN TO SAVE THE OTHER MEN FROM DYING IN VAIN... OR PERHAPS IT WAS JUST AN AESTHETIC DISDAIN OF THE OLD MILITARY PECKING ORDER, PERSONIFIED BY THE COLONEL AFTER ALL THESE YEARS.

AFTER KILLING THE COLONEL, THE LEF'TENANT HAD EVERYONE SURRENDER, BUT HE HIMSELF STAYED BEHIND. HE COULDN'T GO BACK TO JAPAN AFTER WHAT HE'D DONE. HE ONLY WANTED TO SEE FUYUKO. HE COULDN'T FACE HER, SO HE DECIDED TO CARRY ON THE COLONEL'S FIGHT HERE IN HIS STEAD.

ME, I SAW IT ALL. I HAD NO FAMILY—I FIGURED I MIGHT AS WELL STAY ON WITH THIS LEF'TENANT WHO'D KILLED FOR THE OTHERS. ONLY THIS MADE HIM SUFFER MORE. HAUNTED BY AFTERIMAGES OF THE COLONEL'S DEATH AND BY THE FEAR THAT HE'D REALLY KILLED THE COLONEL OUT OF DESIRE FOR FUYUKO, HE SOUGHT ESCAPE IN THE FANTASY OF HIS ONE-MAN WAR.

WHEN I BECAME A MESS KIT FOR HIM I DON'T KNOW, BUT OF COURSE I WASN'T ABOUT TO DENY IT.

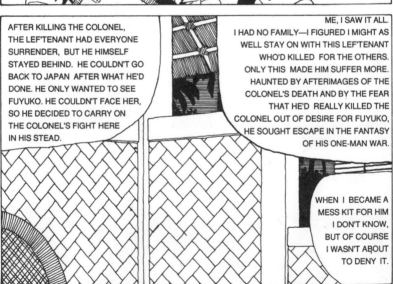

THE NEXT MORNING, THE LIEUTEN'T RETURNED LOOKING STRANGELY AT PEACE.

I'VE DECIDED TO RETURN TO JAPAN AND TELL FUYUKO EVERYTHING.

VERY WELL THEN, FARE-WELL.

UH...NO... PLEASE WAIT, LIEUTEN'T.

THANK YOU FOR EVERYTHING SERGEANT...

LIEUTEN'T, SIR, THINK OF WHAT WILL HAPPEN ONCE YOU'RE BACK HOME...

THE 'MERICANS 'LL TRY YOU AND JAIL YOU FOR LIFE OR HANG YOU OR SHOOT YOU...

I AM PREPARED FOR THAT— I CANNOT STAY

EVEN IF I DON'T SEE HER, I'LL BE IN THE SAME JAPAN WITH HER.

LIEUTEN'T, SIR! PLEASE RECONSIDER AND STAY! EVERYTHING'S BEEN FINE THIS FAR.

I'M LEAVING. LET ME GO!

LIEUTEN–'T

I'VE REMAINED SILENT, BUT I BEHEADED TWO NATIVES ON ORDERS FROM YOU!

DON'T WORRY— I WON'T TELL.

N...NO, IF YOU LEAVE, SIR, THE 'MERICANS'LL COME LOOKING FOR ME!

PLEASE, SIR! I DON'T WANT TO DIE, SIR!

STOP WHINING AND TRUST ME, SER-GEANT!!

BOFF

LIEUTEN—'T!!

LIEUTEN'T!

SERGEANT!

FU... YU... KO...

IT SEEMS TO ME THAT THE LIEUTEN'T LOST HIS SENSES MORE OUT OF LOVE FOR FUYUKO THAN FROM SELF-RECRIMINATION. IT WAS THIS THAT RETURNED HIM TO THE MISERY OF SANITY—THOUGH PERHAPS HE WOULD HAVE BEEN BETTER OFF DEAD. I WOULD BE BETTER OFF LOOKING FOR THAT YOU TOO CAN WIN THE WAR IN 10 DAYS. ME AND THIS _HAPPY_ ALIEN....

First published, 1985
TRANSLATION BY ALFRED BURNBAUM

Michio Hisauchi (b. 1951) is a prolific multi-talented artist, essayist, and occasional TV and film personality who writes full-length novels in comic form. Hisauchi came onto the "art-*manga*" scene in the earlier eighties through his *Perspective Kid* series in the cult magazine *Garo*; these early works are collected in such volumes as *Labyrinth* (1979), *Crime and Punishment* (1980), and *Misery in the Case of the Yamamoto Household* (1982). Known for his wicked eye and fine draftsmanship as well as for his destructured reworkings of history, Hisauchi tosses together everything from Marcel Duchamp to trashy tabloid journalism to commercial advertising. His *Japan's Junglest Day* (1985) inflates the wartime myth of Japan's Longest Day and the by-now cliché of Japanese soldiers marooned on South Pacific atolls, injecting a liberal dose of his own special "physics of misery."

KNEEL DOWN AND LICK MY FEET

Amy Yamada

It's not as if she's some priss who doesn't know a thing about men, but the first time Chika saw me spit in a guy's mouth, she had to run to the toilet. I mean, really. She's the one who came to me begging, Shinobu, Sis, I need to make some money. Help me find a job. What was I supposed to do? I was the same way at first. When I got started in the business, seeing men humiliated like this made me want to puke. But after a few years it's like any job. Your own craft is the only thing you can believe in. If it makes guys salivate and snuggle up, or if it makes them shit before my eyes, it's all the same to me. Men look up to me from all fours and I pity them. I grind my high heels into their pitiful little cocks and watch their faces twist while I drag on a cigarette. And then I say: *Kneel down and lick my feet.*

I hadn't heard from Chika in a while when one afternoon she called to ask if I knew of any jobs. And I said to myself, Just like I thought, things are going sour with her old man. So I asked, but she said, No, things're going great. She sounded cheerful enough. She said his birthday was coming up and she wanted to give him a present, so she needed to make some money. Which made me think, This girl is crazy.

Years ago, she was happy with next to nothing. She'd turn a few tricks and had a nice living. She wasn't lazy either. Worked every day, but she spent all her money on books, records, clothes, and all she'd eat was a little nibble of French bread. I'd scold her and tell her she ought to put a little more in her stomach, and she'd turn to me with a straight face and say, Well, Sis, why don't you introduce me to some nice rich old man? I never dreamed she'd be asking me to find her work so she could buy a present for some guy. Nor could I believe how fast she left her favorite glitzy Akasaka and Roppongi night spots behind. Left her dull black guy, too, and his dumb kid, who she never let out of her sight for a second, just to move to this dead-end base town.

Still, Chika and I had been through a lot of good and bad times together. So, despite my doubts that this hypersensitive girl would make the necessary adjustments, I decided to bring her into this S&M club. With apologies in my heart to her old man. Actually, I've done worse myself. But this line of work is, surprisingly, quite safe, and you don't have to sleep with anybody you don't like. At first it's weird, but once you get used to it, it's like manual labor. You get rid of your frustrations, and you make some money. And it's not a bad profession, either. No other line of work lets you see so many men revert to their natural state. Plus it's nice to have men wait on you for a change. Ginza bar hostesses, by far the bigger fools, put up with more crap for much less money.

The next day Chika came to the club, and the owner —Pops we call him—liked her from the start. She'll be very popular, he said. What an insult! After the years I'd spent polishing her to a fine gleam, when the two of us go to town we get *anything* we want from any man we want!

Chika was Chika, all big eyes and silence at first. She's the lively, joking-around type, but as she listened to what we do here, I could see her sliding into the dumps. As it turned out, that was only because she heard that the first three or four days would be a trial period she wouldn't get paid for. It's the way it has to be. The customers' lives are at stake here. Pops let me teach Chika the ropes. She didn't know the letter *S* about S&M. She'd modeled for S&M magazines plenty of times, but modeling means you don't have to do anything but get tied up and have your picture taken. Neither the "doers" nor the "done to" have any idea what's going on. We know a well-known S&M writer who can't even handle a rope.

There's S&M clubs, and then there's S&M clubs, if you know what I mean. And that's where most amateurs make their first mistake. Some clubs are run by gangsters. The charges are outrageous, and the clubs tend to be filthy. They don't even disinfect the enema equipment before they shove it up the next customer's butt. Talk about breeding grounds for AIDS. In some places, the girls actually have *sex* with the customers. Guys'll call up for the first time and ask, Afterward is she gonna let me do it? As if it were *natural!* The girl who answers the phone is used to this. She tells them politely that queens don't consort with slaves. The fact is, guys who are really after a woman's body can't be called true lovers of S&M. They should just splash cold water on their faces and come back later. Guys who truly love S&M are sincere.

This place is called the Queen's Palace. It's a club for guys who want to get picked on. We don't get many misguided souls who want to tie up women or anything silly like that. So I feel safe. Even someone like me who doesn't really get off on S&M can have a good time. Show me another place where women have slaves in this day and age! Show me another job where you can abuse men and have them thank you for it.

What's more, this place is clean, almost disturbingly clean. All equipment is disinfected after use. The men wear condoms start to finish, the rooms are made spanking clean after each round of play, and, of course, we disinfect our hands with ethanol. So there's nothing to worry about. Still, Chika was frightened of the whole thing—until I got her to put on some black underwear. It's amazing how a black leather brassiere and panties, black seamed stockings, and a black garter belt can make even a total amateur like her look like a real queen. I, on the other hand, wear a French lace camisole and needle-spike heels. Chika likes to play the bad girl. She makes a point of shocking detectives with her black silk lingerie when she's called down to the police department. She actually gets off exposing herself in front of people like that. Try not to look too sweet, I tell Chika, as I open the door to the room where a client is showering.

Let me see—what was it Mr. Yamamoto liked? Oh, I remember, he's the old coot who always takes the full course, *hard*. This might be a little tough for Chika to watch right when she's starting off, but what the hell. Sooner or later she's going to have to do at least this much herself. The sound of the water stops. Mr. Yamamoto is coming out of the shower. In an instant, I have put on the face of the Queen.

I sit on the red velvet throne with my legs crossed. Stark naked, the man approaches. He sits at my feet. He sure does look like a slave. In real life, the guy is president of a big company and spends his time bullying his employees. Chika sits in the chair beside me and watches us play-by-play.

"Queen Shinobu, it is an honor to be your humble plaything today."

"You are a despicable little slave."

"Absolutely, your Highness."

At this point, if the answer is unsuitable, I kick the slave away and shriek, What kind of an answer is that! But Yamamoto knows his part. There's nothing wrong with his answer.

"Well, then, slave, put this on that filthy thing between your legs," I say, throwing a rubber in his face. This is a problem for guys who are too tense or whose sorry little pricks are too small. They can't keep it on. When that happens I clamp it on with a clothespin.

By now I've seen hundreds of pricks, and they're basically

all the same. But the way men are so attached to that one little part of their bodies, the way they're thrilled or pained by whether it's big or small, well, I think it's cute. The only thing a woman cares about is whether the prick is attached to the man she loves or whether it's attached to some other man. Or maybe it's only me. No, Chika says the same thing. What makes one man's dick special is a woman's thoughts, right? I don't care how many pricks I have to look at in my line of work. They just look like a bunch of wriggly vegetables out of some cartoon. Maybe there are vegetables that really look like that—maybe only in fairy tales.

I make a habit of having the slaves massage my legs as I think about what to put on the day's menu. That's part of the game, too. Most men like women's legs, but masochists are crazy about them. Getting to rub a fishnet-stockinged leg gets their mouths watering. And if they start to slobber on your leg and you give them a little kick in the cheek, the job's almost done. The guy's thing, lifeless as a sea slug until then, is standing straight up in a second. Some guys go wild for black high heels and will lick them all over, even the soles. We call this "purification"—but it means that *good* shoes would be a waste. One time I was out shopping with the mama of the club. We were passing by a shoe store, and I said, Look, Mama, let's find a nice pair of shoes. How about these? Don't you think they're great? She just looked at the price tag and said, Oh, Shinobu, they're too expensive. You're just going to let people lick them. Very matter-of-factly, out loud. The shop employees turned and stared at us in shock. The air in the store went cold. Mama and I put on these weak little smiles and walked out of the place.

When I first got into this business, I was just like Chika. I didn't know what to think, but you get used to it. When you get right down to it, there are an awful lot of sadists and masochists in the world. People call this a perversion, but you have to wonder, if there are this many so-called perverts in the world, what is normal? These people know a hell of a lot more about human joy than all those teenagers fucking around without a whisper of love. If it were just a matter of sex, animals can do it. But only people can indulge themselves with a *taste* for carnal pleasure. For some people this is a search for love, but for others it's a thirst for S&M, or romance. S&M is an underground pleasure, but don't you think that's the way sex should be? Everybody has some secret sexual kick. Compared to the rubes who get their kicks from ogling smelly farm girls in trash magazines, the men who pursue their deepest pleasures in the world of shadows are far superior beings. Men who like their women young and virginal don't understand a bloody thing, but what can you do about it?

When I first told Chika about S&M, she thought it sounded great because all she could think of was high-minded stuff like *l'Histoire d'O* and Sacher-Masoch. But when it's a job, you have to cut through that sentimental crap. Make a mistake and you end up with shit on your hands. With a little practice, though, it's no problem. It's easy to learn how many condoms to put on the vibrator you stick up a guy's ass and how to use the tissue paper to clean up afterwards so you don't even have to touch him. It becomes second nature. What's hard is when you have to tie a guy up. There's lots of variations and you have to learn how to avoid those places where, if a rope digs in, you're in trouble. The basic form is called the tortoise-shell truss, but there is no end to the number of advanced techniques. There are pros who specialize in nothing but ropes. By the time you've learned the ropes, your hands are covered with blisters, but you have learned a skill. Me, I can always go to work for a packing company.

So, after having the poor jerk do my merciless bidding for a while, I decide to tie him up and hang him upside-down from the ceiling, his head resting on the floor. Now the fun begins. I sit on his head and abuse his nether parts. Chika says that looks like something she could do, so I let her.

Naturally there's a right way and a wrong way to sit. Properly, you should mount the guy's face—astride his forehead so he can breathe easily. It also keeps the guy from getting the wrong idea and trying to stick his tongue up you. There are some slaves who want to be the Queen's chair so badly they cry. On them, I sit a little harder, give them the extra enchantment of having trouble breathing.

Chika gives out a little squeal of joy as she sits on the guy's face. I scold her, saying, Stop that, you're the Queen, you must be more strict with him. Okay, she says and sticks out her tongue at me. The fool! If she acts too cheerful, she'll put the customer in a bad mood. Take it easy, Chika. A woman is always a Queen. I wrench open the man's mouth and begin to spit in it. A dead hush falls over everything.

"I want to be the Queen's chamberpot."

He says that with such an ecstatic expression that that's when Chika has to run to the toilet. C'mon, I think, we're just getting started. This guy does say the cutest things, though. As a reward, I'm going to punish him but good. You have to leave yourself room to smile. We're no amateurs here. When a slave says things like that to me, it gets me hotter and puts an extra snap into my whip-hand. This guy here is at his peak and will allow himself to do anything. I'm only too happy to oblige. I know all I need to know about that *other* world which doesn't begin to measure a man's *real* character. How bored men and women can get in that existence.

When Chika creeps back into the room, an embarrassed look on her face, the slave is still tied up and upside-down and I'm whipping his back. Look! I say, Queen Chika has returned to look upon your vile body. Got to keep the situation in hand. She apologizes to me, and quietly stands close to see how I use the whip. I've got to teach her how to make a loud noise without leaving a mark. It takes a sharp snap of the wrist. Most girls get a sprain when they start. And most beginners can't control where the whip lands. That can be a problem. Around the ribs, it's easy to leave marks that won't go away. But most people have to go back to their ordinary lives when they walk out of here, so our job is to keep things like that from happening.

Language is one of the most critical things in this kind of play. You need to speak in a dignified manner, but you must also be polite and show respect. Not least of all to yourself. We queens are terribly important personages after all. It behooves us to use words that elevate all our actions. Think about this in an unromantic context, and you can't keep from laughing, saying stuff like Beseech the queen that you might grovel before her honorable legs and receive the venerated punishment. You could chew off your own tongue on those phrases. Slaves who exalt the queen's every action call my piss holy water.

Aside from language, there's one other rule to this game. That is, after abusing the client you have to be nice to him. Anybody who gets hurt all the time is bound to get upset. You have to create a sense that you're punishing the client because you love him. The very whip of love. This is a world of whips and treats. That trade-off is the ultimate taste of the sweetness of life. Technique takes a secondary role. That's why lots of clients say they are completely satisfied with purely verbal play.

But isn't everything like that, really? Love that's only fun makes you soft. A little essence of suffering is what lights the fires of love. Chika is one other woman who understands this very well, so I think she'll get good at this. But it's so true, no?

You know what I really hate? Men and women who think they're having an adult relationship because they can behave coolly to one another. That's the sort of thing kids do when they want to feel grown up. Real adults know what it means to suffer; they've savored difficulty. People who casually sleep together and casually break up don't know anything about love. A real adult, no matter how much he or she wants to sleep with someone, endures not sleeping with them and learns to deal with pain. Sure, sleeping around is just another form of play. And from the most trivial play, a serious love can be born, as both Chika and I have experienced. So it's hard to say. Way back when Chika and I used to play the field, we were something else. We were wanton. We ran our risks and we had our regrets. But one thing Chika managed that I never could—she could always find a good point in a guy and tell me about it. She'd say that some day these experiences would count in our favor, though how she couldn't say.

I tie the guy up good, cross-legged, and shove the rubber dick up his ass. I loosen the ropes to free up his hands and let him masturbate in front of me. We finish right on time. Of course he has to dispose of the condom himself. The sight of a man masturbating with a condom on is pitiful. I talk him through the whole thing. It's a form of hypnosis. At times like these, I think men are quite delicate. If I say the wrong thing at the wrong moment, it's all over for them. If there were a man who could talk to a woman in bed the way I talk, women would come just listening to him. But there aren't many men like that, men who can say enough of the right things in bed. Relatively speaking, foreigners are better at it. Men who can speak in a way that is both obscene and refined, crude and sincere. Most Japanese men don't have it in them. If you find one who can talk, it's usually just a string of words you can't say on television. Not like that Frenchman, whatzisname, Chika, what was the guy's name? The guy who was Jane Birkin's... Yeah, Serge Gainsbourg. No guy like him. Nobody even comes close. It might make things a little awkward, but that's okay. Love can hide a multitude of sins. But no matter how much in love you are, a guy who keeps at it without a word is a big turn-off. One part inspiration and nine parts perspiration. It pisses me off to think of all the guys with no talent for sex getting their way in this world. Their women are just as bad, pretending they feel something. Men might not know it, but there are lots of women out there who pretend to come. It's a simple performance. And men are easily fooled. My women friends are all good women who like men, but there are plenty of them who have never come once sleeping with a man. They have no trouble masturbating to a climax though. It's a shame. They're too easy on their men and that's not right. They should teach them the truth about women's bodies.

"Shinobu, is that girl who was just here a new queen?"

Mr. Yamamoto has changed his clothes, and he's got his company president face back on. I no longer speak arrogantly, am back to my normal voice.

"That's right. She still has a long way to go, but some day you'll be asking for her."

"Well, you'll have to train her well before that day comes."

"What are you saying? All our girls are top drawer."

After the session, it's fun to talk with a client you've gotten to know well. With first-time clients, it's important to be friendly and show them you're not really the frightening bitch they think you are. There are all kinds of clients. I remember one guy who was an orchestra violinist. After his session, he gave a little concert for all the queens who weren't busy. Right there in the room, with pulleys and chains hanging from the walls, he played this *humoresque*. It was so beautiful, the bow moving back and forth in front of the cage. When Chika heard that story she got this faraway look on her face and sighed, Oooh, just like a Kuniyoshi Kaneko painting! Like I'm supposed to know who this artist is....

Another time, as a client was showering after his session, I took a look at the book he left on the table, and it was in some difficult-looking foreign language. As I was leafing through it, the young guy stuck his head out of the shower, and this totally changed bright-boy expression came over him. Your majesty, he asked, do you like García Márquez? Again I ask you, Me? I never heard the name. But when

Chika heard the story she said, Outasight! If only I could have customers like that. I think she meant it.

Plenty of these people seem to have highly developed personal aesthetics.

One customer always brings me a new set of lingerie; another always brings me love letters. But no matter how well I get to know them, very few of my clients ever ask me to meet them away from the shop. Everybody who comes here wants to be entering another world. That goes for me and the other queens, too. Some of us go home to husbands and children who don't know anything about this. Some are straight-laced office workers. Some are just pulling the wool over their parents' eyes. I have a man of my own, and for that matter so does Chika. When I'm with my man, I don't talk big the way I do at work. In his arms, I'm as cuddly as a kitten. People really do have an A-side and a B-side. They're complicated.

Men come here and bare their true selves. And then *we* go home and bare our true selves in our own man's arms. Or maybe those aren't our true selves. We all want the man we love to feel good, so sometimes we flirt in a way that's totally out of character. So maybe our true selves aren't really anywhere but inside us. All people are actors to some extent, except when they're completely alone. That's why, in my heart, I don't believe anything about anybody. But that doesn't mean that I hate them. It's just obvious. No matter how much you trust somebody, that person's acting, at least a little. So all you guys who trust your wives while you go out and blow the company's entertainment budget on some Ginza bimbo better get smart. Before you know it, your ass is going to be in never-never land.

"Well? You think you're up to it?"

Chika answers with an ambiguous smile.

"I don't know. It takes skill to get a big man all tied up and hanging like that. But when it comes right down to it, there's not many things I can do, so I guess I have to try. I've tried all kinds of things. I know there're limits to what I can do. And I know all about what I can't do, the things that disturb me in my heart, disrupt my own time. Being a hostess is okay, but I'm sick of putting up with the abuse when I meet some customer outside the bar. I've had my fill of sleeping with strange men. So in that sense, this line of work seems made for me. One at a time, each time a complete little act. I have a short attention span. Really, I'd be good at office work somewhere, get done by five, but with a pink-collar job like that I could never afford all the things I want."

That was Chika's grumbling analysis. Work that would disturb her in her heart. Come to think of it, when she worked in the bar, she would always run straight home at quitting time and the mama scolded her for that. She has this surprisingly well defined no-trespassing zone. In night-life trades, usually, hearts and bodies flow together and eventually your personal life gets dragged into it. But she clearly rejected that. It was all a joke to her. When she screwed some rich old man to make a little pocket change, she never acted the sweet, young lady, because this was only a temporary withdrawal he'd made from her love bank. She never met him halfway, never played up to him, never gave of herself. When his two hours were up, it was, well, *sayonara*. Just like an American call girl. Not at all like a Japanese hotel whore. And she was the one who decided she would make her money that way. Totally shameless, full of pride. In not playing up to her tricks, by keeping her love for her man, though, she's just like me.

I might raise a frown or two when I say this, but I think that selling your body and working for a company are pretty much the same thing. Just ways to make money. People who need a lot of money have to pick the job that'll get it for them. Chika and I have been that way for a long time. There were always lots of things we wanted. Not that we ever worked in massage parlors or anything, but we've both made money by sleeping with men. Of course, we had our standards. We wouldn't do it with someone who was repulsive. Though it's true that some repulsive people might be considered handsome in ordinary society.

I don't remember ever feeling it was a sin to make money with my body. I only felt it was a sin when I sold, not my body, but my dignity, when business was off and I had to pretend to like some man I didn't like. That can make you puke, really. Well, that was when I was a bar hostess. There seem to be plenty of women who do the opposite, but I don't presume to say anything about them. And that's why I don't like it when people like that say things about women who live like us. Different people have different values.

It seems I didn't have to worry so much. Within a week, Chika was like an old hand. She was quick. She learned the ropes. She even learned to tie a man up and hang him from the ceiling. More than anything, she seemed to like the fact that she didn't have to hang out with the customers afterwards, that each session was a discrete little drama. And she seemed to be indulging her own ingenuity as well. She used music and candlelight, seemed to enjoy her own per-formances. Gee, Sis, she'd say, this work seems to suit me. Men really have a whole lot of sicknesses deep inside. And I'd think of all the men I tossed aside over the years and bite my lip.

Chika is so young, and yet the things she says, her eyes filling with tears, show she understands so much. There are plenty of men, she'd say, who I'm sorry I treated the way I did. I would never have done it if I knew what I know today. Such murmurs of the heart seemed to be her forte. In a way, she couldn't stand anything that would cause her to hate. She honestly seemed to understand the things I had been telling her.

One day, though, when Chika had become as good as any of the other queens, with a long list of clients of her own, she came rushing up to me, white as a sheet, pleading, "You've got to help—I can't handle this guy by myself."

"What are you saying? Nothing should shock you anymore," the club mama and I said as we entered her room.

There we found a young man with a timid smile on his face.

"What an imp! What lowly punishment have you begged the queen for?" I spoke in my regal voice.

"I'm sorry, I'm sorry," he apologized, on the verge of tears.

"What's this?" asked the other queens, who'd all assembled in the room.

"Well, actually, I wanted her to stick me with needles," he answered.

"What? Chika, I've taught you how to do that! What's your trouble?"

"He...he doesn't want the regular needles," she said, opening a box he'd brought with him. In it were hundreds of heavy sewing needles.

"Sir, we don't use needles like this here. We use sterile, disposable hospital needles," said the club mama.

It's fairly common for us to use hospital needles, sticking them in a customer's nipples or through a layer of skin in his scrotum. If you do it with a good strong jab, there's not that much pain or blood. New queens may be a little squeamish, but it's no big deal.

"But that's not what I..." he began to explain, but he had trouble speaking. "I want her...to stick all of these...sewing needles into my...penis."

The queens shrieked in alarm.

"And after that I want her to stick that...writing brush all the way up the...hole in my penis."

The queens shrieked again. Mama was the only one who kept her cool.

"You get an erection that way?" she asked.

"Yes," he said, shamefully.

"You'll bleed a lot. The blood all collects there," Mama continued. "Have you ever done this before?"

"Yes," he said. "So don't be shocked. Rather than do it myself, I came here because I thought it would be better to have a beautiful woman do it."

"I wouldn't do it," the queens said and ran off. In the end, only Mama, who has seen all the bitter and the sweet in this world, and I, who have twice the courage of your average person, were left. Chika, despite her weakened state, sat in the corner of the room and watched as we went to work.

We put the first-timer in a chair, dimmed the lights, and faced him. I sterilized the sewing needles with ethanol and handed them one by one to Mama, who jabbed them into his penis. I wondered if the guy would be all right. The needles he brought were old. Some were rusty.

As Mama stuck him with needle after needle, his prick became engorged. It got harder and harder to put the needles in. If she stopped midthrust, his face twisted in pain. Mama scolded him after each needle. In time, he got a full-blown erection, and the protruding ends of the needles disappeared completely into his prick. I thought to myself, I don't want to be around when they come out, because he's going to bleed *all over the place.*

The more his crotch began to look like a pincushion, the more ecstatic the young man's expression became.

Mama began to speak in a loving voice, in that dim room oozing with insanity. It was enough to make me shiver, in spite of myself. Times like this, I really admire Mama. She's a real pro.

"How's that? This is what you wanted. It hurts, doesn't it? Tell me it hurts. Then I'll forgive you."

"It doesn't hurt. It doesn't hurt at all."

"You really don't know how to listen, do you? If you want to be such a bad boy, we'll have to do this all over again."

"Forgive me. It's all my fault. I won't do it again. I beg of you."

"Too late now. You should have caught on sooner. I can

no longer forgive you. Hand me another needle."

Their conversation went on for a long time, the drama building to a pitch. I glanced at Chika, who was staring speechless at this punishment. There were only a few needles left. Mama also noticed this and seemed to be trying to bring the guy to a climax. I passed the last needle to Mama.

"Look, your prick is full of needles. Shall we cut it off and put it in the sewing box? This is the last needle. When this one is in, your punishment will be finished. You will be mine, utterly."

Mama paused and jabbed in the last needle.

In a burst the man ejaculated. He screamed out: *"Mother!...Mother!...Oh, Mother!"*

I looked at Mama, and she, without a word, was looking at me. Bliss had infused the young man's expression. My chest was filled with emptiness and pain.

"Shinobu, turn on the light!"

I got ahold of myself and turned on the light. The man appeared to be waking from a dream.

"Now we're going to take the needles out. This may hurt," Mama reassured him, "but you're going to be fine."

"I'm used to it," he said.

I brought a towel over and spread it at his feet. Mama waited to get started. The man began talking quietly.

"I was an illegitimate child, and people teased me about it when I was little. My mother—I mean the mother who took me into her house—was the only one who was kind to me. But there were times, I guess, when she couldn't take it any longer. She would call me to the room where she was sewing kimonos, and she would do things to me like we just did. It became a kind of habit. A strange habit. She's dead now. But I can't ever forget her."

With each needle Mama pulled out, the man interrupted his speech. Still, he talked to the end. Around him was a sea of blood. He looked pale, but satisfied.

I commandeered the towel and said, "What will it be,

then? Do you still want the brush today?"

"You mean we can do more?" he asked. "No, that's okay. I'm quite happy for today. Usually when I go to S&M clubs, the women are afraid of me and won't do what I want. No, I'm very happy. Mama, you were truly just like my mother."

Mama smiled and said, "Well, come back again anytime," then left the room. The man bowed deeply.

I thought Mama was fabulous. In this world, being young and cute doesn't mean a thing. I still have a lot to learn.

For all the blood the guy had lost, the bleeding stopped unbelievably quickly. He went into the shower. I was thinking, maybe I'll start to clean up, when I looked around and saw that Chika had fainted. What a sad sight! I left her there and switched on the vacuum cleaner. The sound roused her.

"What a mess," I started swearing.

Chika's eyes gleamed. That sad, frightened look had vanished completely.

"Sis, life is amazing, isn't it?" she said, nodding to herself.

"What do you mean—fainting at the sight of blood and babbling about life?" I said and made her help me clean up.

The man came out of the shower, looked at us, and said flat out, "Oh, Chika, you still here?"

She pouted and looked away.

First published, 1988
TRANSLATION BY TERRY GALLAGHER

Amy Yamada (b. 1959) burst on the scene with the controversial novel *Bedtime Eyes* (1985), which depicted relations between a Japanese woman and a black American soldier. Winning instant acclaim for her frank, unromanticized, often explicit treatment of sex—utterly counter to the typical Japanese euphemistic haze,

Yamada was awarded the 22nd Bungei Prize; the novel was later made into a major feature film. Then followed a string of successful novellas: *Jesse's Spine* (1987), *Fingerplay* (1987), *The Canvas Coffin* (1987), and *Bound Feet of the Butterfly* (1987). Her *Soul Music Lovers Only* (1987) won the 97th Naoki Prize; her latest book, *Ponchan is Here* (1990), is a collection of short stories. Much sought after by magazines for short stories and music commentary, Yamada's street-smart prose is matched only by her reputation as Japan's most liberated woman writer. This excerpt from *Kneel Down and Lick My Feet* (1988) constitutes the opening chapter of the novel.

PEONY SNOWFLAKES
OF LOVE
Osamu Hashimoto

Suddenly the air gets chillier as the road approaches the mountain ridge. Even the cars seem to pant to shake off some air of melancholy, eyes askance at the passing lane.

There are three drive-ins on the ridge. The first, on the left, is an *udon* shop serving homemade noodles Shikoku-style, hence the name Sanuki-tei. Nonetheless, this "country inn" is nowhere near Sanuki; this is not the mountains of Shikoku.

The road curves sharply to the right at the pass, so the drive-ins have been built in a gently snaking line. Behind Sanuki-tei stands the Sangoku Diner. And beyond it, a suburban-type family restaurant called the Lucky Palace. There is ample parking space for all three establishments in front; behind is a cliff. Of the three, the Lucky Palace pulls in the majority of the cars that manage to wheeze their way up the ridge. Next to its neon garishness, easily mistaken for a love hotel, the other two pale by comparison. Sanuki-tei, in particular, looks like a sooty farmhouse, and on nights when fog rises thick from the valley, you could easily mistake it for the Lucky Palace's storage shed.

Sanuki-tei stood yellow in this haze, holding up only the

black-brushed sign of its name. Still, there was one customer
looking out for its warm, inviting steam rising. The time was
just past five in the evening, a little too early for the dinner
rush, but night had already fallen. The fog lamps were wet
with anticipation, like the faces of people waiting for someone to show up. It was that time of day.

A refrigerated truck pulled up in front of Sanuki-tei, and
the driver climbed out. A small, lit sign above the windshield
read "The Shooting Star," but other than that the truck had
no fancy lights. It was simply a big refrigerated truck.

"Come on in!" a cheerful voice called out to the driver.

Sanuki-tei had not a single customer, and its bright interi-
or only made the place seem more lonely; this voice was the
only cheerful thing about the place.

The driver of the Shooting Star swaggered over to a large
center table and sat down, legs akimbo.

"The Stamina Special."

Immediately the words "One order Stamina!" echoed
throughout the shop. *Udon* noodles in a *miso* stew, pork
fried with ginger, a big bowl of rice, and grilled river fish
(sardines, at times)—the Stamina Special was a Sanuki-tei
customer favorite. For long-distance truckers, the mere mention of "stamina" was good for extra mileage.

After a moment, a middle-aged waitress brought tea and a
hot towel to the customer.

The driver of the Shooting Star popped the hot towel's
plastic wrap open. The driver's complexion was pale, unaf-
fectedly so, lacking vitality. The face was well fleshed-out,
ordinary, unimpressive. The eyebrows were narrow, which
was understandable since the driver was female. With the
heat of the towel, a trace of color came to her cheeks.

As the Shooting Star's driver rested her gaze on the corner
of the room, her hands suddenly stopped rubbing her tired
eyes.

"So, you're here!"

A middle-aged woman, who could only be described as

plain, nodded her head in reply. She looked apologetic, painfully awkward, embarrassed at her shyness. She stood hunched, with her back to the dark window panes, coat over her arm. It was a somber dark brown coat—a coat that was not even plain, an "old lady's" coat.

"What—leaving already?" asked the Shooting Star's driver.

The woman nodded once more, perhaps mumbling something under her breath.

"Well, don't just stand there. Come on over!" invited the driver of the Shooting Star. The invitee was Yae Nukada, 52 years old, a housewife and part-time waitress. The inviter was Tomeko Kasahagi, who had a crewcut that, due to the softness of her hair, didn't quite stand up.

Yae Nukada bowed again, clutched the coat to her chest, and shuffled over.

"Old Lady, a beer!" barked the driver of the Shooting Star, although Tomeko was herself as much an old lady as the waitress she addressed, as was also Yae, who stood before her meekly.

"Sit yourself down," Tomeko said. It sounded blunt, but Tomeko had tried to put as much feeling into her words as she could.

Predictably, Yae nodded. She even mouthed a tiny "Yes..." and pulled out a heavy, wooden chair covered in *kasuri*-patterned vinyl.

The "Old Lady" brought over the beer. And only one glass.

"Old Lady, bring us another glass!" said Tomeko.

"But, I...." Yae spoke up, but the Old Lady had already answered "Okay, okay."

Tomeko and Yae sat silently, with the one glass between them until the Old Lady brought another. She was younger than Yae, her co-worker, but she didn't seem to mind being the Old Lady.

"Mr. Honda's running late, no?" said the Old Lady.

"Uh, yes..." replied Yae, with a troubled look.

"What's up?" asked the driver of the Shooting Star, beer bottle in hand, gesturing toward Yae's glass with a thick, round stump that was hardly a chin.

"It's just that...my ride home...still hasn't..." Yae couldn't speak in complete sentences. But maybe she didn't need to: she had gotten it across that life did not distinguish between complete and incomplete.

Yae didn't drive. Because Sanuki-tei was on a mountain pass twenty minutes from town and because trains didn't run there, if for any reason Yae missed the bus she had to catch a ride from someone going the same way. Yae had been waiting for that car to arrive.

Actually, Yae hadn't really wanted to take on the part-time job. The younger brother of Sanuki-tei's owner lived in Yae's neighborhood, and when a regular employee had gotten sick, he had asked Yae to fill in.

Yae's husband worked for a credit union in town. He'd been hired mid-career, but had settled down into a management position and was now awaiting retirement the next year. Their 26-year-old daughter worked for an insurance company in town, and their son was at university in Tokyo. They weren't rolling in money, but they got by. Their daughter contributed a paltry 10,000 yen to the household once a month, unwillingly; it was not a great help, but at least she wasn't entirely a burden. Their biggest expense was the 100,000 yen they sent each month to their son in Tokyo. Even so, the son would graduate within a year and had already secured a job. Yae didn't have much knack for raising extra money, but she knew how to economize. Make do without and they'd get by. For Yae, it was a lot easier to get by on her own than to ask anyone for help. She'd *never* been one to socialize—not her, a woman without a progressive idea in her head.

It was only after getting by for years that she was asked about the part-time job this spring. Rather than reject the idea, her husband thought that if she went out and worked, they'd somehow do a little better.

"Go on. Why not take the job?" her daughter had said, as if she were tired of seeing her mother stick to home like a wallflower.

So it was that Yae went to work ten-to-five everyday. She bought groceries on the way home and managed to have dinner ready just by the time her husband came home. But with the days so short at this time of the year, no matter how quickly she rushed home to take the laundry in, it would already be damp from the night air. And even though they'd been the ones to persuade her to go out and work, if dinner was late, her husband and daughter didn't bother to hide their discontent. "A good-for-next-to-nothing woman and now she can't even do this—what are we supposed to do?" the looks on their faces implied.

During the summer months, at least, their son was home and looked after the house. But now that dusk was creeping in early, a gloom stole over Yae's heart.

"Well, if that's the case, I'll drive you home," said the driver of the Shooting Star, downing her beer. Yae heard these words with considerable relief. It was virtually impossible for her to do something as simple as ask a customer for a ride.

"Glad there's someone," Yae thought, head bent toward the beer glass in her hand. She said nothing.

"What's wrong? Drink up," said the driver of the Shooting Star. "I've got wheels."

In spite of this kindness, Yae had difficulty talking. "Yes...I'm very, very...really...." Her phrases weren't even phrases.

Color rose to Yae's face. Her complexion was bad, her protruding cheekbones sprinkled with freckles. Appealing perhaps on a young girl, but on a middle-aged woman with backaches and pains, freckles looked as becoming as an old *tatami* mat on a compost heap.

It wasn't as if she were blushing from the beer she'd barely touched—although she barely *hadn't* touched it. That blush came like a glimpse of a pale pink peach blossom long after sundown.

Tomeko alone was at ease, grunting like ex-Prime Minister Kakuei Tanaka in his heyday. She ought to have had a folding fan for the full effect.

"Um..." Yae's voice came out sounding like she was mustering up the nerve to borrow money.

"Mm?" The driver of the Shooting Star, who'd been sitting silently with crossed arms, raised her eyes.

"Really...the other day...I don't know what to say," Yae blurted out, her face red to the roots, the veins standing out on her forehead. Actually, this wasn't supposed to be an apology—this was a thank you.

"Oh," said Tomeko Kasahagi, the Shooting Star's woman driver, looking like a drunk snowman under the peach blossoms in full bloom, open mouth ready to belt out a *sumo* song. "Oh, that?" she acted bashful.

"It was the very first time...something like that... really...how can I ever..." Yae Nukada bowed her head lower than low, grateful as a poverty-stricken woman spared the agony of family suicide by a kindly clerk. Lower, then slowly she began to feel long-forgotten girlish emotions rising to the tips of her ears. All this because last Wednesday, Tomeko Kasahagi had given Yae Nukada a pink coral necklace she'd purchased in Wakayama. In a case lined with blue velvet...

Yae had never been given such a present before. No one had even suggested she was the kind of woman who might wear a necklace.

"Aw, just something on sale—it's nothing," said Tomeko Kasahagi.

But Yae, having been told by her neighbor that the coral

was real, knew it *was* something. And even if it had been nothing, it meant something to Yae Nukada. Yae wouldn't have traded it for diamonds.

The authentic coral necklace was pink, carmine pink. Not a thin gold chain. Not some bauble that came in a box of detergent. No, this necklace of pale pink coral with white flecks, strung on silver, had churned up memories of days long gone and justly forgotten. Pink, sweet, and hot—like *aronia* petals blossoming behind your eyelids, like the blood stirring in the breast of a young girl back when Peggy Hayama sang *School Days* and *Fall in Love, For Life is Brief*. These feelings welled up in Yae. After all, pink wasn't just the color of salt plums in a wide-mouthed jar tangled in *shiso* leaves, like something the tide swept ashore.

"Gracious, where did you get this?" a neighbor had asked her. And when Yae Nukada replied, "One of the customers gave it to me," her body quivered with a frisson of happiness, a sensation she'd never dreamed could be hers in life.

When she was alone, she'd laid it on the dining room table. Then, because she knew it would be wasted on her, she put it away.

"One of the customers."

"One of the customers!"

Still, there was only one safe place for her happiness—in the back of a drawer of the tea cupboard.

"You're not wearing it today?" Tomeko Kasahagi asked.

"It's too much for someone like me," replied Yae Nukada, as her hand flew to the collar of her overly youngish print blouse.

Up and down and sideways, lines showed at her throat. True, age first begins to show at the neck, but the yellowing skin under her dark, chapped fingers was arrestingly vivid. Of course, vivid is as vivid does, as all living things are by the mere fact of living.

"Bright things aren't right for me. It'd be wasted..." said Yae, hand now on her chest—as if to say she missed having it on, but to have it on here would seem crass.

"Mr. Honda's here," said the Old Lady, carrying a tray bearing the stamina dinner.

"You getting a ride with him?"

In reply, a flustered Yae lowered her head apologetically.

"I have to go home now..."

The words she'd forgotten until now crawled up her spine. Her face was like that of a waterfowl evicted from the park without notice. A naive Cinderella, fifty-something.

"I have to go home now..."

Not until this moment had she thought of going home. Yet last week, when she received the coral necklace, she couldn't wait. I've got to go home and show this to someone! she'd thought. Only to show it around once and have it end up in the back of a tea cupboard. But today—

She wished *she* hadn't been put away in a drawer.

The woman trucker put on a casual air. Cool as a grand master behind a beaded curtain, she waved her chopsticks as she spoke: "I'll drive you home."

Yae looked up at the Old Lady by her side, seeking her consent. "All right?" she asked silently.

"Now just you wait. I'll eat this up in a jiffy." The driver of the Shooting Star thrust her chopsticks in her ricebowl.

"Well, guess I'll go let Mr. Honda know," said the Old Lady.

"Sorry," Yae replied. Apologies as usual.

The woman trucker wolfed down her food without a word, looking like the mumpsy Otafuku character in a *kagura* performance at a Shinto shrine. A faint pink glow stole over her white cheeks. A real Otafuku.

Yae, contrite at her own extravagance, shrugged, not knowing how to behave.

The town arcade lit up the night like a blaze of autumn leaves. White steam swirling ankle deep, white haze drifting off into the night sky.

The truck door opened and the sounds of the town came to life.

"Take care now," said the Shooting Star's driver, as ·she opened the door. The cab rode high on the refrigerated truck, making Yae huff and puff as she climbed down. A small girl scooting off to kindergarten or a geriatric staggering back to an old folks' home, it was hard to tell—she could have been either.

She stared ahead at the constantly flowing scene of pedestrians passing multicolored store windows.

A horn honked behind her.

"I'll be going," said the woman trucker.

A quick roadside thank-you won't do, Yae supposed, trying to think of something more eloquent. But she could come up with nothing. So Yae bowed her head. Hoping humility would convey the message, she bowed so hard and deep that her back showed.

"This time I'm off to Tokyo—not much in the way of gifts there, though," the Shooting Star's driver spoke outright.

Yae smiled, this time lowering her head only slightly.

"Okay now." That was all the driver of the Shooting Star said, helping Yae on her way.

Like a child letting go of a parent's hand for the first time and heading for the deep end of a pool, Yae stepped into the crowd.

The woman trucker shut the door without a word and stepped on the accelerator as if nothing had happened. In the rearview mirror, Yae's back disappeared into the hustle and bustle. "Take care," the driver of the Shooting Star whispered in her heart.

She sped off, but ran into a red light at the second intersection. Hitting the brake, the woman trucker gazed out the wide windshield. This time she said something out loud:

"Damn, if she isn't cute!"

"Mother, where on earth have you been?" a shrill voice

greeted Yae as she pulled open the door. "Father's been waiting ages!" Her daughter stood there, long hair flowing, still
in her bright red suit, and frowning her bright red lips.

"I had to do some shopping?" Yae replied.

"You're so slow, nothing gets done!"

Yae slowly put the supermarket bag on the threshold and
slowly pulled off her shoes.

Her daughter Sumie fumed off, annoyed that she had to
walk in stocking feet over old floorboards. She stormed into
her room and slammed the wooden door with a bang.

Sumie, who worked for an insurance company, was having an affair with a manager from another company, a married man with children. No one in her family knew this. Even
so, no one dared to suggest that she, at 26, might want to
think about marriage, because to do so would result in her
flying into an uncontrollable rage. Now, the subject was
taboo; to bring it up was like touching an open sore. Still, the
fact was, Sumie wasn't cut out for anything but marriage,
and the lack of talk about mariage served to make her more
lonely.

She had no choice but to throw herself into her career.
Well, not her career as much as her lifestyle. When she
thought of how fashion-conscious she was, how she stood
out in this backwater, the claustrophobic life here drove her
to her wit's end. In truth, however, these feelings only masked
her disgust at the circumstances around her. And to make
matters worse, her manager boyfriend had broken their date
today; for that she was mad at the world.

In the living room, Yae's husband, Keizo, was having an
evening drink while watching TV. The seven o'clock news
was still on. She'd been worried that it was late, but now that
she saw what time it was, she was relieved—and a little
angry.

"What happened?" asked Keizo.

"I had trouble getting a ride home," said Yae.

"Well then, quit," said Keizo, without a trace of emotion.

Yae said nothing and put a small dish of soy-simmered *fukinoto* coltsfoot stalks on the table. Before Keizo was a bottle of beer and a red plastic dish of potato chips. Barbecue flavored. Yae figured that when Keizo asked Sumie for something to eat, she had handed him the chips. Next to Keizo was a pile of cushions. So Sumie had been sitting there, chin in hand, until she came home.

Why couldn't she make something for him instead of sitting there? thought Yae. If she's got the time to sit beside her father and do nothing, then she's got the time to be useful in the kitchen. Better that than taking out her irritation on others, Yae stewed in rare anger at her daughter.

Sumie was totally useless when it came to cooking. But it was Yae who, ashamed to raise a daughter to be like herself, a housewife and nothing more, had never asked Sumie to help in the kitchen. Even if Yae was good for nothing, her more worldly daughter, given the chance, would be able to do something else, or so Yae bravely hoped.

Yae said nothing and went into the kitchen. All the wonderful feelings she'd had bouncing around inside had been crushed the minute she got home.

Ordinarily, words did not spring from Yae Nukada's lips. Neither was she light on her feet. Whatever she was told she fervently repeated to herself and moved around in a jerky trance.

Yae had not a clue how to draw people's attention to herself. She took the customers' orders and carried the trays, all very mechanically. Why would anyone want to joke with her? And even if someone were to drop a casual remark her way, the very idea that she could carry on a conversation with someone she'd just met was out of the question.

She didn't understand that there are all kinds in this world and that all kinds of people could open the door and walk in. And that, in fact, this was what business was all about. The fact that there were all kinds in this world meant a brightness and energy that threw Yae's own lack into such sharp relief that she could not ignore it. Which is why, at first, to return back to her nearly dead-silent home was a relief.

"I just can't get used to it," she'd once let slip to her husband, who responded, "So quit." She got particularly upset by this, when in fact her husband was the type to say "quit" should there be the slightest letdown in the meals she served him.

After that, Yae decided not to think about this—the less anxious she made herself, the sooner the problem would disappear. In time, she found herself caring less about what her husband said, reluctant to return to the depression of home. It may also have been because upon seeing the coral necklace, Keizo said, "Big cheap deal."

"There is no reason to talk like that," she thought to herself three days later.

Once the idea had planted itself in her head, however, there was no stopping her. When the driver of the Shooting Star showed up again at Sanuki-tei, Yae got all light-hearted. After all, she was the only person who admired the way Yae worked. And she was nicer to Yae than anyone else.

"I'll bet she's got a regular fan club," thought Yae, gifted for the first time in her life with bamboo leaf-wrapped fish cakes from Sendai.

"Here, take these," the driver of the Shooting Star had said, handing the fish cakes to Yae. "I was up to Sendai the other day." This was the beginning of September, when summer lingers as long as possible, reluctant to depart. Her words startled Yae, who'd come over to clear a consumed Udon Special from the table.

"Take it," the driver had said to a surprised Yae. "It's too much for one person." And she pressed the leaf-wrapper in Yae's hands.

It was hard to refuse. How nice she is, Yae thought, as the well-muscled driver sauntered out of the premises as nonchalantly as she could.

Someone like that must really be popular with women, Yae mused, but when she mentioned this to her co-worker, the Old Lady cut her to the quick. "What do you mean? She *is* a woman!"

Yae was surprised, but then relieved. Well, that means she's not getting any ideas then, she concluded. And anyway, there'd be others—plenty of younger women gaggling over "him"—no comparisons with herself wanted or needed.

Still, from time to time, the woman trucker gave Yae gifts from her trips, always saying it was too much for her alone.

"Pity, isn't it? She must have her circumstances," ventured the Old Lady. But Yae, confronted for the first time ever by a person of "mystery," was too busy following her fascination to take heed of the words "pity" and "circumstances."

On her part, the Shooting Star's driver was nursing a broken heart. She'd been living with a coffee-shop waitress from Itoigawa, but young women these days—all they can think of is money. Cash. They get used to a little luxury, then before you know it, they've up and run off with some young guy. She was used to losing out, but the one thing she'd never understand was the cold-hearted egotism that allowed young women to trample on someone else's heart. She wasn't angry with herself for seeking furtive romances. No, the driver of the Shooting Star was tired of young women and their indifference.

Somewhere, there's someone to heal my wounds. But what the hell. It's nothing a friendly breeze won't put behind me, thought the woman trucker. And she took off into the wind as she had countless times before.

Then, around the time the maples that bathed in the cool air of the river bottoms took on a fresh, green growth of new leaves, a different sort of breeze touched Tomeko's heart.

Nothing had happened. But by the time she realized that the disregarded paragon of Japanese femininity was there, right before her eyes, her lovelorn heart had taken wing.

Could there be another woman who imparted such sincerity to her hands as Yae did when she served *udon*? When the truth hit, Tomeko began to tremble.

Come on, cut it out! You promised yourself you wouldn't fall in love, Tomeko sat in her truck wiping her tears. Falling for a respectable housewife—where will that get you?

This was in June, when breezes from the pines in Atakanoseki stab at the heart.

But it wasn't until summer had passed and those autumn evenings of untold longing were drawing to an end, that on one rainswept night love's gears began to turn.

"I imagine you're very popular with the young folks," Yae had asked. From across the wide passenger seat. A sad, yearning Teresa Ten number played softly on the radio. It seems Yae Nukada still couldn't quite reconcile herself to the fact that Tomeko Kasahagi was a woman.

But irreconcilable facts were destined to go the way of all irreconcilable facts, that is, toward Yae's happiness. Whether it was the road of womanhood as Yae knew it or the road of womanhood as Tomeko hoped, whatever twisted road it may have been, the big refrigerated truck was hurtling along it on an evening when the few remaining leaves were tinged crimson in the droplets of a sudden rain.

On they sped—not to a motel, but to Tomeko's place of business.

Leave the Sanuki-tei and head downhill, forty minutes or so beyond the town where Yae lives, a little past the intersection with the main motorway, and there will be the depot of the shipping company that contracts Tomeko. In that huge runway of a parking lot will be parked a number of big rigs.

The Shooting Star with its two women on board raced like the wind, and had emerged, suddenly, in a place where there were no rain clouds.

"Oh, what a gorgeous moon..."

A half-moon peered through the cracks in the clouds, casting its radiance over the parking lot.

Teresa Ten, who couldn't have known, was singing:

> *You told me, how could I have known?*
> *It's sometimes best to travel on your own.*

"Damn straight," Tomeko had to agree. Here was a woman who always traveled alone listening to a woman who sometimes traveled alone, and beside her, an innocent woman who never had traveled anywhere. For once, Tomeko found herself agreeing with Teresa Ten, that "sometimes" might indeed be best.

"The *susuki* grass sure looks nice this time of year," said Tomeko. This prompted Yae to say, "Yes, *susuki* grass can be lovely."

Tomeko's depot seemed to float in a sea of *susuki* pampas grass, all the more dramatic for the clouds racing through the autumn night sky.

"Too bad it's raining today," said Tomeko. But the words apparently failed to reach Yae's ears, so she added, more pointedly, "Shall we go then?"

For a drive.

Yae had never been taken on a drive before. Sure she'd been on family trips and vacations, but never would she have entertained the idea of herself going on a drive with someone.

While Teresa Ten crooned,

> *I'm a woman*
> *Who wouldn't mind waiting—*

Yae Nukada daydreamed, "If there were someone who wouldn't mind being my sweetheart...," subconsciously creating a decidedly unpoetic old lady's version of Machi Tawara-style *waka* verse.

Which is how old ladies live—subconsciously. They can't help it. An old lady slips into this subconsciousness so easily, sneaking back to her school-girl days. It's the anarchy of memory.

"Pretty, isn't it." Standing by the truck near the parking lot, Yae Nukada was entranced by the swaying white tops of *susuki* grass that fanned in the moonlight. She was drunk on the autumn breeze.

Tomeko Kasahagi slipped her arm around this defenseless 52-year-old housewife's slender shoulders. As she held her gently, Yae's body temperature rose five degrees.

It was past nine by the time Yae got home.

The large refrigerated truck pulled up alongside Yae's house. The door groaned open.

"Be seeing you," or any words to this effect, were beyond Tomeko.

Yae stood, half inside the cab of the truck, grabbing Tomeko's arm with both hands. "I had a wonderful time," said Yae, back from the first drive in her life.

"Yeah," was all Tomeko could manage. Looking like someone leaning on the entrance booth at the public bath, Yae thrust both elbows on the seat and bowed her head. "Thank you very, very much."

Tomeko nodded silently. A smile lit up her face. Have to smile if it kills me, she thought, cheek muscles twitching. But I'm in no smiling mood. I don't want to leave you.

"See you later," said Yae, closing the door like a preschooler on her way to kindergarten. As she parted from the truck, the engine started with a shivering sob.

Shaking, the big Shooting Star was reluctant to leave.

Yae disappeared from view.

Inside the house was dead silent. "What's going on here?" she'd expected to be asked, but the house was so quiet a hand clap would have echoed. It was so silent, it was frightening, but Yae hadn't quite noticed this yet.

Before she could, a voice loud enough to rip up the floorboards roared out. "Where the hell were you? Meathead!" A thermos bottle came flying at her, knocking down the sliding door. Hot steam rose from the old wood-floored corridor.

The Shooting Star had driven off by now; the clouds grew thick, enveloping the bright moon.

"What is this?" said Yae, clutching the small crepe bag she'd patched herself.

In the next room, Keizo, his expression as dark as ink, his eyes as sharp as needles, was sloshing down cold *sake*. Or maybe he wasn't sloshing it but merely spilling it: the tabletop was sopping. Yae was so taken aback, she forgot to run for a cloth to wipe it up.

Keizo stood up and in one continuous motion made for Yae. Yae stepped back in fright, but Keizo pushed her down anyway. He grabbed her shirt front, forced her head to the floor and began to pummel her.

Yae tried to run, only to be yanked back by her hair and to be pushed down again.

"Ow! Ouch! Ouch!" As miserable as the beating was, this was all she managed to say. Suddenly the door to the further room flew open and in started Sumie. She stopped in the doorway and began to scream, "Stop it! Stop taking it out on mother!"

Keizo rammed Yae's head onto the floor of the corridor and headed back toward where Sumie stood. At a total loss, Yae lay there, cheek against the floor and stared at the thermos bottle lying on the same level. The now-cooled water wet Yae's cheek. Screams and curses could be heard as father and daughter fought it out. Yae scampered to her feet. Her hair was a dripping mess.

"Stop it! Stop it!" Yae threw herself between father and daughter. Keizo began to hit her, while Sumie now tore at her hair.

"Stop it!" she screamed, though she could not tell whether she meant for them to stop beating on her or to stop beating on each other.

Sumie, whose Comme ça du Mode sweater had been pulled out of shape, shouted, "While you were out, Mother, my boyfriend's wife called. Demanded to know what sort of upbringing you gave me. That's what's got to him!"

"What's this?" Keizo rushed toward his daughter like the devil incarnate. "Want to say that again? Some woman starts yelling at me out of nowhere and that's what got to me? Not on your life!" They fought like man and wife.

Keizo raged, knocking down both Yae and Sumie. Yae hit her back on the corner of the table.

"A-ao-agh..." she moaned voicelessly, bursting into tears. Father and daughter continued to fight right over her. Yae did not know what was happening. All she prayed for was the pain in her back would go away.

"Ow! Stop! You don't know a damn thing!"

"Ungrateful brat! I'll teach you!"

What *was* going on here? For the first time, Yae was simply an observer; she had nothing to do with this family anymore. Especially as father and daughter could fight with each other so conjugally.

The next day, the Shooting Star didn't show at Sanuki-tei. Yae knew it wouldn't. It was on its way from Fukui to Okayama.

Her back pained her so much she thought of taking the day off. But because the thought of asking to rest in someone else's home was more painful, when Mr. Honda arrived to pick her up, as he did every morning, she decided she felt well enough.

Her co-worker, Masako Yaoi, the Old Lady, commiserated with her, saying, "It sure is terrible!" A horrible daughter who didn't even ask what was wrong when her own mother was moaning from pain. And a horrible husband who pulled her hair and hit her. A rotten daughter who'd sleep with another woman's husband. And that horrible woman who'd phone somebody's house to complain... Masako Yaoi understood how horrible it all was, and this brought Yae a measure of relief. Now if only Yae's body were younger, she'd have no more cause for complaint.

Winter came and with it her son Kensuke, and a young woman in tow, to go skiing over the New Year's holidays. The young woman had a round face and friendly air. She seemed to be the sturdy type, which put Yae greatly at ease. Sumie had called to tell Kensuke about the family problems. But since Sumie herself didn't know of the extent of her mother's injuries, neither did Kensuke. And Yae didn't discuss it.

As the end of the year approached, Yae asked for time off from the thirtieth of December until the fourth of January. "In exchange, I'll take the late shift starting February," she offered in a low voice over the phone.

"But that means you'll have to work through the middle of the night, you know," the manager said.

"That's all right. I'd appreciate it if you'd let me," she replied.

Kensuke was quiet, but quite reliable. What with his future job all set and his young lady the steadfast type, Yae felt confident he'd do well by himself.

Sumie was another matter. It didn't look as if she would get married for a while, but at least her father was there to take care of her. Yae figured she'd be all right, too. Meanwhile, her husband would be retiring in May, so with more time on his hands, surely he'd help a little around the house.

It seems that Sumie had had her "circumstances" too, which explained why she became hysterical at the mere mention of marriage. Little had Yae known, but now her cheeks flushed at the thought. Maybe the girl intends to wheedle

things out of her father, Yae wondered. It wasn't as if her
father didn't spoil her anyway.

So with that, Yae packed up her things on the twelfth of
January and left. "Thank you very much for all you've done
for me, but I intend to terminate our relationship from this
day forth." It sounded a bit like a retirement request. She
also left a bank book in Sumie's name and the requisite signa-
ture-seal. She'd been saving 50,000 yen a month since June,
and there was now 780,000 yen in the account.

"What's this?" Sumie grimaced when she found it, as if
she'd come across some spoiled food. Perhaps, she didn't
want to believe it was money saved for her wedding.

Carrying her own personal belongings wrapped in a large
cloth and wearing the coral necklace, of course, Yae headed
for the depot near the sea of *susuki* grass—which by now
was nothing more than dry straw—a bride about to embark
on a new life. She was on her own.

Naturally, Tomeko Kasahagi was there waiting for her.

Tomeko Kasahagi had vowed to never join the system. To
always be the lone wolf. But now that Yae was coming to
live with her, she couldn't help but think of things like security and insurance, so she decided to become a full-time employee.

Thus, their life-for-two began.

Tomeko worked two days on, one day off. Knowing that
Tomeko had to get up in the middle of the night to work
made working the night shift easier for Yae. What's more, she
enjoyed the three A.M. calls that Tomeko made from the
road—her "regular update."

In February, they went to see the plum blossoms in Mito.
The blossoms were in full bloom, the crowds genial, and
most important, the person at Yae's side was attentive to her.
Is it fair for one person to be as happy as I? she wondered.

Then in March, a surly Sumie came to visit.

"Here." Sumie handed over a suspicious-looking package

in a plastic bag. It was wrapped in paper with a picture of a fairy-tale temple and some undecipherable English words written on it.

Yae strained to make them out, but not even her bifocals could help.

"Father brought this back from Korea. A preretirement trip with the company," Sumie explained. "It's Korean ginseng."

"Is your father with you?" Yae stood up.

"Are you kidding?" said Sumie. "And this letter came for you. Looks like an invitation to a class reunion, maybe."

Yae's maiden name was written on the back of the long, narrow envelope.

"How long are you going live like this?" asked Sumie.

Yae was reading the outside of the envelope and didn't reply. Or maybe she didn't intend to reply. Or maybe, having been asked without warning and not knowing how to reply, she'd decided not to. The previous day had been so warm, yet today was heavy with clouds, the air chilly, as if winter had returned. Theirs was a two-room apartment, with everything in full view. A small kettle blew jets of steam in the back room.

"And I...," Sumie resumed, as if she hadn't expected a reply, "I don't need this." She pulled out the bank book and seal that Yae had left behind.

Suddenly Yae felt her strength leaving her. "But you..."

"Since when have you ever done anything for me, Mother?" Sumie hissed like a witch. "Just what do you expect me to do with this? You who've gone and done as you please. So you're living with a woman? Two lesbians living together like happy little sows, huh? Everybody's talking about it, wondering what's got into you."

"But, you, you...!" Yae could say no more.

"And she's got a crewcut? Disgusting! Everybody knows about it. Just what is it you're doing? I don't care, but it makes me sick. And you didn't have to leave this behind!"

Sumie grabbed the bank book and seal and flung them into a corner of the room.

"But you...!" Yae frantically watched the seal fly across her field of vision, then turned to find Sumie's eyes overflowing with tears. "You're filthy!" Sumie shouted.

"Forgive me," said Yae, bowing head to the ground.

Yae didn't know why it had come to this. But more than that, she didn't understand why people disapproved of her living like this. She didn't understand why someone should cry over something she found perfectly natural.

Yet aside from that, even Yae could see that her daughter was going through a difficult time. And Yae had been of no help to her, and she had set herself up in a position where she didn't have to be of any help to her. This grieved Yae deeply; for this she'd bowed her head. Thinking of her daughter's unhappiness, and of her own, she bowed her head before her daughter and cried. A small stain formed on the purple heated mat.

Mother and daughter sat there for a while in silence. Only the kettle kept whistling on.

"I'm going home," said Sumie, rising abruptly.

Yae raised her head.

Sumie looked down at her feet. "All women are unhappy," she said.

"You're the unhappy one," Yae said, almost to herself.

"What?" Sumie turned around, aghast.

Mouth open, Yae stared at Sumie.

"*What!*" Sumie demanded again.

"Did I say something?" asked Yae.

"Well, didn't you?" asked Sumie.

"Are things going well for you and...that man?" asked Yae.

"How could things *possibly* go well?" Sumie spat out, almost triumphantly.

"That's true," said Yae, thinking her daughter truly pitiful.

"I'm going," Sumie said again, the strength gone from her voice.

"Wait a minute." Yae rushed to her feet and, hunched over, hurriedly searched for the seal Sumie had flung in the corner.

By now Sumie was standing in the entranceway with her shoes on. Looking at her mother, she reflected, "Still a woman, this one." Here her mother had left home, and rumors of her living with that butch of a dyke were all over. What kind of woman would do such a thing? The very thought of it infuriated her. But now, seeing the old gal searching around for the seal for the savings account that she'd put aside for her—and which might not be of any use to her now, or ever—Sumie had to admit, this woman, she's my mother after all.

She's not disgusting, just out of it. Like all women. Men offer women their useless affections, make a show of half-assed kindness just to get on their good side. No wonder women end up with no place to go, she thought.

Sumie had met her father's eyes when he told her, "Here, take this to your mother." How had this woman, bent over looking for a seal, and that man, who'd sternly asked her to deliver the ginseng extract, ever managed to live together for so long? And what the hell did he hope to accomplish by giving the Korean ginseng to her anyway, now that she was a confirmed lesbian? It just didn't figure.

People don't make sense, was all Sumie could think.

"Take this," said her mother, pressing the bank book and seal back into Sumie's hands. "If this isn't enough, I'm saving more. There isn't anything else I can do for you, so please accept this—for my sake."

"But I don't intend to get married," said the miserable daughter, a troubled look on her face. "If I keep it, I'll just blow it on something else. That's how it is." Her boyfriend came to mind, the way he tried to worm himself away with sweet talk and promises. Oh, how she hated him.

"Just keep it. You might need it someday," said her mother. She clasped her daughter's hand over the bank book and seal. "Now it's time you went home."

"Anything I should say to Father?" the daughter asked.

"That I'm sorry for everything," the mother replied.

Her daughter nodded slightly.

That was how a perfectly ordinary fact was politely dealt with. After all, who knows what Father had in mind buying that Korean ginseng.

That was a real problem. Not even Father knew why. If he did, he probably wouldn't be sitting all alone in the house on a Sunday.

The daughter left Yae's apartment. The mother, alone once more, stretched a little. Lately, her back had improved greatly. Fearing that she'd hurt it again, she stretched again, but no, it was fine.

Yae turned off the gas, then opened the small window above the sink. The view was clear to the mountains, and she could see the scooped-out face of the cliff. Beneath that was the apartment parking lot in which a number of cars stood.

Not that it bothered her that much, but to be told that she was living with a dyke in a lesbian relationship, like two fat sows in their nice little apartment, didn't make Yae too happy.

"Tomeko is such a good person." Yae looked at it as if she were living with an old classmate that she'd known for ages.

She wondered who'd written the letters of her name on the white envelope. Turning it over, she saw the name of her school—the former name, the return address informed her. It made her feel sad.

Outside, time passed, but inside it stood still. Yae, who in spite of everything remained Yae Nukada, had the urge to head out to the hills across the way, lie there under the cloudy sky, and shout at the top of her lungs.

"But what is there for me to shout?"

Yae saw she was standing at the window, clutching onto the frame tightly with both hands.

Maybe I'll just go do some shopping, was Yae's next thought.

Tomeko always wrapped a length of white cotton around her midriff, samurai style. When she was dressed in her work gear, it was hardly noticeable. But with street clothes, in a white turtleneck with a houndstooth jacket thrown over her shoulders, a strange bulge would appear under her arms. Wrapped around her body so tightly, it flattened her front, but the flesh pressed upwards, visible above the belly band. You could even make out the coils of the belly band, although, of course, Yae wasn't the type to look too closely.

Tomeko came home at dusk. Today had been her day off, but she'd gone to the depot to take part in a union meeting. She was in street clothes and had stopped to play some *pachinko* on the way home. She hadn't won anything, though.

There was a slight difference between the work-day Tomeko and the off-day Tomeko. Tomeko the trucker was neither male nor female, just the clean-cut driver of the Shooting Star. But Tomeko at home on her days off was clearly a woman. On her home days, she gave off the scent of a woman, something that Yae, being female, could accept. At her home before, the house seemed to be permeated with Keizo's stink, and Yae had been on edge. But the two woman lived in an elegant tea-time atmosphere. Tomeko liked to drink and drank a lot, but since Yae thought the two of them were similar, she was not threatened by it. After living with

Tomeko a while, it struck Yae that there was nothing the least bit odd about their living arrangement.

"I'm home."

It had been cloudy all day long before drifting into night—a neither here-nor-there kind of day. Tomeko butted the door open with her shoulder and wearily took off black calfskin loafers. She wore a cashmere scarf around her neck. Tomeko took great care with her appearance.

"Welcome home," Yae answered cheerfully.

In the center of the room sat a small *kotatsu* table and on top of this, a pot was bubbling on a hotplate. For Yae, who was a homebody, putting *tofu* on to simmer was second nature.

"Aah, *yudofu*," said Tomeko.

"How was the meeting?" asked Yae.

"Nothing special. Played *pachinko* on the way home and lost a bit," Tomeko answered bluntly.

Tomeko was normally blunt. She'd had a weak complexion, but since living with Yae, a color more expected for her age (she was 18 years younger than Yae) had come to her cheeks. She'd also rounded out a little, become more the old woman, so that the dashing pose she'd taken such pains to cultivate had no place any more. Not that she had any complaints about her life now. It was that the swagger she'd kept up throughout her lonely midnight runs had, for some reason, ceased to suit the new Tomeko. She felt like a retired boxer.

"The bath's nice and hot," said Yae.

"Mm."

The need to raise a clenched fist had disappeared, and she could feel her arm strain. Previously, the belly band had fit perfectly, like a part of her body, but now it slipped up over the smooth, fatted flesh. The white cotton wrap that once looked so sharp seemed more like a girdle.

All was not well with Tomeko.

"You know, somehow, I just don't feel like going to work

today," said Yae, sidling over from the sink to sit down next to Tomeko.

"Something wrong?" Tomeko asked. Sitting cross-legged on the floor at the *kotatsu*, she placed her arm around Yae, who brushed up against her.

"No, nothing really." Yae said, fiddling with her apron. "My daughter came by today."

"What happened?" asked Tomeko, a trace of tension showing on her face.

"Nothing really." Of course, Yae dared not mention the "sows" or the "dyke".

"Starting to miss home?" asked Tomeko.

"No, that's not it. But somehow..." Yae did not continue.

"But somehow what?" Tomeko asked, stroking Yae's shoulder.

"But somehow, I just don't feel like going to work today."

"My, my," said Tomeko, narrowing her eyes.

Yae had been thinking: her life was "somehow" happy enough, only unlike the modern young urban woman, she couldn't come out and talk about it. Nor had she really given herself over to life either.

"Want me to phone them?" Tomeko asked.

"Uh-huh." For perhaps the first time in her life, Yae was being kittenish.

"This woman's acting coy. For the first time since coming here, she's playing up to me." Tomeko gave Yae a big, sucking kiss on the lips.

Naturally, Yae wasn't a virgin and neither was she embarrassed by such things. She wasn't repelled, the kisses didn't bother her at all. But she felt something was missing.

Tomeko had never removed the belly band in front of Yae. Even when they took a bath together, Yae alone would become naked, while Tomeko played bathhouse attendant. After washing Yae's back, after playing with her body, after Yae alone had left the bath, then Tomeko would strip down. But since the apartment bath was a tiny prefab unit, two women in there would have been extremely cramped anyway, no matter how small they were.

"I'd like to move to a place with a bigger bath," Tomeko had said on occasion, but to Yae, their present two-room apartment seemed adequate. She thought that for them, a childless couple, a whole house would be too lonesome; she preferred a small space that allowed her to take in everything at a glance.

To have children come home to an empty house, bringing in their glow like the first streetlights of the evening, injecting an air of life—that was one thing. But the idea of presiding alone over a bunch of empty rooms was unbearable. Since coming here, only this had remained unchanged in Yae.

Tomeko phoned the Sanuki-tei to say that Yae had caught a cold and wouldn't be coming in. Meanwhile, Yae was giggling at Tomeko's side, listening to her awkward speech.

Tomeko hung up and reached out to fondle Yae once more. Yae playfully squirmed out of reach, saying, "Time to take your bath."

"Okay." Tomeko felt awkward, but tried to act cool. Yae stood in place, calm and relaxed. Tomeko just scratched her head "why me?"

Yae did not move. With her chin Tomeko pointed in the general direction of the stove and asked, "Hey, that all right over there?"

"Ah," said Yae, slowly cranking herself up to her feet. She turned off the *yudofu*, went to the kitchen, and removed the lid from the turbot. It was just done, so she turned off the gas. The fan stayed on.

Tomeko stood up, walked to the bathroom that jutted out into the room like a navel, and, screened by the door, took off her clothes.

"Tomeko!" Returning from the kitchen area, Yae called out toward in the bath. She could hear the sound of running water.

"Tomeko?" Yae called out once more, and strained her ears.

"What?" Tomeko's steam-muffled voice sounded within.

"Shall I wash your back?" asked Yae.

All was silent within. The churn of the steam was almost audible.

"I'd like to." Yae said, glancing toward the *tofu*. Over-boiled, probably floating limp and lifeless in the aluminum pot.

There was no answer. A washcloth splashed in the water, implying no need to come in.

All was dead quiet. Except for the droning fan. Yae waited patiently in front of the bathroom door.

Presently, there came the sound of rushing water from within. Then more splashes of the washcloth.

Yae silently opened the bathroom door. Inside, in a space too cramped to allow more that one person to wash at a crouch, loomed a large white back. On the buttocks were two scars from cauterization.

Pouring water over her head, Tomeko turned toward Yae with a heart-rending look.

"Let me wash your back, too," Yae said clumsily, accenting this final word.

Yae took the washcloth, disregarding Tomeko's astonished blinking. Tomeko huddled up. "It's cold."

"Oh, sorry," said Yae, closing the bathroom door. It was a strange, old-fashioned bathroom, the wooden door painted and with a frosted glass window.

With the door closed, the bathroom became all the more cramped. Tomeko made her large body as small as she could in the haze.

"What beautiful skin you have," said Yae, ignoring Tomeko's embarrassment. She began to wash Tomeko.

"Won't you get wet?" asked Tomeko, body still facing forward.

"It's all right," said Yae, though her clothes were getting soaked where they touched the tile wall.

Placing her left hand on Tomeko's rounded shoulder, Yae

rubbed Tomeko's back briskly with the right. The soap bubbles made Tomeko's oily skin seem all the more smooth, so that in the diffuse, yellow lighting, Tomeko's skin gleamed like the coral necklace she'd once given Yae.

Yae's right hand went further down.

The washcloth dropped in front of Tomeko, and Yae, unable to contain herself, cried out, "Tomeko, you have such beautiful breasts!"

Beneath her rounded shoulders were two voluptuous breasts, brilliantly white like the autumn half-moon they'd once seen. Yae fondled one of those breasts with her soapy right hand. This was not the caress of a middle-aged woman. Rather, it was the skilled touch of a dedicated housewife polishing the stove, carefully washing *daikon* or carrots or apples or grapes.

"Tomeko, you really *do* have lovely breasts." Under the tightly wound white cloth of the belly band, the breasts of the woman trucker, far from having being crushed out of shape, had come to fruition at this, the spring of her womanhood.

Laying a cheek on Tomeko's broad and, from a man's point of view, shapely shoulders, Yae repeated, "Tomeko..."

Outside, a sudden flurry of white flakes had begun to fall.

"Look, it's snowing!" Yae said. She had opened a window to cool things down. Large peony snowflakes were falling, layering thickly the dark spring night. Tomeko wore a *hanten*, a short, cotton housecoat Yae had gotten her at the local *kimono* shop, and was squatting at the table, opening a beer.

Yae didn't particularly enjoy her nights with Tomeko—or since the two of them worked nights, the nighttime activites that usually happened in the day.

Compared with men sticking something in you, it was much easier with Tomeko. If only Tomeko wouldn't try so hard to please her. A man's weight bearing down on you she could take, but Tomeko, who was doing her best to bring Yae to happiness, was wearing her out.

She doesn't have to go out of her way to please me. I'm happy enough as it is, thought Yae. But Tomeko, her stubby fingers probing Yae's entire body—"Happiness hiding here, happiness hidden here, too"—was tenacious in the face of largely fruitless labors. On occasion, unable to take it any longer, Yae would raise her voice. Not in a cry of pleasure; it was closer to a cry of dismay at having suddenly lost herself. It was as if the earth had slipped out from under her feet, Yae would explain later. A person her age, getting her body tossed around like that all the time was bound to wear herself out, she worried.

Tomeko, not recognizing Yae's distress, continued to provide the full round of intimate delights.

"Tomeko, Tomeko." Unable to stand it any longer, her only desire to get her feet back on solid ground, a childish Yae would desperately cling to Tomeko. And Tomeko, overcome with affection for Yae, would fervently hold her close and suck from her lips. This especially got to be too much for Yae.

Hence, for Tomeko and Yae, the sexual act always ended with Yae crushed tight against Tomeko, striving with her whole body to hold back a massive runaway truck.

Hardly half a night's worth, was Tomeko's assessment. Whether she was just putting up with it or giving Yae free rein was hard for her to tell, because when she stopped to think about it, her wild-as-the-wind way of life had vanished in the mist. This is what Tomeko thought about on her way home from playing *pachinko* in town, trudging wearily along the gravel road that would never see pavement.

"Just what's going to become of me?" The woman trucker puzzled over what she'd supposedly obtained, that something called "happiness." You could throw it all away or you could let it slide, but by now the heave had gone from this ready-for-anything woman's shoulders.

"Yae, do you dislike me?" the Shooting Star's driver asked out of the blue, taking some salt-kelp with her chopsticks.

"Wha—?" Yae cocked her head in wonder as she placed the turbot on the *kotatsu* table.

"Just thought maybe you were tired of all this," queried Tomeko Kasahagi after downing her beer.

"What makes you say things like that?" asked Yae as she popped open the electric rice cooker. The smell of freshly cooked rice drifted to Tomeko's nostrils.

"Then how come—" Tomoko stopped herself from going further.

Thinking over this life together that had gotten off to such a strange start, Tomeko began to regret that she was only a woman. Tomeko, as much a man as any male, was depressed. Just like a man gets when he starts to brood, straying down that uniquely masculine maze of thoughts and ending up believing that being a man is the root of all his unhappiness.

But if Tomeko weren't female, then what would this all be about? This is what Yae failed to understand. Particularly as Tomeko was *not* a man, but a woman, and one with very beautiful breasts.

Yae served the rice, each grain so plump and white, almost the image of Tomeko's breasts. Yae's cheeks flushed at this thought, or was it because of the steam from the rice? Yae kept seeing Tomeko's breasts in the rice, but that didn't stop her diligent serving.

Tomeko put her hand out to the arm that emerged from the fragrant steam. She took the rice bowl firmly. Yet Tomeko herself did not yet recognize that the arm Yae extended to her was, in truth, the same arm that Tomeko had extended to Yae when she was a part-time waitress. The connection was not in the bamboo leaf-wrapped fish cakes or the serving rice. But if the fish cakes hadn't been given when they were, these white grains of rice probably would never have been steamed up either.

"Let's eat," said Yae, grabbing her chopsticks.

Tomeko silently set the beer bottle aside and picked up her chopsticks as well.

"I'm very grateful to you, Tomeko. You took me in when I had nowhere to go."

"It's not like you didn't have anywhere else to go," thought Tomeko, but if that's the way Yae wanted to look at it, then fine. Silently she started to eat the turbot.

The fish was a little too sweet, the hot *tofu* a little over-cooked. But, as this writer would say, until you can find another place to serve you the same, you've no right to complain.

It was that evening, as huge puffs of peony snow fell, covering everything in a feminine, lesbian world, that Yae said, "Until you get married, Tomeko, I'll always be here."

Tomeko's chopsticks froze in the air, tips trembling, her gaze glued on the chopsticks.

Yae ate silently.

"Tastes damn good," she said.

Like peony snowflakes, these words melted gently in the rice steam.

First published, 1987
TRANSLATION BY MONA TELLIER

Osamu Hashimoto (b. 1948) is best known for his *Peach-Bottom Girl* (1977), which brought him a nomination for the Shosetsu Gendai Award and launched a whole series of student novels. An extremely popular writer—enough to be seen as a barometer of the tastes of the times—Hashimoto emerged from the ranks of the New Left to look back on the seventies' student movement as a comedy of clichés—marking a shift from "wet" romanticism to "dry" appropriation of stereotype. Other works include *The Blossom of Virginity and Soy-Simmered Burdock* (1979), *Repent and Play* (1980), and *Men's Knitting* (1983). Japanese readers of *Peony Snowflakes of Love* (1987) would immediately recognize this story as a sexual inversion on the classic Toei truckdriver-genre film scenario. Hashimoto's most recent book is a compendium of his essays entitled *'89* (1989).

JAPANESE ENTRANCE EXAMS FOR EARNEST YOUNG MEN

Yoshinori Shimizu

He didn't feel like it, but Ichiro Asaka skimmed through the first test problem anyway.

READ THE NEXT PASSAGE AND ANSWER THE QUESTIONS THAT FOLLOW:

Allowing the existence of such a thing as "active stasis," one might well also speak of "passive destruction." This, of course, would be irony. For, as surely everyone knows, the self-absolution of certain intensely intimated convictions may on occasion take on a transparent malice.

By the time he'd read this far, Ichiro's mind was in a fog.

He hadn't the slightest idea what he was reading. Whenever he read modern literary criticism, it was always the same. He could not begin to fathom what anyone was trying to say.

He knew all the words, one by one. He knew what

"active" meant and he knew what "stasis" meant. But when they pulled an "active stasis" on him, he gave up. No image, no thing arose in his mind.

Almost all the problems in the Japanese language section of the entrance exams for the national universities were like this.

Ichiro glanced up quickly at Tsukisaka. He made a "beats-me" face, but Tsukisaka ignored him. Tsukisaka's whole attitude seemed to say, "Hurry up, you're wasting time!"

Ichiro did fairly well in English and mathematics, but Japanese was his Achilles' heel: Japanese was the source of all Ichiro Asaka's troubles as the National University Entrance Exams loomed ahead. He bought reference books and study guides full of sample problems and pored over them, but it didn't do any good. In other subjects, when he looked at the right answer in a study guide, he could tell that his own was wrong, and if he thought about it he could even figure out where he had gone wrong, and how. You learn by making mistakes.

But that didn't work for the Japanese questions. Maybe it was because he had a complex about it, but even when he looked at the correct answer he had no idea why it was right. However many sample problems he tried, he never learned anything. He had no inkling how he should approach the test questions or what formulas he should use, and that was why his grades in Japanese were always bad.

When Ichiro discussed this with his father, his father found a tutor for him: Mr. Tsukisaka.

Tsukisaka was admirably qualified for the task. He was a Japanese instructor at a prep school; he'd even published study guides for Japanese. For all that, he was still quite young, maybe in his mid-thirties. He seemed more like an ultra-perfectionist hot-shot technician at some electronics firm than a teacher, actually.

Today was Ichiro's first lesson with Tsukisaka. Ichiro was to try answering a test problem. He attacked the question with little confidence.

Tsukisaka paid him no attention, so Ichiro continued reading the passage.

> Ebhert Shaftner brought <u>that</u> a ultimate thesis to life-size conception and gave it <u>manifest</u>[1] structure. Humans manufactured and utilized tools to bond themselves to nature, thereby overcoming defeatism via dogmatic stance. <u>The qualitative difference was thus one of disposition.</u>[A] Which, it goes without saying, accounts for the inaccumulation of experiential _____.[A] Thus, if realism can be characterized as objective and rational, it is likewise possible to interpret metaphoric expression as intuitive, hyperbolic, suprarational, and _____.[B] <u>This</u>[b] is actually proven in E. Durkheim's assertion that a god is a symbol of the group and religion tantamount to the group's self-<u>invocation</u>.[2]

Hopeless, thought Ichiro. He was gripped by despair. He hadn't the slightest idea what it could mean, from the first word to the last.

In math he could always get respectable scores. Why was Japanese so utterly beyond his ken? Ichiro was humiliated. Maybe he was just stupid after all. He gave up reading the rest of the passage, which seemed to stretch on forever, and glanced down at the questions.

> I. REPLACE UNDERLINED WORDS 1–4 WITH SYNONYMS.

That should be okay. "Manifest" meant clear, right? "Invocation." Yeah, well, sure. He couldn't think of it right at that moment, but it had to do with religion, right? You know—well...uh...*invocation.* Anyway, it was like praying or something.

Sure, he was embarrassed to admit that there were some words he didn't really know, but not so badly that it really bothered him. Unfortunately, he couldn't say the same for the other questions.

II. CHOOSE WHICH OF THE FOLLOWING BEST
PARAPHRASES THE IMPLICATIONS OF THE
UNDERLINED WORD THAT[a]:

1. That culture sometimes stands in opposition to nature.
2. That which derives from the gap between experience and the self.
3. That, comprehensively speaking, a panorama of events transpired.
4. That expression germane to the literature of Nasume Soseki.

III. CHOOSE WHICH OF THE FOLLOWING
MOST CLOSELY APPROXIMATES THE SIG-
NIFICANCE OF THE UNDERLINED SEN-
TENCE [Δ]:

1. Distinctions of quality depend on the temperament of the perceiver.
2. Quality is quality; quantity is quantity. Only a fool would confuse the two.
3. Humans are diverse.
4. It was as great as the difference between a tomato and a lemon.

Ichiro wanted to cry.

Since he didn't understand the original sentence, there was no way he could pick one with a similar meaning. And on top of that, the sentences he was supposed to choose from were all insane gibberish.

IV. WHICH OF THE FOLLOWING MIGHT MAKE
THE MOST APPROPRIATE TITLE FOR THIS
PASSAGE:

1. Human Beings and the Nation State

2. *L'Automne à Pekin*
3. The Resurgence of Realism
4. The Further Adventures of Mr. Company President

"I have no idea what any of this means," Ichiro admitted defeat and looked across at Tsukisaka.

"Yup. This is actually a pretty tough one. No reason to lose your confidence just because you don't get it."

"Really?" Ichiro was taken aback by Tsukisaka's comment.

"I had you try this one just to see for starters how you'd attack this kind of problem. And what I saw as I watched you is that you have a basic misconception of just what a test question in Japanese really is."

"I do?"

Since Ichiro had never had any confidence in his ability in Japanese, he offered no resistance to Tsukisaka's snap judgment.

"The first thing you do when you get a test question is read the problem. That's a mistake."

"But it says, 'Read the next passage and answer the questions that follow.'"

"That's just a meaningless set phrase. You can't accept it at face value. A test takes place in a limited time frame. In that short time you have to solve as many problems as you can. You don't have time to read all these complicated passages that were only designed to give students a hard time anyway."

But if he didn't read the passage, how could he answer the questions about it? Ichiro swallowed the doubt rising up inside. Tsukisaka's declaration was so full of certainty and conviction that he didn't dare ask.

"And even worse, you actually tried to understand the passage. Am I right?"

"Yes. I did try to understand what it meant. But it was too difficult, and I couldn't."

"That's another mistake. What good is it going to do you if you understand the passage? It's a waste of time to even think about what it might mean."

"But..."

"What's important here is to choose the right answers. Am I right? Understanding the passages isn't going to get you anywhere."

"Yes, but if I don't understand the passage, I won't be able to answer correctly, will I?"

"That's where you're wrong. This kind of problem is a game, Ichiro, and you want to score as many points as you can. It has nothing to do with the essay passage. All you have to do to choose the correct answers is know the rules. What's important is to master the rules of the game."

"Huh?"

Ichiro did a double take at Tsukisaka's cynical pronouncement.

"The people who get this type of problem right start by skimming the questions. Then they glance at the passage, just enough to answer the questions. It's not impossible, in fact, once you really get the hang of it, to answer the questions without reading the passage at all."

Ichiro gasped. This was unbelievable!

At the same moment he thought how wonderful it would be if he could master a technique that enabled him to get the right answers without reading those stupid little essays.

"I see the light's beginning to dawn. You have been playing a game, but you had the rules all wrong. Once you've got the rules down, the questions are a cinch."

"Please. Teach me the rules."

"Right. Okay, let's start from the rule about choosing the right answer on 'content' questions."

READ THE NEXT PASSAGE AND ANSWER THE QUESTIONS THAT FOLLOW:

The origins of the English language are to be found in Japanese.

Thus would I, in one short sentence, summarize what I am positing here.

Needless to say, however, the brevity of that one statement is by no means commensurate to the vastness of the subject. For that matter, never have scholars of comparative linguistics thus far even entertained the notion that Japanese might be the root of any other language.

What are the origins of the Japanese language? Their steadfast powers of thought solely addressed this question. The root of Japanese is Korean, is Ainu, is Tamil, is Mongolian,...*ad nauseam*. Never straying from that all-too-circumscribed, even self-deprecatory frame of reference of the Japanese cultured person, it is only natural that they never dreamed that Japan might have ever been other than on the receiving end of the tongues of other countries.

The entirety of Japanese culture is borrowed from abroad—such is their secret inner belief.

So it is, my advancement of the notion that the Japanese language is the root of another foreign tongue must come as nothing less than a challenge to the hallowed halls of the academe.

—Genzaburo Yoshiwara,
The Japanese Roots of the English Language,
Introduction

I. WHICH OF THE FOLLOWING MOST CLOSE
    LY APPROXIMATES THE CONTENT OF THE
    PASSAGE?
1. If even brief words might speak to unclouded eyes,
    they would have much to tell.
2. Japanese intellectuals are self-deprecatory.
3. Japanese should not feel inferior, but take pride in
    their own culture.

4. My theory will probably not be accepted by academia, but it is great nonetheless.
5. The reason that it never occurred to anyone that Japanese might be the root of some foreign language is that Japanese are not foreigners.

Since he hadn't yet mastered the secret key, Ichiro took the precaution of reading the passage carefully. This one isn't so bad, he thought. He understood most of it.

But it still wasn't easy to pick which of the five answers was the right one. All of them somehow seemed to be saying the same sort of thing as the essay passage.

Thinking it over more carefully, he eliminated number five. It was the only one that he couldn't really make sense of.

Next he eliminated number four. It sounded different from the others somehow, and it was rather petty, actually.

But numbers one through three all seemed right. After a little more thought, Ichiro picked number three. He thought it sounded the most impressive, and it seemed to be what the essay's author was trying to assert.

"I think the answer is number three."

"And what makes you think that?"

Ichiro explained his reasoning process. Tsukisaka listened without comment, favorable or otherwise. As he was talking, Ichiro began to lose confidence in his choice.

After hearing Ichiro out, a faint smile crept across Tsukisaka's face, and he spoke.

"A typical mistake. You've fallen right into the trap the person who invented this problem set for you."

"You mean there are traps?"

"Of course. The goal of the people who write these problems is to catch as many students as they can and trick them into giving the wrong answer. That's the first thing you have to realize. Test questions in Japanese are *designed* to make you make mistakes."

"Oh."

Thinking back on his experiences up to now, Ichiro saw how this made sense.

"So now let me explain the rule that you have to use to answer this kind of question."

"Please."

"The first thing to remember is this. When questions about content have four possible answers, you can usually divide them into Big, Small, Further, and Out of Focus. When there are five, then you have to add the category Wrong."

Ichiro copied the five categories into his notebook as Tsukisaka explained.

"Big means that the answer inflates the meaning of the essay passage. In this case, Big is number one. It organizes the content of the essay and expands it into a more general statement. That means that as a general principle, this one is true."

That sounded right.

"Next is Small. That's number two. Small picks out and focuses on one part of the essay. A Small answer is always right there in the essay, but the trick is that it's not all that's there. There's more to it than that. Now the beginner usually falls for one of these two patterns, Big or Small."

Since I chose number three, maybe I'm not a beginner after all, Ichiro thought, with a surge of pride.

"Be careful not to get caught by either Big or Small. In other words, you've got to be on the lookout for an answer of the same scale as the essay itself."

Ichiro nodded. Tsukisaka's instructions were perfectly clear.

"Next is Further. That's number three here. The one you chose. This is the one that people are likely to fall for when they give the problem a little thought."

It had been a mistake after all.

"This one develops the main idea of the essay one step further. If you read it again carefully, you'll find that there is no statement like the Further anywhere in the essay itself.

In the essay it says that Japan's intelligentsia are self-deprecatory as regards foreign countries, but it never says that they should take pride in their own culture or anything like that. Number three presents a conclusion that you would expect to draw from the essay, what you would imagine the author's opinion to be. That's why people who have at least partially understood the essay are likely to choose the Further. But what you're being asked to do is choose the sentence that's *closest* to the meaning of the passage. It doesn't say to choose what the author of the passage is thinking."

"The secret is not to think about what you're reading, right?"

"Exactly. Or to put it another way, there's no need to give the person who wrote the essay passage any more credit than he's due. Just concentrate on what's there on the page. You've got to watch that. This is just another trap set for you by the person who wrote the problem."

"I can't believe how many times I've fallen for this kind of stuff up to now, taking these problems seriously."

"Great. Once you've realized that, everything's going to be okay. Right. Let's get on to the next one. Skip number four and look at five—that's the Wrong. This is a simple mistake, and actually very few people are fooled by it. The sentence itself is contradictory and screwy. They just put this one in to take up space. We don't need to worry about this kind. The next one is Out of Focus—number four. Hmm. In this problem it's 'My theory will probably not be accepted by academia, but it is great nonetheless.' This is Out of Focus. By that I mean a sentence that seems to be a little out of sync, it has no clear connection to the essay. Yes, this sort of thing *does* appear in the essay, but it's not really the main idea."

"Excuse me, but if this isn't the main idea, then why should you choose it as the right answer?"

"Hold on, now. In this kind of problem, the right answer is this far-fetched, Out of Focus type of answer. The answer to this problem is number four."

"What? You mean the one that's Out of Focus is the right answer?"

"Read the instructions carefully. It says to choose the sentence that's closest to the content of the essay. It doesn't say to choose the one that best summarizes the essay. It makes perfect sense, if you think about it. If there was a sentence that properly summed up the essay, most students would get the answer right. But that's not what tests are designed for, now is it?"

Tsukisaka's words came as a violent shock to Ichiro. He felt as if he had been kicked in the head.

It had never occurred to him that the Out of Focus answer might be the right one. Otherwise, too many students would get the right answer—what a horrible fraud this all was!

"It's rigged."

"That's Japanese test questions for you. For example, if you were going to summarize this passage correctly, it would probably go something like this: 'My theory will not be accepted by Japanese academics, whose thinking is perverted and who are self-deprecating as regards foreign countries, but it is really a great theory.' That's about it. Number four has most of that in it. It leaves out 'perverted thinking' and 'Japanese,' but otherwise it's all there. And it's phrased in such a funny way that it seems too petty or too self-serving or something to be the right answer. But if you're asked to pick the sentence that's closest to the content, this has got to be it. The person who wrote this problem purposely twisted it Out of Focus to confuse people taking the test."

Ichiro was lost in thought. So it was only to be expected that he would get these kinds of problems wrong, only natural that he wouldn't be able to understand even when provided with the correct answer. The problems were designed from the start so that none of the answers would seem right.

"But if you master the rule that I have taught you,

everything will be fine. First you divide the sentences into Big, Small, Further, Out of Focus, and Wrong. Once you've gotten the hang of that, it's easy. Then all you have to do is pick Out of Focus. It'll be right."

"Hmmm..."

Ichiro began to trust his tutor Tsukisaka. It was refreshing to hear his confident voice offering such a clear analysis of all these things that had been swirling amorphously around in his head up to now.

"I understand what you've just said. But if I follow this formula, I still have to read the passage, right? Before, you said that there was a way you could get the answers right without even reading the passage. Could you please teach me that?"

"Well, well. You haven't even completed the basic course and you want me to skip ahead to the advanced lessons?"

"Oh, that's not allowed? That's okay. I just thought that would be a lot easier for me."

"Well, all right. Today I'll make a special exception and reveal to you the secret technique for answering the questions without even reading the essay."

"Oh thank you, thank you!"

"But you have to realize that, even though it's a highly effective technique, it isn't fail-safe. You can't expect to get one hundred percent of the questions right without reading the essays. Some Japanese test questions are poorly designed things, written by second-rate teachers, so taking those into account the best you can expect is eighty percent correct. You should only use this method when you simply don't have enough time."

"All right, I'll remember that."

"Okay, here goes. The method is based on two rules. The first is Eliminate Long and Short.

"Right. Eliminate Long and Short."

"In other words, don't even read the longest and shortest answers among the multiple choices. Just eliminate them."

"Really? You can tell by the length of the sentences?"

"Yup. Because these multiple choice sentences were designed to trick the test takers, the test writer doesn't want the right answer to stand out—as one that's too long or too short would. That's what the writer is thinking, you see. In this problem, for example, number two is the shortest. And numbers one and five are about the same length, the longest possibilities. So you eliminate one, two, and five without even reading them."

"Then three and four are left. But they're about the same length. So even if I got this far, I could still make a mistake. Number three expresses a very positive opinion, but number four is self-serving and petty, so I'd probably end up choosing number three."

"That's where rule number two comes in handy. Eliminate the Logical Choice."

"Huh? The Logical Choice?"

"Eliminate the Logical Choice. That means cross out the one that sounds logical and right and true. I'll bet you already know the reason. The test is trying to catch the students by getting them to choose what *seems* right."

"I've fallen for that so many times!"

"Beginners often get caught on this one. But you don't have to worry about that any more. If you know these two rules, you'll choose number four, without even reading the essay."

This guy is amazing, thought Ichiro. He explains the way to answer those slippery Japanese test questions as if he were teaching you how to take apart and reassemble a machine. What used to be a foggy, intangible mass had been made comprehensible in its sharpest outlines.

Ichiro had always been pretty good at subjects based on logical reasoning, like mathematics. Once he had absorbed the logic and rules that Tsukisaka taught him, his grades in Japanese improved suddenly and dramatically.

Take, for example, the following problem:

When we read the phrases "One hundred geese flying in a single line" and "The warm quiet of the evening sky," we are carried away to some unfathomable _____ of the distant skies.

CHOOSE THE BEST WORD TO FILL IN THE BLANK ABOVE FROM THE FIVE CHOICES BELOW:
a. Mystery
b. Emptiness
c. Longing
d. Sorrow
e. Contemplation

First there was a poem, and this question was related to its interpretation.

It wasn't an easy problem; the *old* Ichiro would have puzzled about the right answer a long time. All five possibilities seemed just fine to him.

But Tsukisaka taught him this rule: Mysticism is a trap; go for Sentiment.

Mysticism referred broadly to any mystical or metaphysical kind of words. "Mystery," (a), and "Emptiness," (b), came under this heading. For high school students, these words had a very broad meaning and a strong appeal, so they were likely to choose them. Which was exactly what the problem writers figured.

According to Tsukisaka, while of course there were poems and essays that expressed a mystical feeling or a magical beauty, the sort of people who wrote problems for the Japanese language examinations were not on the intellectual level to appreciate them. As a result, they would not appear in test questions.

What the problem writers understood and liked and used in their test questions was pretty elementary stuff—longing for home, dreams of distant lands, the sadness of being alone, the pains of youth—all that Sentimental schlock. So when you came across this kind of problem, without even reading the poem, you would choose from (c), (d), or (e). Now (d) was just too drippy, and (e) reeked of the intellectual. So by adapting and applying the Eliminate Long and Short rule, you knew at a glance that (c) Longing was the right answer.

Could it be true, wondered Ichiro as he looked at the answer in the study guide. There it was: (c) Longing.

His respect for Tsukisaka rose. Why didn't I meet him sooner? he thought.

With Tsukisaka's method, if you made a mistake at least you could understand how you had done it. You had simply erred in the way you applied the rules.

Ichiro loved to study now. He even came to like Japanese, which he had hated so much before. When he saw through the traps that the test writers had set for him and sidestepped them with ease, he felt the same exhilaration he felt when he dodged and outran a pursuer on the soccer field.

Ichiro became good at Japanese. Finally the day came when he was ready to attempt that most perverse of problems, Summarize the Passage Above in <u>X</u> Words.

Before they started, Tsukisaka offered a brief introduction.

"These problems where they ask you to summarize the passage in thirty words or explain the meaning of the underlined sentence in fifty words are really ridiculous. They are the dumbest of the dumb."

"Really?"

"Absolutely. If you could say it in thirty words, of course the original authors would have said it in thirty words! They couldn't—that's why they wrote something longer. Let's say these are the directions to your house—'To get to my house you get out of the station and go right. Follow that road for about thirty minutes until you get to a corner with a watch shop. Turn left there and keep going until you get to a bank. Right past the bank is a tobacco shop, and my house is across the street from it, the one with the hedge.' Could you summarize that as 'You can walk to my house from the station'? That's what these problems are asking you to do. They're completely arbitrary."

"I see."

"You can't tell the truth in a certain number of words, and that's it. For example, just look at this problem."

And Tsukisaka pointed to this question:

> THE AUTHOR USES THE EXPRESSION "AN INSTANTANEOUS FLASH OF ART." EXPLAIN HIS MEANING IN THIRTY WORDS.

"Now let's pretend that the great painter and sculptor Taro "Big Bang" Okamoto was answering this question. It would probably go something like this."

Flipping through his notebook, Tsukisaka showed Ichiro a paragraph that he had obviously prepared beforehand, faithfully imitating the artist's inimitable style of delivery:

> *Harumph.* What we call art has nothing to do with any constricting, nit-picking theories. Living human beings, their life force, perhaps you could call it, the *energy* of the human creature gushes forth instantaneously. It is the product of an explosion, *ha-rumph*—not a "flash" or anything as puny or dim as that. And the person who creates it makes it without knowing, without understanding what he's doing. That is what art is. Art must be something that people see and think What on earth is this? *Harumph.* (ninety-seven words.)

"As you can see, Mr. Okamoto was unable to explain the phrase in thirty words or less. Of course, when you compare what he wrote with the thirty-word summary of some university professor or cram-school instructor, there's no question which is better as far as content goes. Okamato's is superior. But on a Japanese language test, his answer will be marked wrong."

"In other words, there's no need to try to say what's true or even anything very intelligent."

Lately Ichiro had become quite expert at seeing what made those test questions tick.

"That's it. A very sharp insight. The high and low of it is that these are stupid problems, and you'll end up the loser if you take them seriously. Let me give you three points to observe when answering this kind of question."

And with that Tsukisaka explained the following three points to Ichiro.

"(1) Employ a diversionary tactic by sprinkling your answer with words and phrases from the original.

"(2) Make yourself sound like a fan of the author; write as if you were writing him a fan letter.

"(3) Don't give any specific examples; just list a long string of vague, abstract expressions and wind everything up with 'and so forth.' (Refer to forms and announcements from your local government office for good examples.)"

Example:

> In the future, it is to be hoped that, aiming as we do for life-long education, universities and other institutions of higher learning will initiate research in areas concerned with education and learning that exploit the unique characteristics and abilities of adults, thereby creating a scientific basis for lifelong education and exploring suitable curricula for adult education aimed at a wide variety of free and independent students, and meeting the learning needs of contemporary society.
>
> —*Report of the Ad Hoc Committee*
> *on Educational Evaluation*,
> "Outline of the Evaluation Process," No. 4.

"Got it. Bad writing is better. You suck up to the writer and write something so muddy that no one knows what you're saying." Ichiro announced in confident tones.

"That's the rule. I mean, when the question's stupid, the answer has to be stupid to be correct, right?"

With that preparation, Ichiro tried a perverse Summarize In X Words problem. As he expected, it was not as easy as the other problems, which you could answer as long as you knew the rules. Ichiro was naturally of a logical frame of mind, so before he knew what he was doing he had written an answer without any gross contradictions or misstatements, taking pains not to go over the allotted number of words.

But his efforts gradually paid off. Finally, Ichiro reached the level where he was able to answer even this kind of question. The original was about ten pages long; here is a summary:

The heroine Sugako Miki lost her beloved brother in an accident at sea when she was a little girl, and she has been haunted by his memory ever since. When she was seventeen, she met the rugged fisherman Umekichi and, seeing her brother in him, fell in love with him. Her father's strong opposition to the match and her sister's attempted suicide made things extremely difficult, but eventually the pair were married. But just then the war started and the day after their wedding Umekichi was sent off to the front. Left alone, Sugako opened a craft workshop, but because of the political situation it was closed down by the military. The officer Yamamura had sinister designs on Sugako and pursued her relentlessly, but she was rescued by her childhood friend Mitsutaro. Eventually a son, Umeo, was born, the fruit of her single night of wedded bliss with Umekichi. At last the war ended, and with it came news of Umekichi's death in battle. The grieving

Sugako was encouraged by Mitsutaro to open a weaving workshop. She displayed a talent for business, and her little classroom grew into a large school. Mitsutaro asked Sugako to marry him, and she accepted. Then, on the day of the wedding, Umekichi reappeared—the report of his death had been false. Though Mitsutaro and Sugako were already officially married, their relationship remained pure. Sugako's sister returned to live with her and eventually fell in love with Mitsutaro. Sugako divorced Mitsutaro and remarried Umekichi, who had become the president of a shipbuilding company. Then Sugako's mother died of cancer. Her father became senile. Her son turned into a juvenile delinquent. Her husband's company went bankrupt. Her school was taken over by someone else. Taking her husband's hand, Sugako looks back over her life and considers its vagaries as she prepares herself to start over from zero.

I. IN SIX WORDS OR LESS, WHAT DID THE
   HEROINE SUGAKO THINK WHEN SHE
   LOOKED BACK OVER HER LIFE?

Ichiro had an immediate answer for this most difficult of problems:
"A lot of stuff happened."

"Superb! *Five* words! And you've summarized precisely what she thought about her life," Tsukisaka praised him.
"Is this right?"
"Yes, it is. It's perfect. You have reached the highest level. I have nothing left to teach you."
"B...but, Mr. Tsukisaka!"

And that's how Ichiro Asaka came to get good scores on his Japanese tests. The new year arrived and the time for the university entrance exams drew near.

Of course Ichiro got into the college of his choice. He had always been good in English, and once he was able to get good scores in Japanese, nothing could stand in his way.

Ichiro composed a letter to Tsukisaka, to whom he owed so much, to share the news and express his thanks.

His letter was eloquent testimony to the fact that expertise at answering questions on Japanese tests had no relation whatsoever to skill at using the language. If anything, it suggested that being able to answer those questions correctly led to a degeneration in his Japanese skills.

This was the letter:

> I have learned that one of the joys of life is the joy of achieving a goal you have set.
>
> Did you perhaps teach me that?
>
> Or did you accomplish the task of sending one more person, whose ability you nurtured and cultivated, out into the world?
>
> Or finally, thanks to you, I have passed the entrance exams, and I'll never forget what you did for me.
>
> If you were to select from the five sentences above the one that was closest to my feelings right now, which would it be?
>
> Anyway, when I remember you I think of all kinds of things, which I could never summarize in six words or less, but if I had to I would say: I owe it all to you.
>
> As far as my future is concerned, which of the five phrases below best describes my feelings:
> 1. The world is an uncertain place.
> 2. I am determined to persist in my efforts to succeed.
> 3. I just want to sit and stare and not think about any thing.
> 4. I'd like to have some fun, finally.
> 5. Mystical and melancholy.

When I reflect upon it, that paradigmatic experience known as the examination, as an abstraction of our present reality in which truth and fiction carry out a fantastic and endlessly repeating excoriation of our *Weltanschauung*, has taught me _____. The _____ is, probably, the fact that you can do it if you try. In our amusement, just as in a religious sacrament, we seek both solace and courage.

I.   BY THE WAY, ARE YOU MARRIED?
II. MAY I COME VISIT YOU?
III. WAS I A GOOD STUDENT?

CHOOSE THE MOST APPROPRIATE ANSWER FROM AMONG THE FOLLOWING:
1. Ichiro was a very good student.
2. Ichiro was a lousy student.
3. Ichiro had personality problems.
4. Ichiro was a forgettable student.
5. Ichiro was an arcanely objectified student.

First published, 1988
TRANSLATION BY JEFFREY HUNTER

Yoshinori Shimizu (b. 1947) is most often associated with the idea of pastiche. He assumes the exact verbal color of everything from scholarly tomes to bestsellers to advertising pamphlets with painfully absurd results. Primarily a writer of short stories, he is best known for his collections *Soba and Kishimen Noodles* (1986), *Eternal Jack and Betty* (1988), and *Growing Down* (1989). *Japanese Entrance Exams for Earnest Young Men* (1988) won the Eiji Yoshikawa New Writer's Award.

GIRL

Mariko Ohara

The city was an overripe fruit about to drop.

Rotting outward from deep in the core, its putrid flesh was held by only the barest shell.

Once the city fell, no one knew what would become of it. If things degenerated any further, even hell would close its borders. For the city's inhabitants, there was no escape.

Gil probed a long tongue into the bottom of the Venetian cut-glass stemware for the last of the nectarine pulp. Sitting with his platinum-mink–encased genitals exposed, he could sense the attention he was drawing. Every nerve ending in his body tingled, almost painfully, from the repeated caresses of staring eyes.

Gil knew his own charms better than anyone.

The smooth, honey-colored curve of his back from his shoulders on down, his wisp-cinched queen bee waist, his wind-teased shock of straight blond hair, and only slightly darker, his amber-hued eyes.

Even more, he knew, his was a beauty in motion, a fluid grace to his movements that had been there from birth—the same as his mother's.

Ordering another drink, Gil surveyed the premises from his high stool at the bar. The several faces he met fairly dripped with desire. He felt like spewing up the contents of his stomach. Of late, he'd had no appetite, no sex drive, no nothing. All he could do was to keep drinking, like this, bathing his tissues in toxic drams.

When he redirected a transparent sigh back toward the counter, a half dozen glasses of the divine nectarine liquor stood before him.

"Curser?" he called the bartender's name feebly.

The drinks, she answered, were from that customer and that one and that one and...

"I don't want 'em."

"That so?" Curser's voice was terribly businesslike. Too cold for the likes of Gil, who had come here lonely, unbearably lonely.

The six glasses, having absorbed the multicolored lights of the bar, were reflected on the polished ebony countertop. A pathetic tableau, simply lovely.

Gil fancied cut glass. It elicited a resonance in his delicate soul. So like him: edgy, hypersensitive, close to the point of breaking.

He drank half his cocktail and drowsily stood up. Sliding off the stool seemed less a rising motion than a slip.

Now even more eyes were trained on him. Not a few of them recognized him as Jill Abel.

He tossed the out-of-sorts Curser a tip, hoping to elicit a smile, but she only relaxed the occupational deadpan for a split-second. Her peachy cheeks barely quivered.

Fighting the undertow that threatened to suck him down into a sludge of despair, Gil forded the dimly lit room through swirls of dirty purple smoke. The drinks had gone to his head. He was a deep-sea fish creeping across the ocean floor. A mild attack of human-detox came over him. Suddenly, reality siphoned off. Everything—people's faces, feet, voices—everything drifted far, far away.

He collapsed.

Someone had tripped him, he knew, intentionally, but he was helpless to do anything about it. His left elbow hit hard, the pain returning him to his senses for a brief instant.

"You okay?"

The John who'd tripped him was lifting him in a gentle embrace, caressing his genitals. Must be slipping, he thought, letting some guy he'd never even seen before climb all over him. Mustn't get too aroused...would be my own fault...my guilt.

"How 'bout it, like now?"

How many times had he surrendered to the momentary rapture of being touched there? That utterly irresistible shudder of pleasure.

Inadvertently, he pushed the guy's heavy breastplate aside.

The John was disoriented at first, then flew into a rage.

Gil grabbed for the back of a chair and pulled himself up to his feet. With the John clinging fast to his collar, Gil's soul began to flood with tears. Have mercy, have mercy...

Expecting a beating, he braced himself and pleaded.

"Forgive me, I beg of you."

At which, the fists that were pumped up with rage fell limp, sapped of all strength. The John lowered his voice to a deflated whisper of pity.

"Beat it, Jill. Didn't know you were such a wimp."

Denied even the violent side of human relations, Gil once again set his feet lumbering toward the exit.

While he waited for the ancient relic of an elevator, a woman careened out of the bar. Gil was leaning against the cracked wall, eyes closed, but from the scent and sound of her presence, he'd conjured up a full mental picture of her.

"Hey, it's here. You getting in or not?"

"Go on ahead."

Gil cracked opened his eyes to confirm his image of the woman. But what he saw made him gasp. It wasn't a woman;

it was a girl. No, not simply a girl. Her skin, soft and creamy white. He felt the urge to touch her, ever so gently. Just a little. Just a touch.

"Oh?"

With that, the girl boarded the massive freight lift.

Gil looked on as the door slid shut in slow motion. Always missing the boat. Always too timid, too shy, knocked out of the running, out of sync with the world.

His excitement, far from subsiding, blended into a curiously colloidal state as he waited for the next lift.

The hellbound elevator—floor carpeted, walls and ceiling in burgundy velvet—lurched into descent, carrying him with it.

Depressed, he waited for the door to open, then slinked out. But when he looked up into the acid rain that came pattering down on his head, his heart squealed.

"'Evening. We meet again, I see."

And here he'd been thinking she'd gone. A tumult roared through his breast.

"Y...you waited?"

"Sure."

The girl turned abruptly and started walking, her bright toothy smile hovering in view. Gil scrambled after her. His stupor was dissipating posthaste.

"Where're you going?"

The girl flashed her enamel lovelies to his question.

"Home."

"Where's that?"

"Where I live."

"And someone's waiting for you?"

Gil began to feel frustrated. What did this female mean, leading him on?

"I'm unattached."

Gil caught up with her, to walk alongside her through the black wind. The girl looked angelic in profile. But weren't angels boys? A girl, the image of a boy.

The girl wore skintight black leggings and a black shirt

draped over as far as her wrists. Black hair, black pupils, black to the tips of her shoes. What little skin that showed radiated a phosphorescent glow.

Gil detested jerks who designed clothes that showed off a body's lower parts in such graphic detail. And he felt nothing but contempt for himself for having chosen his show gear.

Street level was deserted.

Who, especially this late at night, would be out walking in the cold and wet with no umbrella, no aircar? Nobody on the street, however, also meant no stick-ups, no nick-and-runs.

The hundred-storied buildings glimmered like glitzy chandeliers. Gil loved their cheap sparkle. He loved this rotting city.

Without warning, the girl touched Gil on the arm.

"You...human?"

Gil returned the girl's driven black-eyed stare and thought, So she didn't know, eh? Didn't know he was Jill Abel, the dancer, spent excretum of the city's dazzling decadence, high civilization tottering on the edge of collapse.

"Umm."

"Well, then, you're...male?"

Gil's chest boasted two voluptuous mammalian protuberances. Much bigger than the girl's own budding breasts. And at the same time, he displayed a male organ swaddled root-to-tip in fur.

"Yes. I'm a man."

He answered honestly.

"Looks more like a tail."

She smiled as she spoke, then broke right back into stride, so quickly that Gil didn't even notice the vermilion peck planted on his pale cheek. All the same, he walked at a slower pace for a while.

The girl's home was forty-seven floors underground. Tiny, but a cozy enough little hole. An egg-shaped room after the latest fashion, with an oval bed, slightly too big for one person, suspended close to the ceiling.

"How d'you get up there?"

To ask was to be shown: the girl lowered a ladder by remote control.

"May I?"

The girl laughed.

"Fine by me, but maybe you'd like to shower first?"

Gil nodded humbly, as if he'd had the shit beaten out of him. He stripped off his clothes, received a towel embroidered with the name "Kisa," and stepped into the immaculate bathroom. For a moment, he stood there blankly. There could be no doubt about it. The girl was a whore, named Kisa. A streetwalker. That's why she'd lured him here...that was the whole of it...that and nothing else.

After his shower, the entire bathroom turned into a drier. He watched in the mirror as his golden hair tossed in the whirling gusts of hot air.

His implanted breasts maintained their picture-perfect form. He'd had the cosmetic surgery done that time he'd played the Sphynx. The attributes proved so fabulously popular, it seemed a shame to lop them off.

The Sphynx's mother was half-maiden, half-serpent, known as the Equidona. The Equidona gave birth to all manner of horrible monsters. The Chimera, the Gorgon, the Kelberos, then later the Dragon, and lastly the Sphynx.

Thoughts of "Mother" made him suddenly want to vomit.

Beautiful, shapely breasts, never once intended to nurse a child...well, fair enough...

Stepping out of the bathroom, he was surprised by a four-legged white robot, standing by with proffered bathtowel.

"Not bad, huh? Built this baby myself."

Gil looked Kisa in the face, then gazed back at the robot.

"From a kit, a Flexi?"

"Customized. Even speaks. Goes by the name 'Sphynx'."

Gil shivered and covered his breasts with the towel.

The two-foot-tall Sphynx looked like a blanched dynosaur skeleton. On voice-command from Kisa, it started to walk, bones rattling, one foot set out in front of the other, barely holding together.

"'Excruciating.'"

"No, really! It's my baby. Tell me how cute it is."

Kisa laughed enchantingly, like a fairy sprite...yes, that was it...Mother was something of an enchantress. Which explained his attraction to the girl. That had to be it. That, and that she was a pro. He had her pinned. Right on the mark.

"Why don't you shower, too?"

"Okay."

There came the slightest rustling as the girl peeled off her slinky black silk shirt.

Gil was speechless. Her skin virtually lit up the room—as if her dermis enveloped a white inner luminescence.

The girl slipped, silky as her shirt, into the bathroom. Gil heard the steamy sound of the shower, as he crouched down to the floor.

"Sphynx! Gimme a drink."

Sphynx turned its face composed of a cyclopean red lens and a single speaker toward Gil.

"Many different beverages are available."

"Anything's fine."

Sphynx's random tables came up Scotch. The robot walked on four legs, the two front limbs serving as arms for manual labor. The hindlegs had no fingers, whereas each foreleg had three.

Drinking his liquor down straight, Gil grew sleepy. He tucked a cushion behind the small of his back. The silver-gray walls—affixed with a number of exhausted electrophoto transmissions—were all dreamscapes.

Meadows and ocean and springs and other pedestrian fare. The singular absence of either human or animal figures struck Gil as out of character for a girl. Still, Gil thought the scenes pleasant enough. And then it registered—the girl wanted to escape this world. But for where? For some completely other, secret world. Perhaps the girl possessed such a secret world in her mind.

The girl appeared, newborn fresh, brilliant with life, with a vitality so rich it overwhelmed Gil. Like walking white electricity. Delicate white fingers forever energized.

The girl slipped a white nightgown over her electric body.

Gil did not rouse from where he lay propped by the big cushion. The electric girl drew near. His body tingled. When he reached out to put an arm around her shoulders, the girl gently stayed his hand. Her touch sent an shock coursing down his spine.

"For some reason, lately, I've been thinking...remembering things that happened a long time ago...when I was a child..."

"What sort of things?" Gil half-sighed. Had it been any other female, he probably wouldn't have thought to ask her life story.

"You...an Earthling?"

"Yes."

"I always used to look at Earth from where I lived."

"Oh?" Gil responded. "They say that from far away it looks like a jewel."

The girl betrayed a trace of a smile.

"When I was a child, I often fought with my brother. About who'd be the first to take that blue planet."

"Younger brother?"

"Older."

"Who's still fine, I trust."

"If he was, I wouldn't be talking like this."

Whereupon the girl broke away from him and stood up.

Gil had no idea what was going on, but he knew he'd said the wrong thing. He sat up.

"No, that's a lie," said the girl.

Feeling hurt for no reason he could understand, Gil trained his eyes on her.

"Will you leave?"

This wasn't a question; it was an order. Untangling his legs, he managed to get to his feet. The blood vessels in his head throbbed as if squeezed.

"I get it. You're expecting some stud."

That came out nastier than he'd intended.

Kisa froze into a statue. But now her marble hands were opening the door and pointing the way out.

"My roommate's a woman, thank you."

Gil felt ripped asunder. This girl had come here all alone from some poorer outworld. She looked pure and innocent, but surely she'd been hurt—badly—deep down inside. People like her spatter their poisonous lies everywhere. Trip you up, betray you, beat you so bad you can't get up again...Gil flashed back on his own battle-scarred past and cringed. The thought of going through all that again gave him the chills.

"I get the picture. I'm leaving."

As he stepped out from the comfort of that womb-like interior, the girl called out to him.

"Wait. What's your name?"

"Jill Abel."

The girl's expression told him the thread of recognition had connected.

It was nearly dawn by the time he got home, but his cohabitant Remora was still awake, watching the news on the wall-sized screen.

Remora was genetically male, the proof being that the fingers of his left hand, all six of them, had been remodeled into cocks. When asked, why the left hand? his only reply was that if it had been his right hand, he wouldn't have been able to hold his chopsticks.

"Lookit lookit! A sideswipe spaceship collision!" Remora shouted at the top of his lungs. "Lookit lookit look! Bad meanness or what! It's Sirius!"

On the screen in the black oceanic depths of space, a half-crushed silver hull drifted "shipwrecked." Disemboweled scraps of sheered metal glinted in the light of a distant sun.

"Dirty outworlders! Bet it's some 'droid plot!"

In spite of himself, Gil's expression lightened at this irrepressible outburst—yes, there were good folk on this planet, even if they had no education, no refinement, no table manners, even if they were bigots to the core. Telling the most blatant lies, only to find himself deceived in the end, Remora remained tough through it all. Remora might have been a fool, but wasn't everyone a fool?

Floating useless in the void, the half-dismembered corpus looked strangely erotic.

The darkened room gave them the illusion that they themselves were lost in space.

"Hey, you heard the latest sex rave 'mong them outworlders?"

Gil took a seat next to Remora, who placed a hand, the right one, on Gil's knee. Remora was squirming with delight, dying to fill Gil in on the gossip. Come what may, Remora was the man who knew all the latest dirt.

"Haven't the foggiest."

It was the invitation Remora was hoping for. His face lit up, his gorilla's bulk shaking.

"They swim out in the zero-G and jack sperm globules all over 'emselves just like fish."

Cheap thrills. Gross, but the idea did get him off, Gil had to admit.

"Sort of a urological partita, hmm?"

"Huh? Howzat?"

Remora's vocabulary didn't extend that far.

"Kinda like a golden shower spree."

Remora chortled with pleasure. His face was illuminated by the twinkling afterglow of the spaceship debris on the screen.

"Then, looking straight at Gil, Remora said, "What gives? You don't usually get excited like this."

Gil blushed.

"Well? C'mon now! Something happen to you out there tonight?"

As he spoke, Remora slowly eased Gil into a reclining position. They hadn't been like this in so long. Remora trembled in his skin.

"*Girl*, I thought you'd never get it up. That's better...and here I was thinking it was time for my tide to be going out."

"Don't go."

Gil's pretty face distorted in a grimace. He couldn't help pitying a guy so insensitive it'd be *sayonara* once the physical part had gone. Yet he knew that if Remora really did leave, Gil would be the one to grieve; it made him desolate. And so the two lovers tumbled deep into the cosmic sea.

Later, as they were falling asleep, Gil told him about the girl.

"Means she's got a thing for you, is what. Pretended not to know you so's to get close, I bet."

"Then why'd she give me the brush-off?"

"To sink the hook," snapped Remora. "Within a week she'll surface. Have confidence."

Confidence? That wasn't it at all! How could he hope to explain to him?

"But anyway," Remora went on, "c'mon, an outworlder? Not your style. Do yourself a favor—throw this one back."

Remora was a die-hard outworld-hater. Probably got dumped real hard by some bitch when he shipped out on the interplanetary routes. Or else, maybe he was hiding a past—maybe he'd been an outworlder himself until his twenties, and so he hated his own origins. Just like Gil detested being a dancer.

Resting in Remora's massive arms, Gil confessed, "I don't know. I'm not sure."

"'Bout what?"

Remora sounded gruff. He hadn't expected Gil to unearth

what he'd already taken for a dead issue.

"I don't know...what she's up to...what sort of female she is..."

"Whether she gets it on with her roommate?" taunted Remora, grinning. "Like us?"

Gil wrestled out of Remora's embrace. Gil's mouth seemed to fill with disdain. Heedless, Remora only drove home his hard feelings with a dare.

"How 'bout a bet then? A thou' sez you blip her within the month."

What was this ape saying? That wasn't what he meant, not at all... Gil rose, hands over his mouth, to go vomit out the acid disgust stinking in the pit of his stomach.

While Gil barfed, Remora recounted details of his own exploits with women.

Gil realized he'd broken their rules, betrayed their understanding: he'd brought his outside affairs back home. Remora may have been crude and blunt and just plain dumb, he may have conducted himself badly, but at least here—within the confines of these walls—they had to keep a trust, or some semblance it.

The following day, Gil woke up past noon to find Remora gone. His precious spaceship crewman's helmet was missing.

Gil gazed at the shelves of cut-glass trinkets that covered one entire wall. His head throbbed, the glare pierced both his eyes.

He couldn't hold back. He cried, which made his head ache more. Only afterward did a silent, long, fine sleep come over him.

Drugged out of his skull, Gil commuted to the Rox Star Club every night.

Except for when he was on stage dancing, he always had someone around, whom he slept with later. Always someone different. For eight months he had no want for anything, and yet he had nothing but need; it was as if a dam had burst.

Physically, he ought to have been exhausted, but dancing gave him a mysteriously sharp clarity.

He would usually find himself in a private craft, hard at it with some woman he didn't know. Today Gil noticed that the craft was driven by a real human, not a robodroid, so for appearance sake he tried to make conversation.

"Y'know, every time I pass here I wonder. What do you think they're building there?"

The lot next to the Rox Star Club had been under construction for some time. They were actually building something—something new was surfacing in the midst of this festering, sore-scarred city.

"Really wouldn't know." The driver obviously didn't want to talk. The aircar came down for a smooth landing on the Club roof. Totally blasé, Gil pushed aside the woman's paws and climbed out first. The woman was furious. She was pretty enough, but compared to the girl whom he couldn't forget, women like her didn't rate.

Nauseous, he downed a handful of pills without water. A few minutes later, his brain began to decompose, and everything dissolved into the far, far distance—the stone-faced driver, that embarrassing socialite glitterbox of an aircar, the night town atmosphere laid out before him, the gleaming skyscrapers blocking out the miniature planetarium dome of the heavens, the woman screaming like a hysterical mother. Everything retreated, the whole scene intact, out of reach, safe and inviolate.

Gil kept dredging up thoughts from his murky consciousness—Remora's prediction that the girl would show within a week, that within a month he'd have her. But when Gil had gone back to her apartment, she'd already moved.

Time passed. Seasons blurred one into the next. He'd worked his way through a parade of partners. After all this, he was sick of himself—and yet the filthy, sinful image did become him. Still, something in him, some effluent that foamed up from his silted heart, yearned to be saved, if only for one faint, glimmering moment.

Have to find her...have to find her... The urge grew and grew, as day after day his ragged body was grounded into the dirt. His gray matter was melting. Only his physical movements sparked with electricity—like the city.

Gil advances to stage center and bends in a deep bow. A full house showers him with applause.

Costumed in golden feathers, he crawls out of his mother's womb. His mother is an insect, an enormous spheroid eggcase covered in honey-colored fuzz. The genetically engineered freak wiggles its giant abdomen, and Gil half-emerges. Smeared with emulsion, Gil's golden plumage glistens. The insect suffers. It rages, beating Gil, the cause of its suffering, against the ground with primitive spite. Gil is knocked nearly unconscious. Gil and the insect explode with equal fury, bolts of pure hatred arc and colide.

Writhing and squirming, his torso freed at last, hands flat upon the slime-plastered stage, Gil saw her. His heart forced its way up into his throat.

That face! Out of an audience of thousands, he spotted her in an instant. That face—radiant, electric, white!

Gil extracts his legs from the insect womb. Too quickly, in fact, for huge quantities of blood spill out over the stage. The insect writhes and spreads its parafin wings. The wires that hold them in place begin to cut into the thorax.

Soaked and sticky with blood, Gil leaps from the stage and runs. Hundreds of hands reach out to touch him as he sweeps past. Gil simply knocks them aside. He isn't a violent person—not ordinarily—but at the moment, anything in his way is his enemy. He is a golden beast charging through fields of shoulder-high grass.

Meanwhile on stage, the mother insect, body severed in two, losing cascades of blue plasma, screams in its last throes of death.

The audience rises to its feet, thrilling to the new direction of the performance. Rochster, the theater owner, peers into his closed-circuit display, calculating the cost of repairing the blood-soaked stage.

Gil latched onto the girl. Gripping her by the shoulder, without a word, he proceeded to lead her outside.

Only then does the audience suspect that something is amiss. The crowd shouts. The guards fight them back. The woman next to Gil tears at his costume, railing at him insanely. A guard moves in to protect the star, but women batter him down. Gil's only thought is to shield the girl—and to dash for the nearest exit. When hordes of women rush after Gil and the girl, the security crew slams the heavy doors, letting the two escape.

Gil grasped the girl's beautiful electric hand.

"At last..."

Kisa smiled, running apace.

"You're sopping wet."

"Keep running. It'll dry."

"You stink of blood."

"I was just born, after all."

The girl led Gil into the construction site next to the Rox Star. The frame of the building was all that had been erected. Hushing their breath, they looked up to see the night sky. The chandelier heavens.

Inside the skeletal structure were several rows of benches. Sitting down, the two of them locked gazes, audibly, golden eyes to black eyes.

"Do you...what *do* you feel toward me?"

His voice trembled and caught. Never in his life had he asked such a mawkish question. Kisa laughed.

"These two months passed clear for me."

And prior to that? Gil swallowed the question. But what about himself? What the fuck had he done these last two months?

Clothed all in white, the girl looked even whiter. Had her birthplace never seen a sun?

"Unless I purged myself, I didn't think I could see you."

Gil's heart ached. For someone the likes of me? How defiled could she have been before? What hell had she been involved in?

"You see, I..."

"Don't tell me."

Gil commanded the girl to turn and face him. He didn't care: so she was a prostitute, a lesbian, a swindler, someone who hurt people so bad they'd never right themselves again. Maybe she'd plummeted into despair, laboring under misery that had been with her since birth.

Kisa wound her long black hair around Gil's neck as she held him. This was good. Perhaps this is what a mother's embrace was like.

"I must tell you, I..."

"Yes?"

"My roommate threw me out."

"But why? No, I don't care," Gil cautiously withheld his words. "Have you no place to go?"

Kisa shook her head on Gil's shoulder.

"Come home with me, then," he offered, giving thanks that Remora had chosen to leave.

Suddenly, a large shadow fell over them. Looking up in alarm, they saw a gigantic pterodon glide across the night sky. An idiot had let out his pet to roam the city.

A breeze wafted through the skeletal structure. It tussled Gil's hair, which was now completely dry.

Kisa gave Gil a squeeze.

"Know what this is, where we are here?"

"No."

The girl grinned. "It's a church."

"A what?"

"The M/F On-Call Network Church."

The Mothers and Fathers Church? Gill had heard of it—supposedly it was run by an organization of psychics. They homed in on souls in crisis, places in need of love, wounded hearts, battlefields of all kinds and they came forth to heal. To treat, sometimes to scold. Materialized from millions of light-years beyond...

So this is what it was. An actual old-fashioned church, with rows of pews, a crucifix and altar.

What in this city had they sensed calling out for parental love?

Gil left Kisa, made his way over to the unfinished statue of Mary, and bared his chest. A face—the girl's face—burrowed into the fullness of Gil's breasts. He heard Kisa's voice asking, could he really give milk? He didn't know. Why didn't she just suck?

Thirteen years later, the city in all its decadence was destroyed by two filth bombs, sending two hundred million inhabitants to hell.

Gil and Kisa had long since parted ways. Yet the Mothers and Fathers worked to save as many people as they could in the years before the city breathed its last. The light they provided was small, but certainly it was there, shining deep in the shadows of the city.

A light made visible by the dark.

If the darkness is deep enough, even the briefest light leaves a brilliant afterglow.

First published, *SF Magazine*, 1984
TRANSLATION BY ALFRED BIRNBAUM

Mariko Ohara (b. 1959) is first and foremost a science fiction writer. Her writing style, however, is not so easily pinned down: it floats among the fatuous voice of girls' comics, the repartee of a comedy of manners, and the flat, understated tone of a mystery novel. Other works include *The Galactic Mailman Always Rings Thrice* (1988), *The Monitored City* (1988), and *Mental Female* (1988). Ohara admits to writing *Girl* while listening to Tina Turner's "Private Dancer."

THE YAMADA DIARY
Masato Takeno

I had no idea there was game software like *The Yamada Diary* on the market—let alone that it was a "role-playing" game. Nor can I explain my buying the software on impulse. Pure chance? I'd like to think so.

The whole episode began with my skipping school, which I wouldn't want to believe I was fated to do. But as to why I bought the thing at all, who can say? That's just the way it happened.

That day—the day this unobtrusive software title went on sale—I happened to be in town quite early. This was the very first time I'd cut classes without my folks' knowing. Early in the morning I went to collect my pay from an after-school job, leaving the entire rest of the day to kill before going home. With no particular destination, I strolled along the avenue in front of the station near where I worked. Ten A.M. The town, having seen off its parade of business types on the commuter train, seemed to breathe a sigh of relief.

I had no reason to go pick up the tidy sum that would still be left after subtracting the installment on the TV in my room. It's just that, well, I had this dream about the after-school money. Final exams were coming up and schoolwork was taking its toll on my sanity when, in a dream, another "me" appeared to egg me: "Spend your take! Spend your take! Go out and play! Go out and play!"

(There are always two of me when I dream. One of them is an unseen me; that is, the dream-self that acts like my waking self—babbling, fuming, overreacting, crying, complaining. The other me is a me I can see, a figure that has my form and stands in for me.)

Half out of reckless abandon, with hardly a thought in my head, I didn't board the usual school-bound local. Instead, I caught an express and went straight to my after-school job. Cutting classes without permission was suicide, I knew, yet when the train sped past my high school stop, I merely gripped the handstrap and watched the students get off the other train. Soon I was walking downtown. The upcoming tests were a drag, like sinker-lines behind me. Strangely enough, I didn't feel particularly anxious or resigned. That's because I put all the responsibility on the other me in my dream.

Still, the fact of the matter is, once I had the cash in hand—and this is typical me—I didn't have any idea what to do with it. I just stuffed the money into my breast pocket and went sauntering off aimlessly.

As I passed the big-name discount camera store in front of the station, I saw that a line of seventy or eighty people had formed, waiting for the store to open. This was a weekday, yet junior high school kids, even grade-schoolers were lining up at the storefront computer game counter. Me, I'd graduated from computer games long ago, but here I was, totally irrational, getting drawn into the excitement. A sorry trait.

Computer games now outsold cameras, I knew, but this many people in line meant some new software must have been hyped in a big way. Not being up on the latest game info, I had no idea which. Little difference did it make; I shuffled over to the end of the line. And there I stood, thinking this buying games wasn't going to get me anywhere, thinking I had to stop impulse-buying, when just then two salespersons came out of the store. While one of them raised the heavy shutter, the other proceeded to announce over a loudspeaker the brand-new software items that would be going on sale.

Very probably, it was the sheer insipidness of the product names versus the length of the line that hooked me. I decided to stay put among the ranks inching their way forward. There *had* to be some good reason. Why else would this many people stand in line for such dumb-sounding games? What flash features would they have? The names were so nondescript, I could only imagine. All too soon, however, any fantasies I might have entertained came to naught.

When I reached the head of the line, I found there were two stacks of pre-wrapped packages set out. Little did I know, the rapidly dwindling pile on the left contained the ultra-spectacular, intergalactic "shooting" game, *Saber of Althagoras*, with no less that four-hundred enemy characters. On the right were a mere three packages. How could I tell which game was in which pile? I pulled a five-thou note from my pay envelope and pointed to the one on right.

The salesperson promptly bagged a game cassette from the righthand pile as I looked on blankly. Thus did the computer game software called *The Yamada Diary* pass into my hands.

I immediately beat a path for a bookstore, furious at myself for having made that ridiculous snap purchase. A little distraction was what I needed.

The science and philosophy section and—a little more useful to me—computer-game fanzine corner were totally without customers. This was supposed to be school hours, after all. I checked the covers of sixteen computer-game monthlies; most ran big features on either *Saber of Althagoras* or on *Psyland III*, in which you ventured deeper and deeper underground in search of buried treasure. Any mention of *The Yamada Diary* was relegated apologetically to tiny print in a lower corner.

Dilligently, I thumbed through one magazine after another, scanning the contents page. Out of all the publications, the only four that did carry something on the *Diary* briskly claimed that they had "featured *The Yamada Diary* before it went on sale." One, at the most two paragraphs—a bare minimum for the fiercely competitive publishing business.

I did notice something odd, though. All the other software reviews ran with brilliant, full-color repros of game screens, but for this game, there wasn't a single photograph. The four *Diary* reviews were text only.

Had I ever blown it! The realization hammered in even harder, but for some reason, that clunky title still intrigued me. Who's to say it wasn't in fact a fantastically great game? Not knowing a thing about the game only encouraged me to imagine as I liked. All four spreads bore the same, identically worded promo copy—no doubt cranked out by the software company—which told me nothing about the game itself. There was no description of what kind of game it was, taking place in what sort of virtual world. The catchphrase veered completely off the mark of anything that might entice or appeal:

> *First ever! A revolutionary new role-playing game that simulates your very own everyday life! A no-finish "never-ending story"—just out!!*

End of text. Pitiful. It kind of made me sad just reading it. Whoever heard of a no-end role-playing game? I hadn't a clue what that meant. And in any case, it didn't exactly make me burn with any gotta-play-quick-and-find-out urge. A sinking feeling came over me as I closed the last magazine and returned it to the rack.

The cassette-sized game instruction book included with *The Yamada Diary* was poorly thought-out, too. Incomprehensible. Practically worthless:

«STORYLINE»
Yamada is an ordinary student who goes to an ordinary high school. He is seventeen.
Yamada always wakes up when his alarm clock goes off at seven-thirty. Five minutes later would be disastrous. He would have to fly out of the house with his hair still mussed from sleeping.
At high school, Yamada is not really a go-getter; neither is he the type bullies pick on. If anything, he is the kind of student that no one in his class even notices. Yamada does not belong to any extracurricular clubs, so he goes straight to his after-school job before going home. He works for very low hourly wages because he is a high school student.
Yamada gets depressed about his day-after-day routine. But there is nothing he can do about it. Yamada likes computer games. When he has free time, and even when he does not, he plays computer games.
One day, Yamada has a dream. In the dream, Yamada dares to...
And so, Yamada sets out on a journey of adventure.
Use your skill to move Yamada and lead him toward his great adventure.
Your adventure begins—*now!*

A lot of help that was.
I inserted the cassette in the computer slot and switched on the power anyway. A fanfare blared and in bold letters, *The Yamada Diary* came up on a blue screen. The fanfare went on and on. All right already, hurry up and start the

game. My jaded ears ringing, I pressed the START button.

The screen cleared, followed by a three-second display of white letters on black.

«YOU ARE YAMADA.»

Hmmph, in most computer role-playing games, players are free to input whatever protagonist name they wish. Pretty pushy, I thought as I waited for the next screen.

The white letters disappeared and the black screen slowly filled with fine color-graphic dots that gradually formed a cross-section of a house.

The upstairs room on the right was flashing. «KIDDIE ROOM» the tag read, just like—mere coincidence?—the plaque on my own real-life room. There inside slept a figure, apparently the main character. The speakers began to issue a *beep-beep-beep*, *beep-beep-beep*, *beep-beep-beep* approximating an alarm clock.

«WAKE UP?» pulsed the YES/NO choice. Not knowing what to do, I hesitated maybe for twenty seconds, at which point the Mother figure appeared in the room and the speakers began yelling *Get up! Get up!* over and over again, a voice simulation. Whereupon the Yamada character popped up, automatically.

The awakened one-hundred-thirty dot Yamada once again faced COMMAND OPTION hell: «BRUSH TEETH» «EAT BREAKFAST» «GO TO TOILET» «GO TO SCHOOL». Wanting to avoid that nasty «GO TO SCHOOL», I tried selecting another COMMAND so as to have him «EAT BREAKFAST» first, but as it turned out, the OPTIONs weren't options; they had to be dealt with in a fixed order. Heedless of my frantic efforts to resist, it was «BRUSH TEETH» «EAT BREAKFAST» «GO TO TOILET», leaving the «GO TO SCHOOL» COMMAND to last. Apparently nothing would proceed further unless I made that selection, so I had no choice but to press [A], the key I usually use to fire missiles, setting it in OPERATE mode.

Yamada went to school.

«GOING TO SCHOOL»

But once in school, nothing special happened. Six hour-long classes later, Yamada was without anything to do but go to his after-school job.

«GOING TO WORK»

His place of work figured as an uninspired still screen—a real skimpy production—an unidentifiable storefront. At this point, a value of one «UNIT DAY LIFE POWER» has gone down. After work, Yamada's co-workers invite him to «GO DRINKING» «GO DRIVING» «GO PICK UP GIRLS», but what with his «UNIT DAY LIFE POWER» running low, it seems he'd better decline and go straight home. Back in his room, Yamada finds he probably only has enough «UNIT DAY LIFE POWER» left to «PLAY COMPUTER GAME», so he toys with his computer console a while, then goes to sleep.

In a dream, I am carrying a ringing alarm clock on my back. The thing is huge and monstrously heavy. I drag my feet, yet with each step I take, in the dream I'm thinking, "This has to be some kind of symbol. Gotta be. What can it mean? What can it mean?" I get all excited, huffing and panting, practically limping, meanwhile another me is looking on askance, wordlessly keeping pace.

From the darkness toward which I seem to be walking, the alarm clock on my back, my Mother's foghorn voice bursts in with "Get up!" I wake up.

Overslept more than twenty minutes, I had. There was no time to eat breakfast or brush my teeth or go to the toilet. I dashed out of the house with my slept-on hair standing straight up, more than a little confused about the overlap of reality and the story in the game.

This was getting complicated: I'd had a good-as-real dream, and in the dream I was playing the game; then on waking, I couldn't tell if I were playing the game or dreaming or playing the game in my dream. The crazy mix-up in my head was pulling the real-life me in there with it. I wanted a reality-check, some kind of sure-fire test. Here I'd walked half way to the station and it felt more like I was walking the game's protagonist. I was half under the illusion that this was still a game-in-progress.

The Yamada Diary occupied my thoughts, threatened to swallow me whole. Or more to the point, for literally the first time in ages I found myself totally absorbed—and that was the truth. This thing had me spooked.

The game was utterly lacking anything to make it exciting. No matter how long you kept at it, all that came up was the same old storyline: up-in-the-morning-off-to-school-go-to-work-play-computer-game-fall-asleep...over and over again. I'd gotten the hang of the after-school job, so fewer points ticked away from my «UNIT DAY LIFE POWER», but I only ended up wasting all the remaining «POWER» points on the computer game. Which meant that Yamada found himself stubbornly glued to the game-inside-the-game, unable to hack its inner workings. For in spite of pouring the better part of my «UNIT DAY LIFE POWER» into game-playing, Yamada was clearly frustrated in his attempts to crack it. «YAMADA IS IRRITATED» read the display; I was irritated too.

I had to hurry in order to catch the none-too-frequent bus to the station, yet I was lolling along. I was barely out to the main avenue, when this brilliant yellow jumped out at me. There by the newly constructed studio condos, in a tiny, tiny, concrete planter, two lanky shoulder-high sunflowers made a show of stretching upward toward the sun.

Straight on in front of that, standing at the edge of the pavement was a girl. Her drop-handle bicycle propped sideways against the guard rail, she sat side-saddle and was sketching the sunflowers. She was drawing away, never once lifting her face from her sketch pad.

Ah, yes, July already—suddenly the season struck me. I'd

noticed the sunflowers several days before; it was the girl who was summer to me. Still half-asleep, all confused over some crazy mixed-up dream-game—or was that a game-dream?—I began to take interest in the girl. What was with her? Didn't she have to go to school? She had to be about my age, well, probably. But why did she want to sketch sunflowers, right here of all places?

I had the sensation, ah, this has to be reality; the girl's being there was so out of the blue and—for me—completely unreal. And yet, the impact was as real as could be. It didn't make any sense. A reality plastered solid with real-looking imitations might also have this extreme sense of unreality. For although things other-than-real are surely meaningless, they still might give every appearance of a certain reality. In any case, caught up as I was in appearances, my wits were not as sharp as they could have been. I guess I was hooked on the unreality of this game.

In *The Yamada Diary*, when Yamada get ready to go to school, the house graphic suddenly changes to a school graphic. But if there had been a «GOING TO SCHOOL» screen showing him walking this avenue, would there have been sunflower icons? And right in front of them, there to be passed by, some simulated girl character? I had to wonder.

At school, I learned there was another kid who had purchased *The Yamada Diary*. Some joker who—it only figured—went by the name of Yamada.

Even so, in a school of nine class-groups per academic year, I had no idea which Yamada, out of all the other Yamadas, he could be. My source of this info, Ken, the resident networker, just said, "Know who else bought it? Yamada, like in the title." And at that, he'd shifted into high gear and zoomed out of the classroom. He was busy; he had to keep abreast of the latest tricks to the new *Saber of Althagoras* that were all the buzz since the day before. Every day he'd race around between classrooms, gathering info on computer

games. Being the single solitary networker servicing the com-
puter-game-fan needs of an entire school, he had his work cut
out for him. Here it was, almost exam time, and still he went
chasing around whenever breaktime came.

There were many reasons why Ken was the sole game-info
networker at school, but basically no one else wanted the job
because it earned you zilch. He was always toting three college cribbooks of "Networker Notes," which contained, first
of all, who had what software, along with each respondent's
birthdate (a special birthday gift to each info-service sub-
scriber!), family background, hobbies and interests, even personality traits (only here did Ken express his own opinions).
The painstakingly logged data was complemented by updates
on which game software each wanted, a realtime market
report that kept him continually on the go.

From there, it was a short step to brokerage, engineering
software exchanges, and lending schemes. Among high
school students, the computer game addict was often subject
to a cold looks from peers, so it was not always possible to
hang out a sign. That being the case, Ken was a guardian
angel to all closet game-junkies, helping them get the goods.
By the same token, this garnered him not only position and
status, but also some measure of authority.

On the one hand, you see, the closet game-junkies got a
channel of accurate, realtime information, which obliged
them to report honestly to Ken on any game software they
themselves purchased. On the other hand, once cut off from
his rather unilateral interventions, you'd become an outlaw,
only able to operate via telltale leaks in Ken's near-perfect
network. Such "closet-closet" cases had to be reckoned with.

As it happened, this Ken was a classmate of mine, but my
user-membership in the info-network didn't count for much.
The paltry fourteen games to my name correlated to a
neglible presence in the software-exchange market. When I
told Ken, hey, I'd bought *The Yamada Diary*, he merely put
on this finally-got-around-to-buying-something-new-eh? sort

of look and said, "I'd hate to try plotting your software-pur-
chasing curve." Then, allowing not one word in edgewise, he
spit out, "Thought Yamada'd be the only one who'd buy
that."

The homeroom monitor was writing the final exams
schedule on the blackboard, promting a chorus of gasps and
sighs from the entire class. Actually, everyone had known it
was just a matter of time, so it all went down quickly. Fine,
another ten days until exams.

When it came to exams, an info-dealer like Ken was
nobody. Around exam time, everyone was a changed person
and left him no room in which to operate. While certainly no
one welcomed exams, the general mood at school—if only
out of spite—was to shift into overdrive.

Under these pre-exam circumstances, however, Ken pre-
vailed upon his networkees: he collected black exam-info,
thus revealing his dealings for what they really were. And of
course, Ken the networker never allowed the least glimmer of
this rather special information to slip out to the rest of us.

To no one's surprise, you never heard of any exam-info
dealers.

Mother enters the room. Not studying for exams? she
asks. I thought it over a bit, but went on playing my computer game.

Mother has a regular fit. What have I done now? I
thought to myself, but kept at my game. Mother seethes,
scattering letters'n'quotes all over the room. «BITCH BITCH
BITCH». Unthinkable in real life. So Mother gets angry, so
what? Then, just when I'd begun to think this repetition
would never end, she snaps out of her tirade at nine o'clock
on the dot, announces that she is «GOING TO WATCH
TWO-HOUR TV DRAMA» and withdraws downstairs to
the dining room.

Eager to check if any change had come over the cycle, I
pushed a button to call up the data display. Among all of

twenty-four data banks on Yamada, I detected that the «UNIT DAY LIFE POWER» supply was slightly depleted. Other than that, the «DISSATISFACTION» index, which nothing had affected one way or another so far, was up by one digit. That was the whole of it; nothing more or less.

The Yamada Diary was so utterly normal—"more normal" than everyday life—I got the feeling you could wait forever and never see a hint of anything exciting. Still, I was caught up in it. Precisely because I'm not the type to plunge into fantasy-world dream sequences. This suffocatingly realistic-in-all-its-dead-dull-detail theater of nothing-doing was just my speed and I knew it.

Did I say speed? This was paralysis. Anytime now, anytime—yet wait as I might, there was nothing to the game. Only the pointless back-and-forth of house and school and job. Before long, I was scheming up ways to pry Yamada loose from his daily rut.

Slowly at first, imperceptibly, little by little...Then irresponsibly, I proceeded to subvert the game, turning Yamada into a sloppy, haphazard character. It was so easy, because everything took place within clear-cut confines, a dimension apart from my own. People could curse a streak—what did I care? It was only a game. I'd show them, set my vector on a warped personality, not even not caring. No matter what the Old Lady thought, no matter that friends gave you grief, the object of this derision was always Yamada—the "me" in the game—not me myself.

Interestingly enough, it was input into the game that exams were coming up for Yamada, too. A big display «__ DAYS TO EXAMS» appeared, occupying one wall of the «KIDDIE ROOM». From that point on, Yamada's activity options came to include slightly more radical COMMAND choices. Suddenly they were just there, these COMMANDs that weren't there before. And without the least hesitation, I took them up, directing his activities down these new branches. Say I forced Yamada to blow the exams. What would happen then? My pulse ping-ponged at the prospects.

Yamada did no studying for his exams; I had him do nothing but play.

Just once, I selected the «STUDY» COMMAND. But all that happened was Yamada sat at his desk, grim and silent, and studied for hours. No fun at all. After that, I never touched that COMMAND again.

That evening, desperate for some lead toward the "great adventure" of song and «STORY LINE», I made Yamada search the «KIDDIE ROOM». Clues, after all, were the essence of role-playing games—or so I'd seen written in a book of game tips.

A treasure map or magic lamp was bound to pop out from a drawer or behind the bookcase. Was I ever disappointed! Fish through drawers and for what? Your usual crap: a textbook and pen case and scissors and pencil sharpener and ruler and knife and seven notebooks. Thinking, hmm, just maybe, I clicked the display «BEHIND THE DESK», but the total find there was «THREE GLOSSY PORNO MAGA-ZINES».

All the same, I was determined to set this *Yamada Diary* on course to an adventure worth the name. This became a primary goal, driving me to grab at anything in the hopes it might prove a clue.

One time around, I skipped out on the after-school job and tried to talk some information out of the family.

Navigating over in front of Mother, I pushed a button and the COMMAND MENU appeared. I slid the arrow to «CONVERSATION» and pressed the button again.

«WHAT IS IT?» asks Mother.

Of the dozen responses possible, all were trivial requests: «MOTHER, A BUTTON CAME OFF MY CLOTHES» «MOTHER, GIVE ME MONEY FOR BOOKS» «MOTH-ER, WHAT'S FOR DINNER?». . . . I had to try them all. But in each case, Mother only gave a perfunctory reply, followed by the phrase «DO YOUR SCHOOLWORK». End of discussion.

I next tried the Old Man, who was perpetually drinking beer and watching baseball on TV. The possible conversations were four:

«WHO'S WINNING, FATHER?» «GIANTS, 4-1.»

«MY ALLOWANCE, PLEASE, FATHER.» «TODAY IS NOT YOUR ALLOWANCE DAY.»

«WHAT AM I SUPPOSED TO DO WITH MY LIFE, FATHER?» (This looked promising, but no—) «BECOME A PRODUCTIVE MEMBER OF SOCIETY.»

«GOOD NIGHT, FATHER.» «GOOD NIGHT.»

I went downstairs to find the place completely dark. Past ten at night and I was the only one home. Father nearly always missed the last train out here to the 'burbs and had to catch a late-night taxi home, so it was rare to find the tube broadcasting baseball in the living room.

Mother, moreover, had ladies' meetings. At least four this week. I knew she'd be out; I'd heard her say so at breakfast. I'd headed straight up to my room after work and didn't noticed the note on the dining table until I turned on the kitchen light: *Will be home late tonight—Ritsuko.* One line, in Mother's near-print script. Over which I scribbled «BITCH BITCH BITCH», quote marks and all. If only she'd written all in caps, I thought for no good reason, as I boiled water for my instant cup-noodles.

The next morning, the girl was in front of the sunflowers again. I stopped in my tracks directly across from her, yet she seemed totally unaware of me. As before, the girl was pegged in position, face hidden behind her easel.

That's when it occurred to me: if I said something to her, how would she react? But the more immediate question was, how could I strike up a conversation with someone I didn't know? I wasn't the type. Suppose I spoke to her and she didn't give me the time of day? What if she thought I was a nut?

I walked on past the girl. I could have kicked myself, well, almost. I wavered back and forth between the me who was mad at myself and the me who turned passively aside and made excuses. This way and that I walked, like a bump-'em toy. I jerked past her, a pathetic street performance, wishing somebody would take a game control lever and deftly maneuver me out of there.

The girl, for her part, kept on sketching with this don't-know-what's-with-you-but-leave-me-out-of-it sort of air. The slight glimpse I caught of the side of her face bore a note of sadness.

As soon as I entered the classroom, Ken the networker came over to my seat. He'd been waiting for me and seemed a bit worked up. *The Yamada Diary* had been taken off the market, he stammered.

"Won't know the details till I read the 'zines, but it sure sounds like there was some heavy-duty programming glitch, 'cause they don't recall products after they've gone on sale unless they're way wrong. Minor bugs they just let go, ordinarily..." Then he leaned in close to offer an even more precious pronouncement. "Anyway, this is massive—for you, too. Even if they do issue a new edition, yours'll be at a premium as a first edition. And since they're talking bad sales, the scarcity factor could shoot the value on your software straight up. Might make it worth more than *Althagoras* or *Psyland III*—top software, but they're everywhere. And here at school, it's just you and Yamada holding. That's going to zap the exchange-loan market. Fun fun fun."

"Hmph," I retorted, not letting on much interest.

"Anyway anyway, I want a full rundown on this *Yamada Diary*. To me and me only. Got it? Word yesterday was it's way strange software, so a daily report on just how far you've penetrated, all right?"

He had his nerve, I felt like telling him, especially right before exams, but I left it at "Roger!" Nice and straightforward. Then I had a thought: he'd be the one to ask about the game.

"Tell me. About this game, somehow, I can't seem to get the play to advance at all. What am I supposed to be doing?"

The junior networker grew visibly impatient with me, who in spite of holding the possibly-soon-to-be-worth-a-fortune *Yamada Diary* was giving him this strictly amateur question. But, okay, he'd humor me; he'd put it in layman's language, calm and deliberate.

"First, you find the hidden item and you access it."

"Hidden item?"

On my way to my after-school job, I peeked into the game software corner at the big-name discount camera store in front of the station. Just like Ken said, they'd put up a notice that *The Yamada Diary* had been taken off the market. Even so, the notice was a meager scrap of paper compared to the printed *Sold Out* handbills pasted up for other software.

Work was hectic. The fast-food shop was overrun with a steady stream of junior and senior high school girls. They kept us busy for hours on end, which gratefully brought a temporary amnesia about the exams only eight days away. I swear, though, the high-pitched spiel put out by that girl with the dainty little hand gestures who takes the orders at the counter, her voice careening overhead, the racket in that place—it was enough to start me on a long distance race in my head. "I can't wait to get home and play my game." The marathon runner was panting harder and harder.

Five hours on the job, and just when I was about to leave for home, the manager stopped me. This was after I'd gone to the changing room, taken off that tacky uniform, and caught my breath. My head was already monopolized by *The Yamada Diary*—I was kind of in a hurry. What did he want? Backtracking to the work area, the manager grabbed the shift schedule and pointed to a blank column. He was still one hand short for tomorrow.

As a rule, shift requests were supposed to be submitted by the middle of the previous month. I thought I'd requested not to have to come in the week before exams, starting tomorrow. The manager looked distraught. The guy who was scheduled to come in had up and quit; he'd ruined the entire shift assignments, pleaded the manager, showing unusual weakness.

"Oh all right," I said, like it was no big deal, just to console him. Something I wouldn't have been caught dead doing until now. And what, ahem, about my exams? A feeling of panic came once it was too late. The manager toddled off back into the shop. I just stood there. This flip-flop schizophrenic behavior of mine was all because of *The Yamada Diary*, I swiftly shifted the blame. Sure, I'd been in a big hurry to get home and play the game, but even more unconsciously, it seemed I was overcompensating for Yamada's guilt feelings after his boss chewed him out for skipping out on work in the previous night's game.

Time-wise, I'd had my math book open for maybe thirty minutes.

Without realizing it, I was humming the electronic game theme music while solving formulas. I just wasn't into studying. I took a second "break," and sat myself down in front of the game console. Each thirty minutes of study earned me a whole one hour and twenty minutes of *The Yamada Diary*. What the hell—with fear and trepidation, I heaved a big sigh and switched the game on.

The snowstorm on the screen changed to the title field of eye-catching primary colors, the familiar fanfare flourished, and what relief! I was back where I belonged—in my virtual world.

I hit the START key, a fifty-*kana* syllabary chart floated up into input readiness. I keyed in the «RESTART INCAN-

TATION» I'd jotted down when I cut short my game not thirty minutes earlier, running the cursor arrow through the fifty syllable-sounds in the prescribed nonsensical order—*nu-po-ko-me-hi-ko-mi-shi-ki-fu-ji-su*, then pressed [A]. Presto! Right before my eyes, the me-called-Yamada was ruminating over his studies.

As Yamada's exams approached, the display window showed various data changes. The «DISSATISFACTION» index kept inching upward; even the «BIG BANG POWER», the use of which was still a mystery to me, started to move.

Unable to find the hidden item, I could only attack the game via standard play. No doubt, the tension and frustration building up toward these exams would give rise to "adventurous" developments in the «STORYLINE». That far I could see. These expectations drove me deeper into the game. What if I made Yamada space out on his tests? That would turn the tide but quick. I could hardly contain myself.

As expected, on exam day, the COMMAND OPTIONs whether to take or not to take the exam appeared. Without any hesitation, I pressed the key to move the cursor to «FORFEIT EXAMS».

«I'M HOME.»
«I JUST GOT A CALL FROM YOUR TEACHER. WHY DIDN'T YOU TAKE YOUR EXAMS?»

Yamada's Mother is furious. There appears a list of Yamada's OPTIONs: «APOLOGIZE» «IGNORE» «EVADE» «SONG-AND-DANCE». I'm expected to pass over the «HIT HER» COMMAND, but instead I zap the thing.

Whammo! Onomatopoeia flies across the screen like in a cartoon. Mother falls over.

Next move, I opt for «HIT HER AGAIN».

Biff! Boff! Pow! Mother gets knocked down in nothing flat, only to pop right back up like nothing sharp.

«YOU'RE NO CHILD OF MINE! HOW COULD YOU? HOW COULD YOU?»

Bitch bitch bitch, bitch bitch bitch.

«UNIT DAY LIFE POWER» depleting. «DISSATISFAC-TION» rising. «ALLOWANCE» running low. «TRUST-WORTHINESS» down. «BIG BANG POWER» up. Nice nice nice. I savor the changes in the data, completely innocent of what the effects might be.

Yet no matter what dastardly tricks I played, one data indicator, «NORMALITY», refuses to budge from zero.

"Oh...uh...Hi, Mom."

"What's this now? At your game again. Do you really think that's a good idea? Not studying? Today, I was with Mrs. Araya, Manabu's mother. And she said Manabu was all in a dither this week getting ready for exams."

As if shadowing the game Mother, my mother burst in my "Kiddie Room," firing her verbal machine-gun, but not daring to come between me and my game screen.

So she'd been with Mrs. Araya? And which of her many "meetings" was it today? Ah yes, the Citizen's Initiative—or whatever—to turn that nearby housing project site into a park. A place in our town for children to play. How nice. The girls probably had themselves a grand old time crooning their Ryotaro Sugi in that *karaoke* sing-along basement bar across from the station. And at their age, too! In these nightspots, these adult playgrounds, you should hear the noise pollution. My mother, the songbird!

She had on her sober face, but her speech and footfalls were those of a drunk. The intoxicating mood had possessed her.

"Here I am doing my darnedest to provide facilities for playing outdoors in the sunlight and all you do is sit in this dark room playing that *beep-beep-beep-beep* game of yours."

She flicked on the room light. The sudden fluorescent flood hurt my eyes, jerking me back to reality.

"Are you listening?"

I saw a list of phrases in my head. Lots of them. In as little time as it took to maneuver a joystick and push a button to select one of the phrases, a lovely, hollow response issued from my lips.

"I understand, Mother. I will stop playing the game right away."

Which didn't strike her one way or another in her drunken state. She left the room. If only the phrase, "Hoof it out of here, loudmouth!" had surfaced among my OPTIONs! And such a prime opportunity! I chased the impulse: how'd it have been if I said that?

Seeking an answer, I took another look-see at the «KIDDIE ROOM» in the game. Mother was still bitching away, scattering letters over the computer screen in an inexhaustible simulation of rage.

The following day, Yamada is called upon by his teacher and forced to take make-up exams. There is no «FORFEIT» COMMAND. So on continued the game, an indistinguishable succession of rerun days.

So much for Yamada's "adventure."

It was another five-days-and-closing-fast to the real-life exam. Class time and breaks alike found me asleep at my seat for lack of sleep. The desktop wasn't much of a bed, but the English teacher's slurring Japanese-English made a great lullaby.

"You must be studying your ass off," remarked Sugawa, a duly impressed classmate. And well he should have looked so amazed: I'd just slept through the entire morning and barely showed signs of rousing with the noon recess bell.

"Been at the game full-time, *after* after-schooling. Uses up all my Unit Day Life Power," I told him.

"You're still half-asleep," he said, grabbing up his study kit and trotting off to the library.

Strangely enough, during these classtime dozes, I didn't dream.

Simultaneous with the recess bell, Ken the networker
made a mad dash out of the classroom, only to come scurrying back unexpectedly. And that wasn't all: where typically
around this time he would have toted a handful of cheat-
sheets culled from other classrooms, today, for some reason,
he carefully cradled his regular Networker Notes. As soon as
his eyes met mine, he made a beeline to my seat and pro-
duced some photocopies from his schoolbag. His eyes looking suspiciously vacant, Ken emitted a nervous *he he he*. Was
he overstressed to a frazzle himself?

He drew close, but only so close, almost deferentially.
Spooky. Positively unsettling. "So tell me, how've you been
coming along with *The Yamada Diary* since yesterday?"

What a change! From "I want a full rundown" to
"How've you been coming along?" I smelled manipulation.
This much I'd gathered: Ken was scheming to get at my
scarcity-value software and secure an even higher standing
among his networkees. He planned to gerrymander the lending order, withhold certain key *Diary* details for a privileged
few, and play all sorts of little tricks sure to piss people off.
Yet just when Ken had gotten so close to sewing up the
school's info system, a kid by the name of Sabu had declared
himself an info-broker. This upstart, who'd been kicked out
of the network for snubbing Ken, was in cahoots with Yamada— the owner of the sole other *Yamada Diary*—and now
threatened to form a whole new network. The heat was on
Ken, and all in the space of these past few days.

Ken was at a loss, grasping at straws—me, namely—
thinking to lasso me to his side. Hence this last-ditch scam.

"Here's the inside scoop on Mr. Tsurumi's Classical Japanese," he whispered in my ear. "Got it via channels in B
Group, so it's gotta be good for pretty high marks. Quick!
Hide it, hide it!" Before I could stop him, he was flicking
photocopies into my desk. "This oughta trim off some study
time, so you can concentrate on your game, eh?" he grinned
lasciviously.

"One good turn deserves another, eh? One good turn," he repeated, grovelling like some despicable traveling salesman as he left.

Ken was desperate: If I didn't crack *The Yamada Diary*, his whole empire would be in serious trouble. I pulled his photocopies out of my desk and leafed through them. Meanwhile, Sabu, together with Yamada as his inside source, was probably making steady inroads into *The Yamada Diary*, carving out major new channels among the school's info-system subscribers.

Nonetheless, my *Yamada Diary* and Yamada's *Yamada Diary* seemed to be taking slightly different courses. Granted, my game still had not gotten all that far, but already the arena wasn't shaping up like the game Yamada played. In his hands, the *Diary* charted a different direction. According to reports leaked from Sabu's side, Yamada's "Yamada" undergoes a complete "self-improvement," from which unfolds a "love" story.

His Yamada's days repeat an ongoing routine. This much was the same. But at some point, the other Yamada falls frantically in love. The girl is a nameless female he meets on his daily route to school. She is on his "mind" constantly—in school, at work, back home. She, for her part, seems neither particularly bothered nor interested (such apparently was Yamada-the-player's dogmatic reading). Yamada-the-game-character is at an impasse. How can he chat her up? This motivation underscores all his actions; winning her becomes the adventure of the hour.

One day, he skips school and waits for her all afternoon in front of her train station. She, however, does not show. Night comes on. He's about to give up and go home, when he sees a girl being assaulted by some nasty-looking brutes in a back alley. He must rescue her. He bravely challenges the attackers, when what should happen but a gleaming «HIDDEN ITEM» materializes on the pavement. He accesses it, and the gang blips off the screen. Enter a second heroine. The plot thickens; the "love" story escalates into the grand realm of romance.

As different from my story as clouds and mud.

My mother entered the room. Right when Yamada is arguing with Mother. Aghast, she—my mother—switched off the TV without a word.

"What are you doing?"

"What am *I* doing?" she snapped, turning on the light. "You have exams in five days. What's gotten into you? This is not like you, this is crazy. You've never done anything like this before."

"Crazy? Me, crazy?"

"Yes, crazy. You do nothing but play that game. I don't care how wrapped up you are in the game. Before exams you've got to get control of yourself."

"Examexamexamexamexamexamexam," I chanted. The spell had no effect on my mother.

I went to my desk and opened a textbook for the first time that day. Then I waited quietly for my mother to leave the room. This was the only spell that worked with her.

For five minutes after she left, I hesitated. Then I crept back to the game console and switched the monitor on, this time turning down the volume. The game console had not been turned off, so the OPTION-branching scene of Mother and the «KIDDIE ROOM» floated up immediately, impatiently.

I moved to choose a weapon from Yamada's pitiful arsenal of possessions: «THREE GLOSSY PORNO MAGAZINES» «PEN CASE» «TEXTBOOK» «KNIFE» «BIG CARRY-ALL» «RADIO-CASSETTE PLAYER»... I selected the «KNIFE» as best for my purposes. *Click-click-click-click*. That, I guessed, was the sound of the blade sliding out. Mother proved awfully formidable with her «FRYING PAN ATTACK.» *Bang-bang-bang, bang-bang-bang. Ouch-ouch-ouch, ouch-ouch-ouch.* Yamada's «UNIT DAY LIFE POWER» depletes rapidly, until finally it hits zero, and Yamada keels over like a cockroach doused with bug spray.

The whole screen vaporizes. I waited for the next screen with very little expectation, and wouldn't you know it, the scenario merely returned to the morning alarm-clock reveille. I felt cheated. Try to kick up some action and you go nowhere; your points shoot straight to zero and you wake up back at the same first screen in the daily routine.

Which for Yamada meant «GAME OVER». That is, «DEATH».

Yet at the same time it was «GAME START». The alarm clock clanging away, Mother reappearing to deliver her tidings of great joy.

Get up!

After school, Yamada goes to his part-time job. Day after day after day. By doing his job, his «UNIT DAY LIFE POWER» goes down. In compensation for which, his «ALLOWANCE» goes up. But that's it—the repetition yields only more of the same.

This was what I was thinking the whole time I was at my real job. There was no point to having Yamada work. Make him quit, make him quit—I indulged the idea as I plunged a wire-mesh basket of frozen potatoes into hot oil. I pretended to keep an eye on them, but my thoughts kept churning away: what *would* happen if I did just that? I must have really spaced out, because I jumped when the timer for the potatoes went off. All at once, shop noises came crashing in on my ears.

What the hell was I doing here? The potatoes tossed and bubbled in the deep fat. My job was to lift the wire-mesh basket and drain off the oil, then salt and pack the fries. But I simply stood there, dumb and motionless, as if waiting for a COMMAND. I just stared at those pitiful potatoes, writhing there in that pool of fat, practically pleading for help.

After work, the manager called me in. There on the table

was a plateful of blackened remains. The other student part-timers passed by, looking first at me, then at the manager who stood stiffly with his arms crossed.

"What, may I ask, is the meaning of this?"

"Umm..." I disowned, as if it had been someone else's doing. "Just daydreaming, I guess."

"Just daydreaming can cause real problems."

"I'm sorry." You bet I was sorry. One side of me was cowering. And yet, I was split down the middle. If this were *The Yamada Diary*, what would I do...? *Blam! Blam!* Onomatopoeia exploded through my head.

"Of all the... 'I'm sorry' isn't enough. Not this time. I mean, what am I supposed to do? Why even have you around? It's beyond me. I'm paying you, aren't I?"

Bitch bitch bitch, bitch bitch bitch.

"Okay, so don't pay me."

"What did you say?" The manager turned a pressurized purple.

Right then, a graphic-dot mental image of myself blossomed in my head: I was pressing a joystick button, shouting «GET LOST» in quotes.

"Shut up!" I blurted out. What *was* I doing? Was I challenging that idiot manager? Was I mad at that idiot me-in-the-game who egged me on? The manager glared at me in astonishment, his eyes bulging out of their sockets. I could feel a shock wave ripple through the part-timers who looked on.

I hedged, though my gut reaction was to cut loose with the abuse, scream something with a little more authority. I was the one holding the control lever, after all; why stick to such dippy curses?

I was late getting home because of all the trouble. I went straight to my "Kiddie Room" and revved up *The Yamada Diary*. I made Yamada quit his job. Why hadn't I thought of it earlier? This left Yamada with nothing to do but go straight to his «KIDDIE ROOM».

Time. Time until it's time for bed. Time accruing instead of «ALLOWANCE». Time for the prince of the «KIDDIE ROOM» to retreat to his throne.

First published, *Kaien* magazine, 1988
TRANSLATION BY ALFRED BIRNBAUM

Masato Takeno (b. 1966), the youngest contributor to this collection, won the 5th Kaien New Writer's Award for his novella *Square Dining Table* (1986) while still an economics student at Hōsei University. This was followed by *The Yamada Diary* (1988), excerpted here, and most recently by *True Love Movie* (1989). His cool control and oblique viewpoint already evidence a considerable degree of authorial maturity, while his grasp on the *otaku* "computer kids" boom shows him to be an astute observer of his times.

About the Translators

Alfred Birnbaum, born in Washington, DC, in 1957, calls Tokyo his home. American by passport, he has lived in Japan since childhood and travels extensively, contributing regularly to Japanese and European magazines on popular culture and media. A graduate of the University of Southern California in East Asian Studies, he is translator of Haruki Murakami's *A Wild Sheep Chase* and the forthcoming *Hard-Boiled Wonderland and the End of the World* (Kodansha International).

Terry Gallagher was born in Brooklyn, New York, in 1956. He studied art history at Brown University and at the University of Freiburg, West Germany. He first visited Japan in 1977, and has lived there about half the years since. He works in Tokyo as a journalist.

Jeffrey Hunter was born in Kenosha, Wisconsin, in 1952. He attended the University of Wisconsin, receiving a B.A. in communication arts and a Ph.D. in Buddhist philosophy. He lived for thirteen years in Tokyo where he worked as an editor and as a translator of literature, Buddhist texts, and architecture essays. His translation of *The Pilgrimage of Good Fortune*, by Mutsuro Takahashi, is forthcoming by Gay Men's Press, London. He lives in New York where he works in publishing.

Mona Tellier was born in Portage la Prairie, Manitoba, Canada, in 1957, and grew up in Thunder Bay, Ontario. She studied political science at Simon Fraser University in British Columbia, then moved to Tokyo for eleven years, studying, working in advertising and production, and writing for English-language magazines. She lives in Barcelona, Spain, where she writes for several Japanese-language journals.